6.50

Watercolour Workshop
with
Jack McDonogh

Watercolour Workshop with Jack McDonogh

step-by-step demonstrations
of how to paint watercolour landscapes

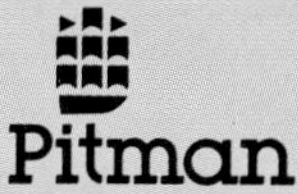

Pitman

PITMAN PUBLISHING PTY LTD
A Longman Company
Kings Gardens, 95 Coventry Street
Melbourne 3205 Australia
Offices in Sydney, Brisbane,
Adelaide and Perth

First published 1987
Reprinted 1989

Edited by Elizabeth Flann
Designed by Lynda Patullo
Photographs by Brian Howlett
Set in 12/13 Caslon Roman
Produced by Pitman Publishing Pty Ltd
Printed in Hong Kong

National Library of Australia
Cataloguing in Publication data

McDonogh, Jack H. (Jack Henry).
Watercolour workshop with Jack McDonogh.

Bibliography.
Includes index.
ISBN 0 7299 0068 1

1. Landscape painting – Technique. 2. Watercolour painting – Technique. I. Title.

751.42'2436

Acknowledgments

This book is dedicated to all the friends I have made through my classes in watercolour painting at the Mitchell College of Advanced Education, Bathurst. It was because of them that I wrote my first book and it was because of them that I have continued to write books.

My thanks to you all and to my wife Colleen for her help with the texts.

Thanks are also due to Brian Howlett for his excellent photography.

Special thanks to Royda Jaques for her assistance with the typing.

Contents

Foreword

I am delighted to accept the request from Jack McDonogh to write the foreword to his second book on watercolour painting. His first book on watercolours has been a notable success and I am confident that this one will be the same.

Through his teaching, his paintings and his books, Jack is now widely regarded as a master teacher–artist. He has through a lifetime of effort earned the respect of all.

Apart from the pleasure he gains from painting, Jack McDonogh has dedicated years of his life to bringing the same pleasure to people who want to paint in watercolours. He has been teaching painting and creative arts since the late fifties, first with the Adult Education Department of Sydney University in combination with the WEA, and then since 1973 in the Mitchell School of Creative Arts, which he established when he was head of the Creative Arts Department. This school of creative arts has become part of the Mitchell College tradition, attracting students from all states of Australia and from New Zealand.

Although Jack retired as Head of Creative Arts at Mitchell College in 1977, he is still very active in teaching watercolour painting in the Mitchell School of Creative Arts as the Honorary Resident Artist of Mitchell College and has been honoured by being made a Fellow of the College. He encourages the beginner to join his classes. As Jack says, 'I want to give people another reason for living and a very pleasant hobby.'

This book I believe is a logical sequel to Jack McDonogh's first watercolour book and I wish it all the success it deserves.

Melvin E McMichael
Principal
Mitchell College of Advanced Education
Bathurst NSW

Introduction

This book has been written with one aim on my part and that is to help the beginner in watercolour painting.

My first book on watercolour painting *Australian Landscapes in Watercolour* was written to introduce the beginner to the fascinating world of art, as was another book of mine *An Introduction to Pencil Sketching*.

In the first watercolour book I took the reader from the very beginnings of learning to paint watercolour landscapes, showing techniques I use for stretching paper, composition, and painting the various elements of a landscape, the trees and clouds and reflected light. In this book I do not dwell on the various techniques used but mention where they help me in painting a landscape. So this book is to be seen as a follow-up to *Australian Landscapes in Watercolour*.

Let me stress as strongly as I can that this book was not written with any idea on my part that the methods used are the only ones or the correct ones. It is my way. There are as many ways to paint watercolours as there are artists, so study every artist's work and learn from them all. My aim is to start you painting.

In most of the paintings in this book I mention that a pencil outline is first drawn. With this point in mind, let me tell you how I plan my watercolours.

I generally start with a pencil sketch of the selected scene and two or three photographs. Back in my studio I make further pencil sketches to work out the composition, light and dark areas, etc. When I feel all is correct I first paint what I call a miniature (21 cm × 17 cm) of the scene, and the only difference between this painting and a full sheet painting is the size of the brushes used. All the colours and techniques used will be the same in the miniature as for the larger version. If I feel the small painting looks correct, I can then approach the larger painting knowing that all my problems have been worked out. Even with this plan I still keep my fingers crossed that all will work out well.

In other words, what I'm saying is that your pictures have to be planned. Rarely will you succeed with an unplanned painting. Watercolour can be a very difficult medium—this is agreed by all artists—but it is certainly a most exciting one. Things can be done with coloured water on paper that no other medium allows. The watercolourist is invariably living dangerously, mainly because we cannot paint over our mistakes when using transparent watercolours. So the lesson is to plan carefully. If you do, you will have less failures and save a lot of watercolour paper and paint.

I'm a great believer in learning to paint or draw the various elements needed in landscapes before you combine them in a picture. By this I mean practise painting trees, clouds, reflections and so on using the backs of discarded sheets of watercolour paper (I have plenty of paper for this work). I still spend time doing this sort of thing, painting gum tree trunks and breaking waves, and it certainly gives me confidence when I come to make the final painting.

The paintings shown in this book were all painted within a mount with a viewing size of 31 cm by 24 cm. This allows a half sheet of paper stretched on a board to have a painting at each end of the board (see Figure 5). I suggest you paint the pictures to the same size. Painting watercolours to half sheet or full sheet size requires more skill. As your experience and confidence grows you can move to the larger sizes. I still recall my first try at a full sheet painting—the paper looked like a half acre paddock. Strangely enough, with experience this size doesn't present any problems.

And finally let me say, from one who knows (and every watercolourist I know agrees with me) be prepared for the fact that you are going to have failures sometimes. Please do not let this worry you; it is part of the life of the artist. When you finally paint a picture that pleases you it makes all the failures worthwhile.

And remember it's a case of practise, practise, practise. There is no easy road to success. Best of luck and my great wish is that this book can help you.

I enjoyed writing it.

Good painting,
JACK McDONOGH

Part 1: Before you start

Materials and equipment

PIGMENTS AND PAINT BOX

The choice of the way you place or hold your paints for painting is a very personal thing. I find that the ordinary metal box shown does all I require of it.

The paints I use and recommend are Winsor and Newton watercolours, Artist's quality. Although you can see I have pans in thc box, I buy my colours in tubes and refill the pans as needed from the tubes.

Colours I use sometimes, but not in this series of paintings, are alizarin crimson, cadmium red and french ultramarine blue. You will notice I have no black or white in the box. I never use these pigments.

In summer months I keep a wet tissue in the paint box to keep the paints moist.

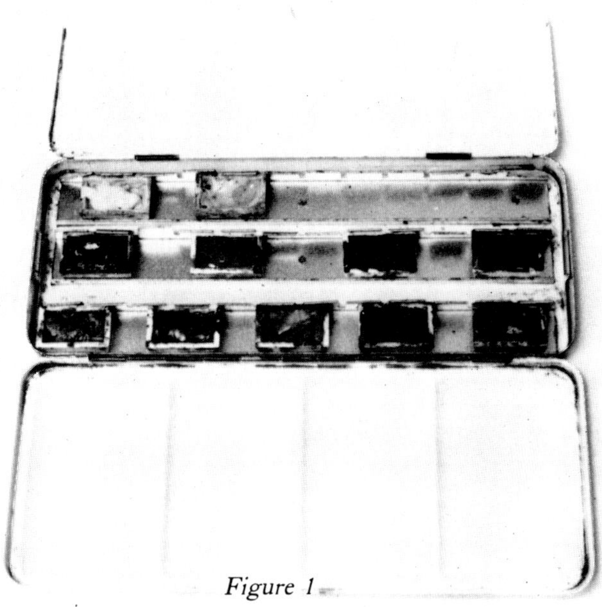

Figure 1

Cadmium Yellow Pale	Indian Yellow			
Payne's Gray	Cobalt Blue	Antwerp Blue	Winsor Blue	
Raw Sienna	Raw Umber	Light Red	Burnt Umber	Burnt Sienna

Figure 2 Arrangement of colours in paint box

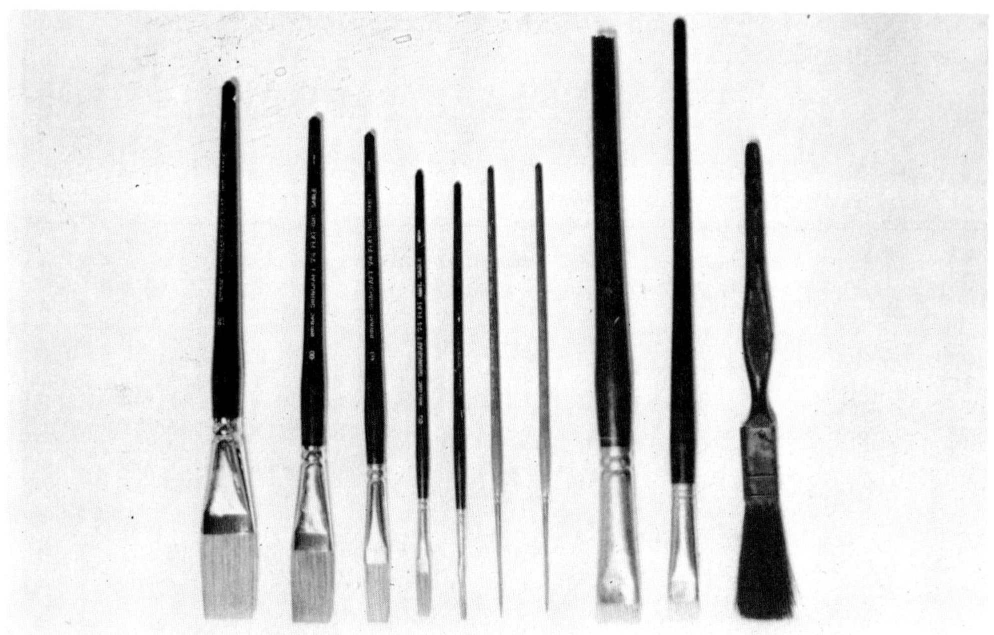

Figure 3

BRUSHES

Flat brushes

Roymac Signcraft 74 flat imitation sable

No 12	No 8	No 6	No 3	No 1
25 mm	20 mm	12 mm	7 mm	3 mm
(1")	($\frac{3}{4}$")	($\frac{1}{2}$")	($\frac{1}{4}$")	($\frac{1}{8}$")

Round brushes

Roymac Signcraft 75-L pure sable

No 1 No 2

Lift-off brushes

Oil colour brushes with bristles cut to 1 cm long

20 mm 10 mm

The use for the lift-off brushes is explained in the notes before the section dealing with the paintings.

Varnish brush

12 mm ($\frac{1}{2}$") ordinary paint brush

Actually a clean, battered old one does a better job than a new one. Always keep this brush dry. It is never dipped into the water. I use this brush to show grassy edges on washes.

The brushes used for painting should be washed in clean water after each painting session.

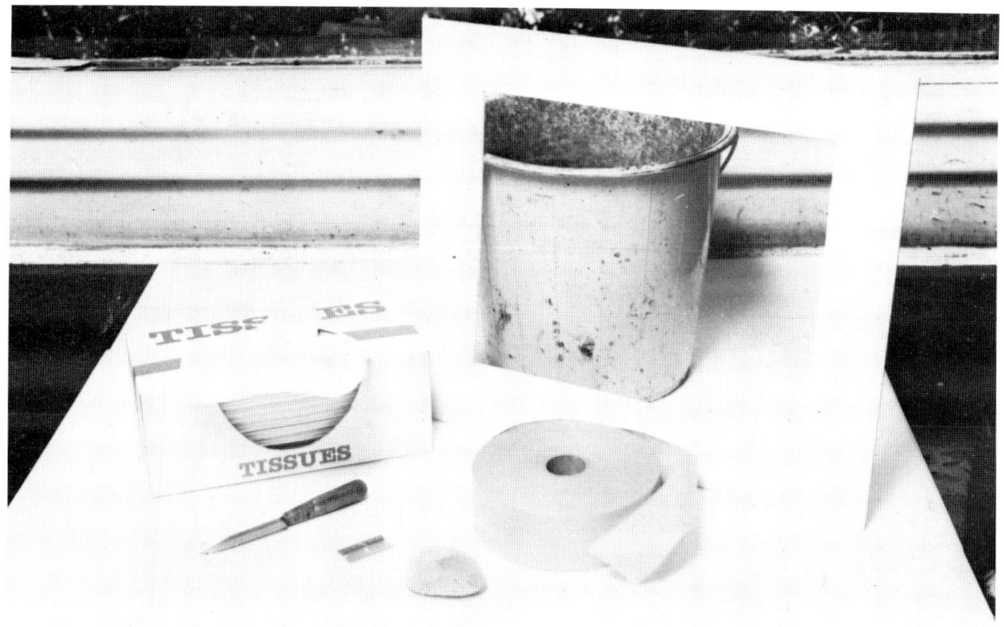

Figure 4

ACCESSORIES

Accessories you will need include:

paper tissues
razor blade or scraper blade
vegetable knife—non-serrated edge
6B pencil
cosmetic sponge
bucket
roll of gummed paper—40 or 50 mm wide

I use the razor blade to scratch highlights on dry paper or to push it into wet surfaces to give earth textures.

The vegetable knife is used to give textures in wet surfaces.

The cosmetic sponge is used to wet the surface of the paper prior to the 'wet-in-wet' technique or when well wrung out to 'lift-off' shed roofs, etc.

The tissues have a lot of uses from lifting colour to cleaning up.

The gummed paper is used for stretching the watercolour paper.

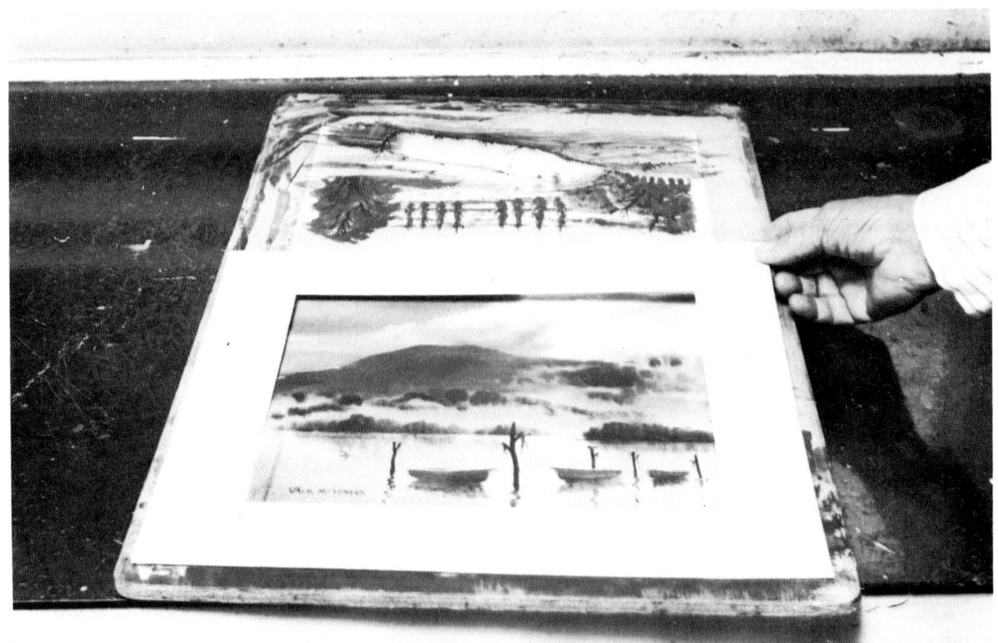

Figure 5

PAPER

The paper used for all the paintings was ARCHES, 185 GSM Rough. Half full sheets were used and two paintings made on each piece of paper (see Figure 5).

The paper was stretched on five ply boards. Stretching means that the paper was soaked in cold water for about fifteen minutes then attached to the board with strips of gummed brown paper and laid flat to allow to dry.

MOUNT

Size of mount—outside measurements:
43 cm × 35 cm
inside measurements:
31 cm × 24 cm

The mount can be made from any white cardboard. I have several mounts I use when painting, to fit the miniature, quarter sheet, half sheet and full sheet sizes.

Some notes on techniques

STRENGTH OF COLOUR

A point to notice in my style is that I rarely paint the final strength of colour required in the first instance. I usually paint a lighter wash at first for such things as leaves, shadows, tree trunks or water scenes, then strengthen these again when dry in the final development of the picture. In saying this, let me also say that I rarely retouch the clouds. Sometimes I have had some very good effects by painting another cloud study over an already dry one. Carefully put clear water over the study and paint the new layer of clouds. You might try this some time.

BRUSH SIZE

I cannot overstress the need for you always to use the biggest brush capable of doing the job you want done. The height of frustration can easily be reached by using a No 1 flat brush to paint a cloud study on a full sheet of paper. It is a pleasure with a No 12.

'WET-IN-WET'

Most of the application of paint to the paper in my paintings is done on a dry surface. On other occasions, such as painting clouds, I always use what is known as the 'wet-in-wet' technique. Simply put, this is painting colours into a wet surface on the paper. I mention every occasion for which this technique is used.

Getting the right amount of water on the paper is critical with this technique. Too much water is just as bad as too little. It has to be just right. What I generally do is to have the board flat then apply the water to the paper with a sponge, or with my largest flat brush. I then hold the board vertically on its edge and let the surplus water run from the paper. When I think it is right I lay the board flat again and start painting.

There are two ways I introduce the colours to the wet surface in the 'wet-in-wet' technique. The usual way is to add the colours after being mixed in the pan of your paint box,and don't forget to make them a bit stronger than you think you will need because the wet surface will help to weaken the colours. The other way is to pick the colours straight from the pans and mix them on the wet surface. I will often pick two colours up with the same brush. This method gives very strong colours in the finished painting. You will see where I have done this, but unless specially mentioned I want you to assume that I have pre-mixed the colours in the paint box. Most of the normal lightest clouds are painted in this way.

MIXING COLOURS

Watch when you are mixing colours in the pan of your paint box.I always find it best when mixing two colours to put the lighter colour in first. A good case to explain this is the mixing of light red and winsor blue. These two colours can make a thousand variations of greys with a little extra or a little less of each other, and they are my usual colours for clouds. The mixture requires very little winsor blue, which is a very powerful colour. So put the light red in first and the smallest dabs of winsor blue until you arrive at the colour you want. Of course, if I were painting stormy clouds, I would reverse the procedure.

A point to remember if you are using a pre-mixed colour when painting 'wet-in-wet' is to mix the colours before wetting the paper. The paper can dry out before you have found the colour you want.

Always have some pieces of watercolour paper by you, when painting, to test your colours before applying them to the paper on the board.

Remember that watercolours are much paler on the paper when dry than they are when wet.

TISSUES

I like to keep a clean tissue in my non-painting hand when doing the strengthening washes. It is a great safety valve. If I have overstrengthened I can pick up the offending colour immediately with the tissue. If this is done straight away no trace of the offending paint is left.

LIFTING-OFF

You will find that, in some paintings, particularly the seascapes, I mention that I 'lift-off' colour. This is done with the 'lift-off' brushes as shown with the other brushes earlier in the book. 'Lifting-off' is always done on a dry surface. Simply dip the brush into clear water and rub firmly into the area to be lifted. If enough lift is not obtained, wash the brush and repeat the process.

Dry the area straight away with a tissue.

PAINTING POSITION OF THE BOARD

I always paint with my board flat on the table. At times I tilt the board for special effects. This is mentioned in the steps.

EXCESS MOISTURE IN BRUSH

Quite often I find, with the flat brushes particularly, when I pick up colour from the mixing pan the brush is just too charged with water and colour to do the job I want. So I give the piece of paper for testing one brush stroke before I apply the paint to the picture. This removes the surplus moisture.

WATER

I always use a plastic bucket to hold the water when painting. A four or six litre plastic icecream container is satisfactory. Keep changing the water in your bucket or water container. You cannot get good colours from dirty water.

USE OF MOUNT

You will notice I have a mount displayed earlier in the book. When painting I advise you to keep checking your painting within the mount. Apart from isolating the painting from the board surrounds the mount shows you how the picture will look when mounted and framed. When nearing the finished stages of a painting I find myself checking the painting within the mount very regularly.

CLEANING UP

I strongly suggest you clean the pans and mixing areas of your paint box after the completion of each painting. Quite often I will clean the box after each step.

DRYING

You will notice how often I tell you to allow the picture to dry before doing the next step. In winter, particularly, waiting for the paper to dry can take a lot of good painting time. To speed up drying I keep a small electric radiator in my studio and hold this over the painting. This quickly dries the surface.

Part 2: Step-by-step paintings

Sand dunes

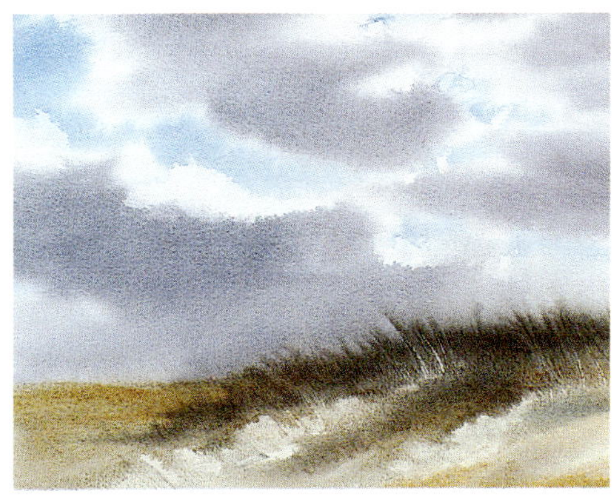

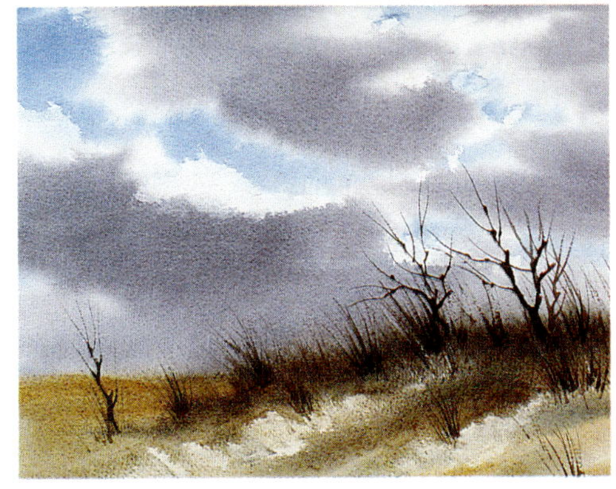

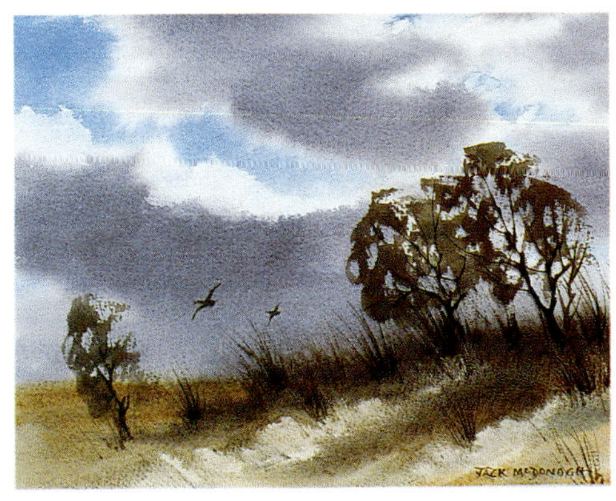

Sand dunes

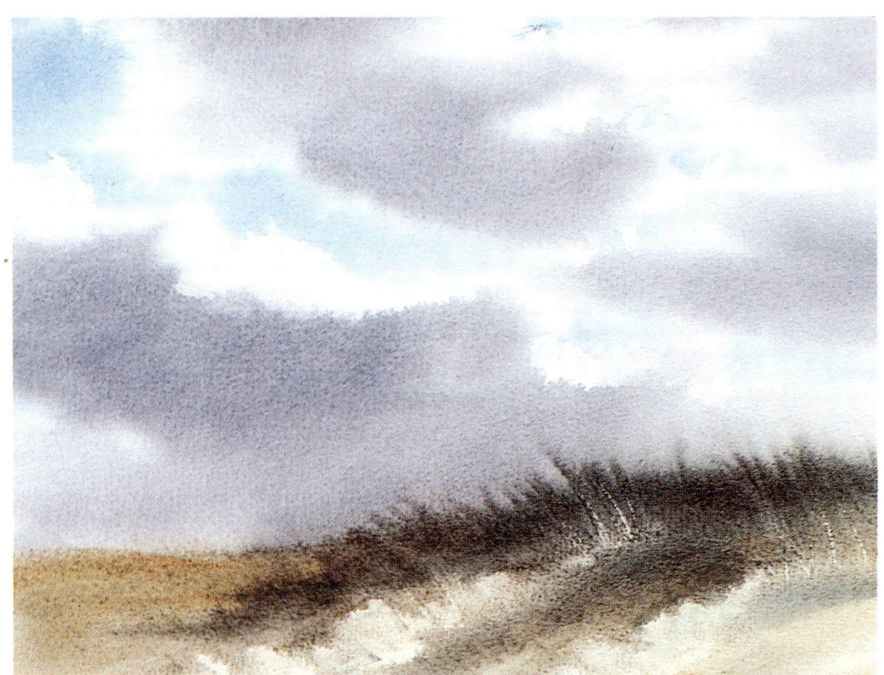

STEP 1

In this painting I shall explain how I paint the clouds. In the pictures following, where similar clouds are used, I shall give the mixture used and when to paint the clouds. Step 1 is painted 'wet-in-wet'.

A No pencil outline required.

B Mix colour for the clouds with a mixture of light red and a touch of winsor blue. At the same time have a pan with some pre-thinned antwerp blue ready. Test the colours. Make them slightly darker than required when dry.

C Cover entire sheet of paper with a thin coat of clear water.

Apply cloud colour leaving gaps of white paper. Paint some of the antwerp blue into the white areas. If needed 'lift-off' some sky colour and cloud colour at the top of the clouds with a tissue.

D While still wet paint some raw sienna straight from the box on the left side of the picture. Then some burnt umber to the right side of the picture. Bring some raw sienna into the foreground.

E Add a stroke of antwerp blue into the burnt umber. With the dry varnish brush rake upwards to give a grassy edge.

F Make some textures with the razor blade and some strokes with the knife through the grassy area.
Allow to dry.

Sand dunes

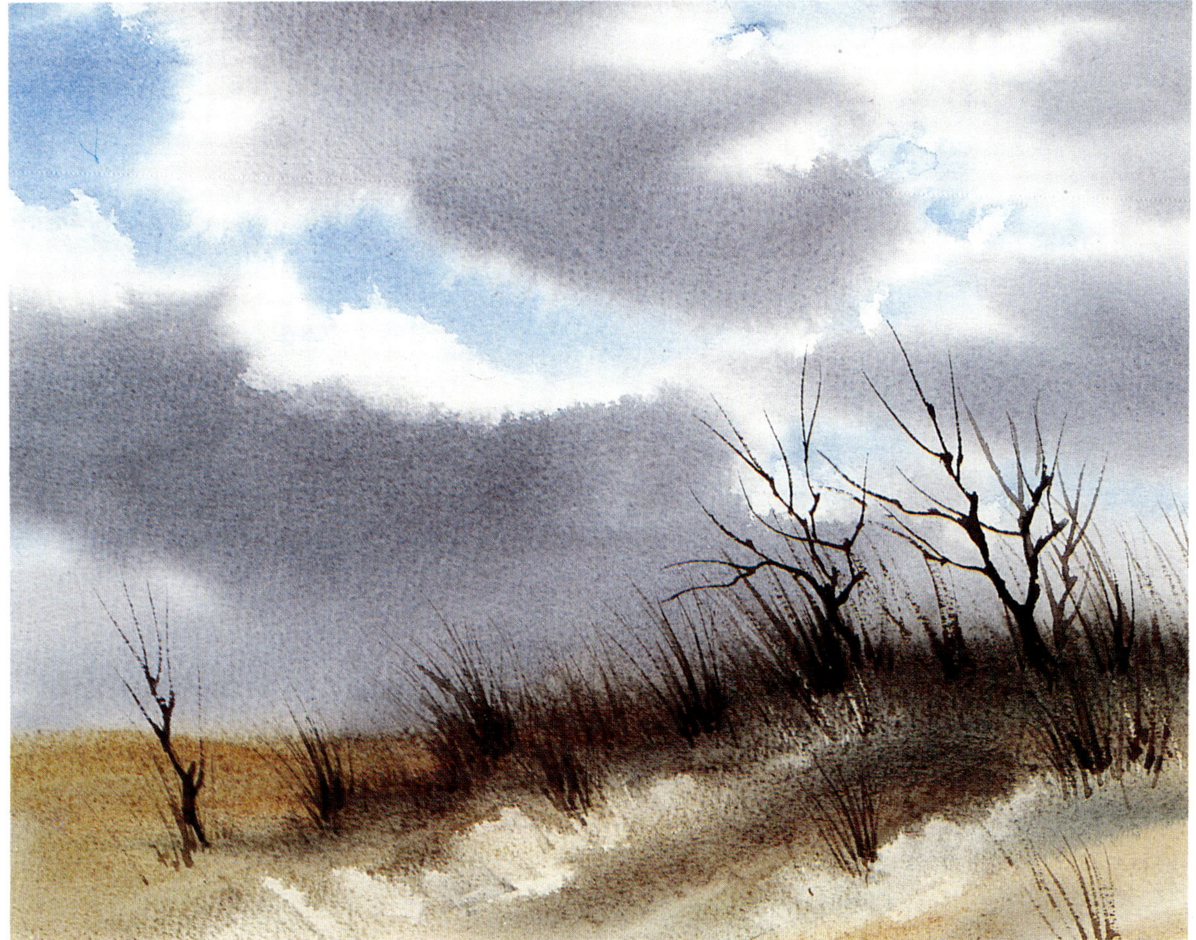

STEP 2

A With a small round brush add some strokes of grassy edge using burnt umber.

B Paint trunks of trees with a mixture of burnt umber and a touch of antwerp blue.
Allow to dry.

Sand dunes

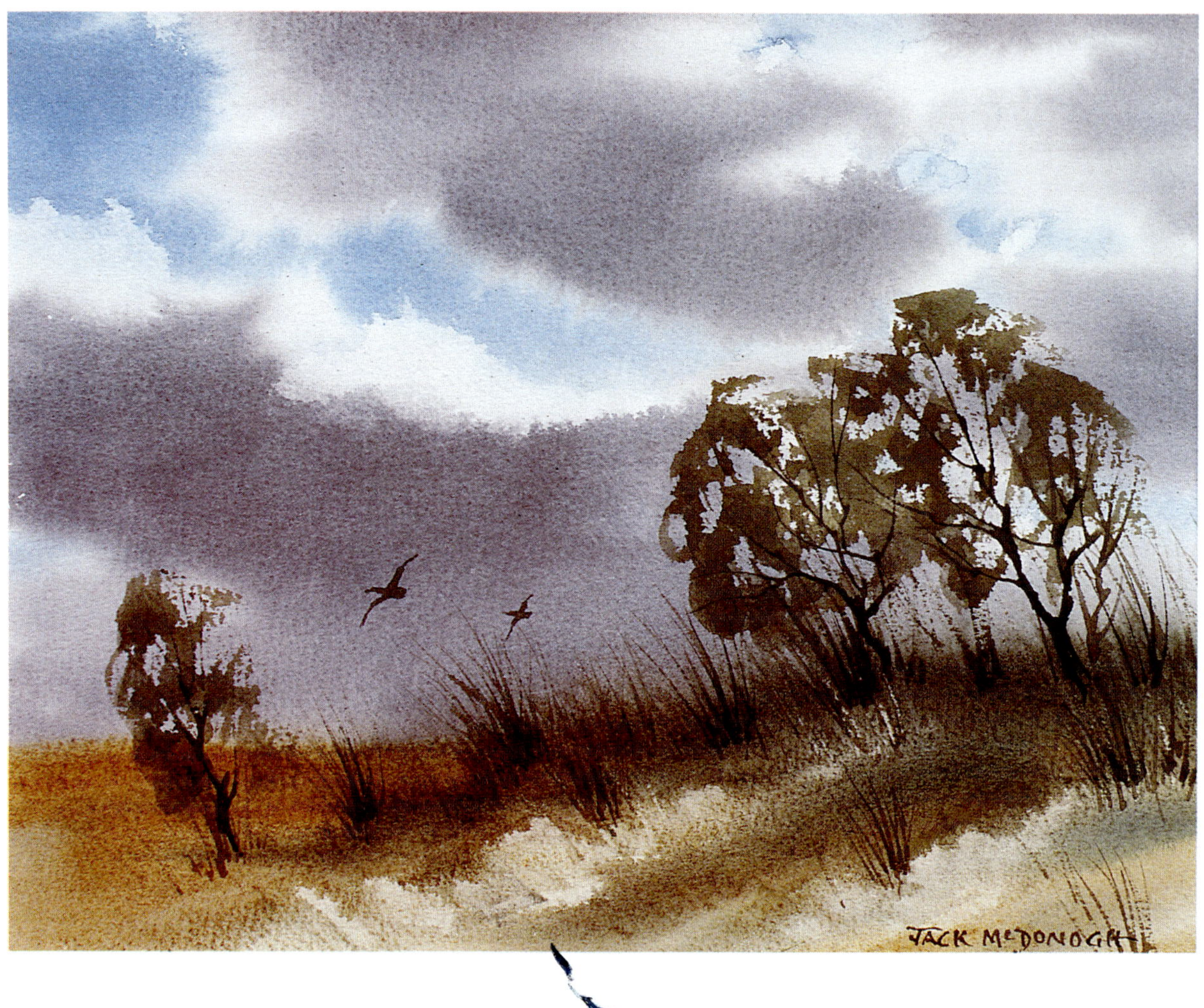

STEP 3

A Paint leaves on trees using raw umber with a touch of antwerp blue. When dry strengthen parts of the leaves with the same mixture.

B Paint bird with a thinned burnt umber.

The gum tree on the hill

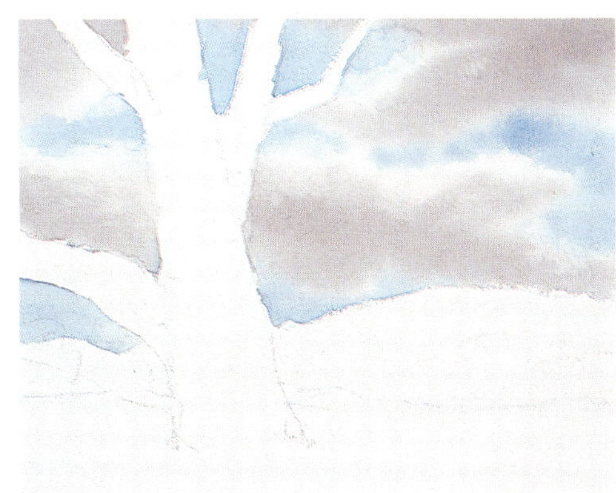

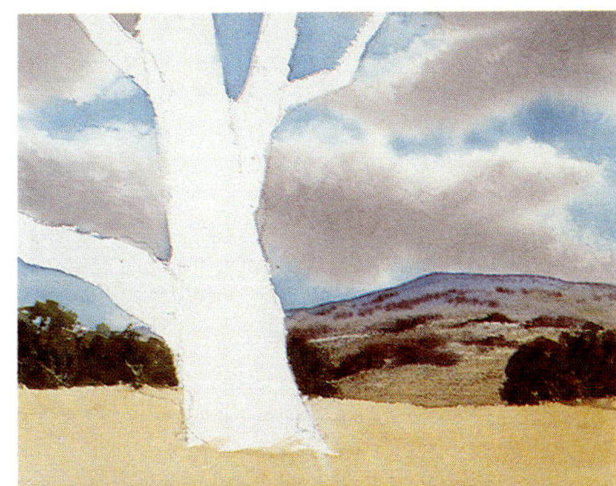

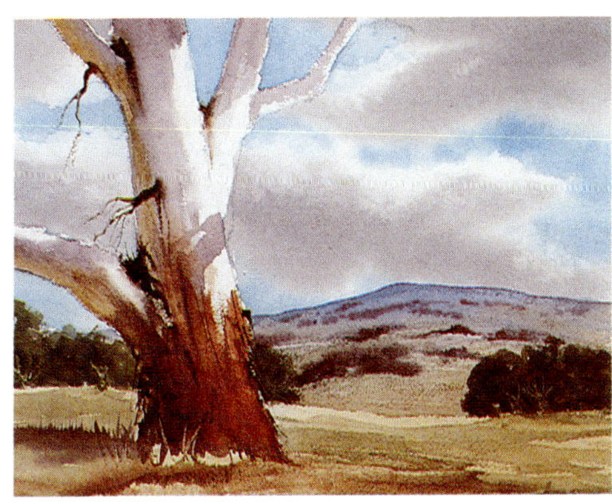

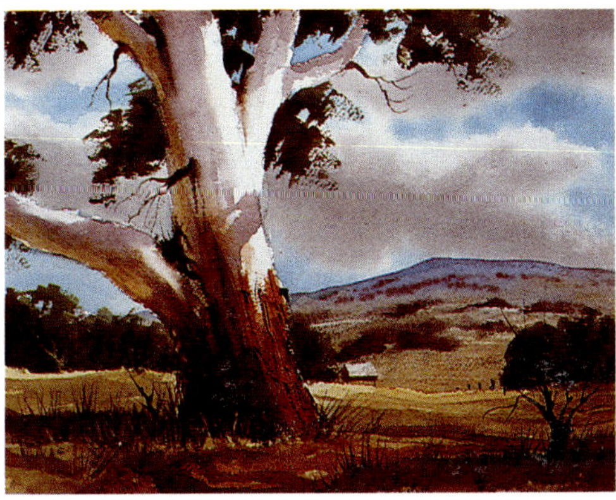

The gum tree on the hill

STEP 1

A Pencil outline of the scene.

B Apply clear water carefully over the sky area, leaving the gum tree shape dry.

C Paint clouds using a light red and winsor blue mixture. Use antwerp blue for the sky area.
Allow to dry.

The gum tree on the hill

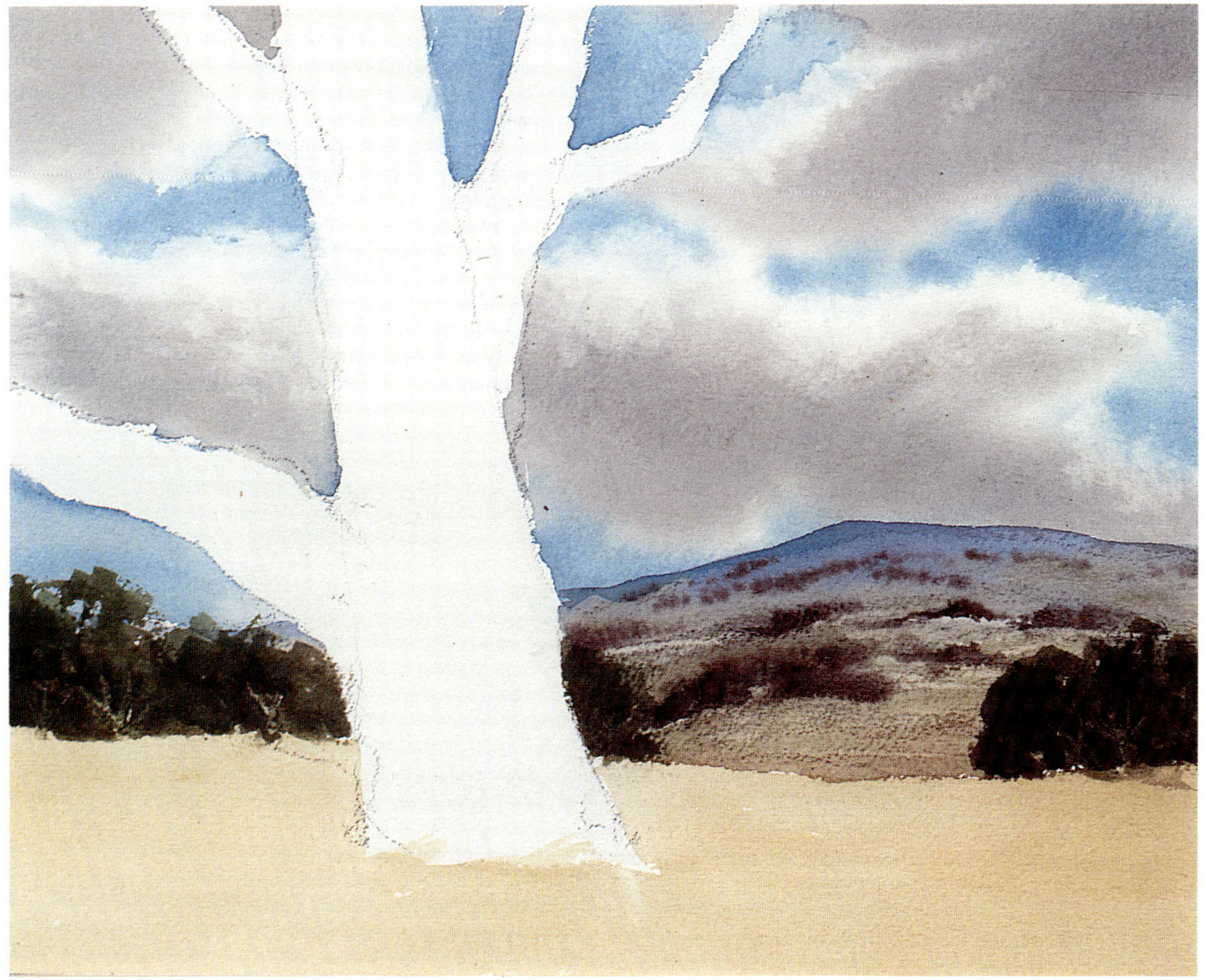

STEP 2

A Paint distant hill with cobalt blue and bring this about half way down the area to be painted. Now work some raw umber into the cobalt to indicate grassy areas and bring this to the edge of the foreground. While this area is still damp add distant trees with a strong mixture of cobalt blue and light red. Use a small round brush.

B Paint middle distance trees using raw umber with a touch of antwerp blue.
Allow to dry.

C Paint foreground with a wash of raw sienna.
Allow to dry.

The gum tree on the hill

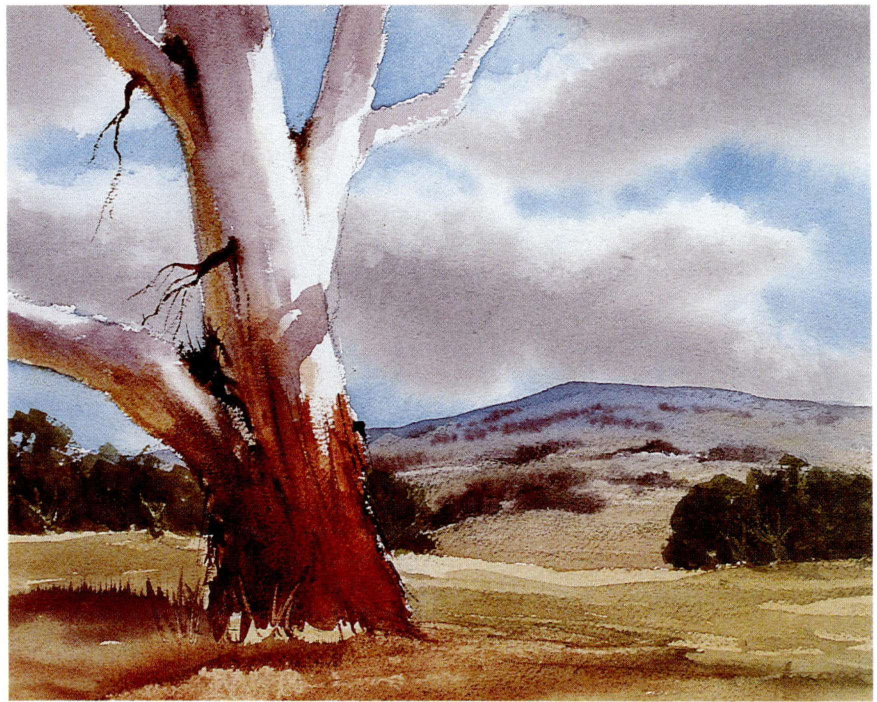

STEP 3

In this step be very careful not to lose your white areas on the trunk.

A The trunk of the tree is painted on a dry surface. Paint shaded areas with a mixture of cobalt blue and light red.

B While this is still wet add some raw sienna on the back edge of the tree to indicate reflected light on the trunk.

C While still wet add some burnt umber at the base of the trunk on the shaded side and then some burnt sienna on the sunny side. Texture with some knife strokes.

D Use some burnt umber with a touch of antwerp blue to indicate where limbs join trunk. Paint the dead dark pieces coming from the trunk with the same mixture. Some strokes of this mixture can be added to the shaded side of the trunk at its base.
Allow to dry.

E Paint a wash of raw sienna with a touch of antwerp blue over some of the grassy foreground. Add some burnt sienna while wet near the tree and texture with the razor blade.
Allow to dry.

F Shadow behind tree using a mixture of cobalt and light red. Use varnish brush on shadow edge while wet.
Allow to dry.

The gum tree on the hill

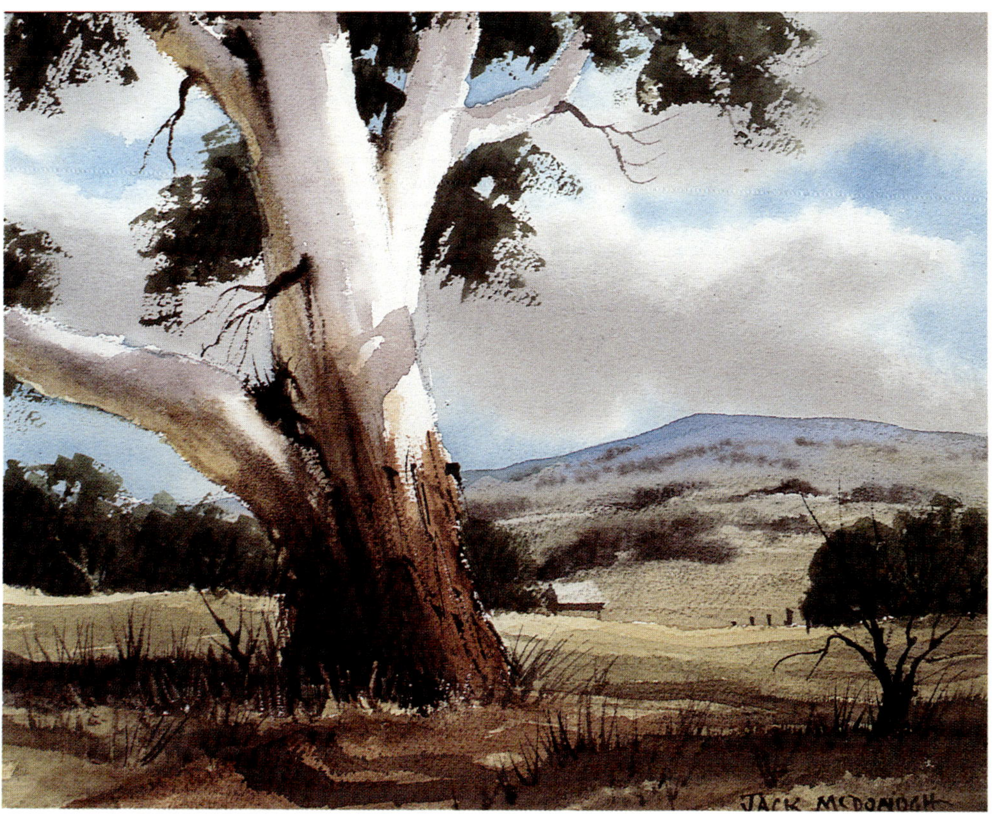

STEP 4

A Paint some cobalt blue (not too strong) into the shaded areas of the middle distance trees.

B Paint leaves of the tree using raw umber with a touch of antwerp blue.

C Add more burnt sienna to the foreground and texture with the razor blade.
Allow to dry.

D Strengthen shadow behind the trunk with more cobalt blue and light red. Make shadow darkest just behind the trunk. Use varnish brush on edge of shadow to indicate grass.

E Paint shadows into foreground using cobalt blue and light red mixture. Use varnish brush to show grassy edge. Note how shadows follow the contours of the earth.
Allow to dry.

F Strengthen leaves in some areas with a mixture of raw umber and a touch of antwerp blue.

G Add twiggy little trees. Use burnt umber with a touch of antwerp blue. Add extra grass strokes with the same mixture.

H 'Lift' and shade shed.

Gums along the road

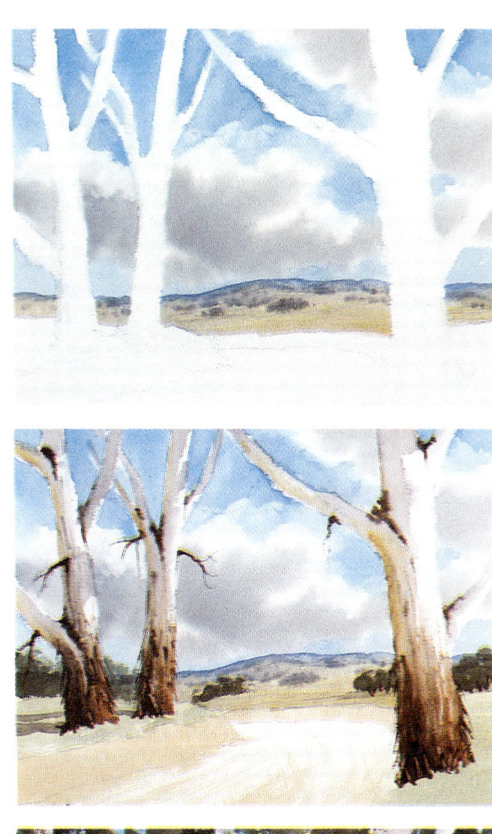

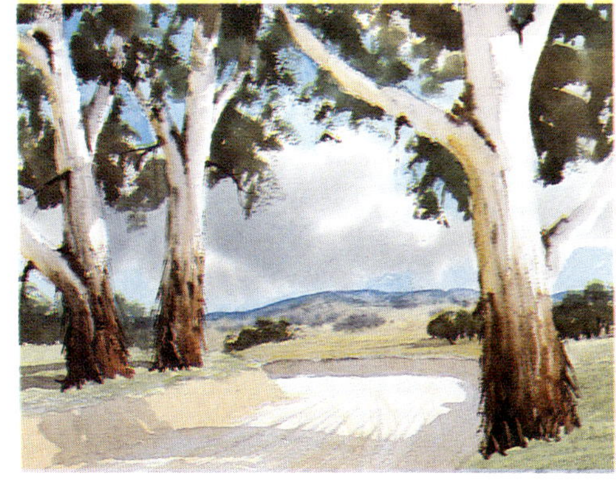

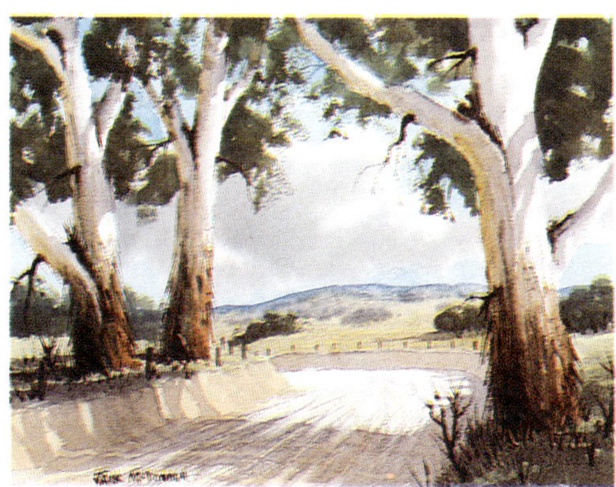

Gums along the road

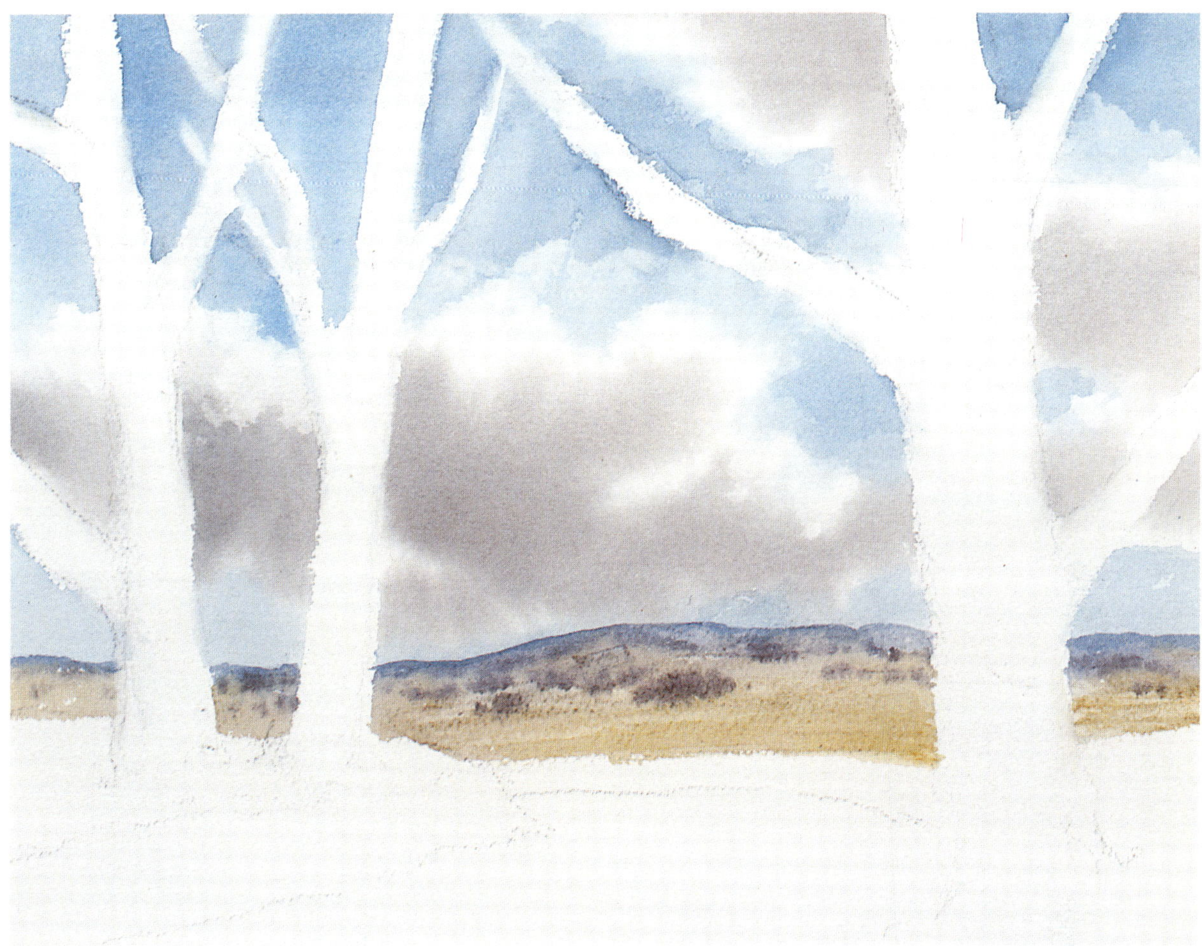

STEP 1

A Light pencil outline of the scene.

B Wet sky area and paint clouds using a light red and winsor blue mixture. Use antwerp blue for the sky area.
Allow to dry.

C Paint distant hills with cobalt blue, then work some raw umber into the still wet cobalt blue, then work some raw sienna to where the wash stops.

While still wet, with a small round brush add the distant trees with a strong mixture of cobalt blue and light red.
Allow to dry.

Gums along the road

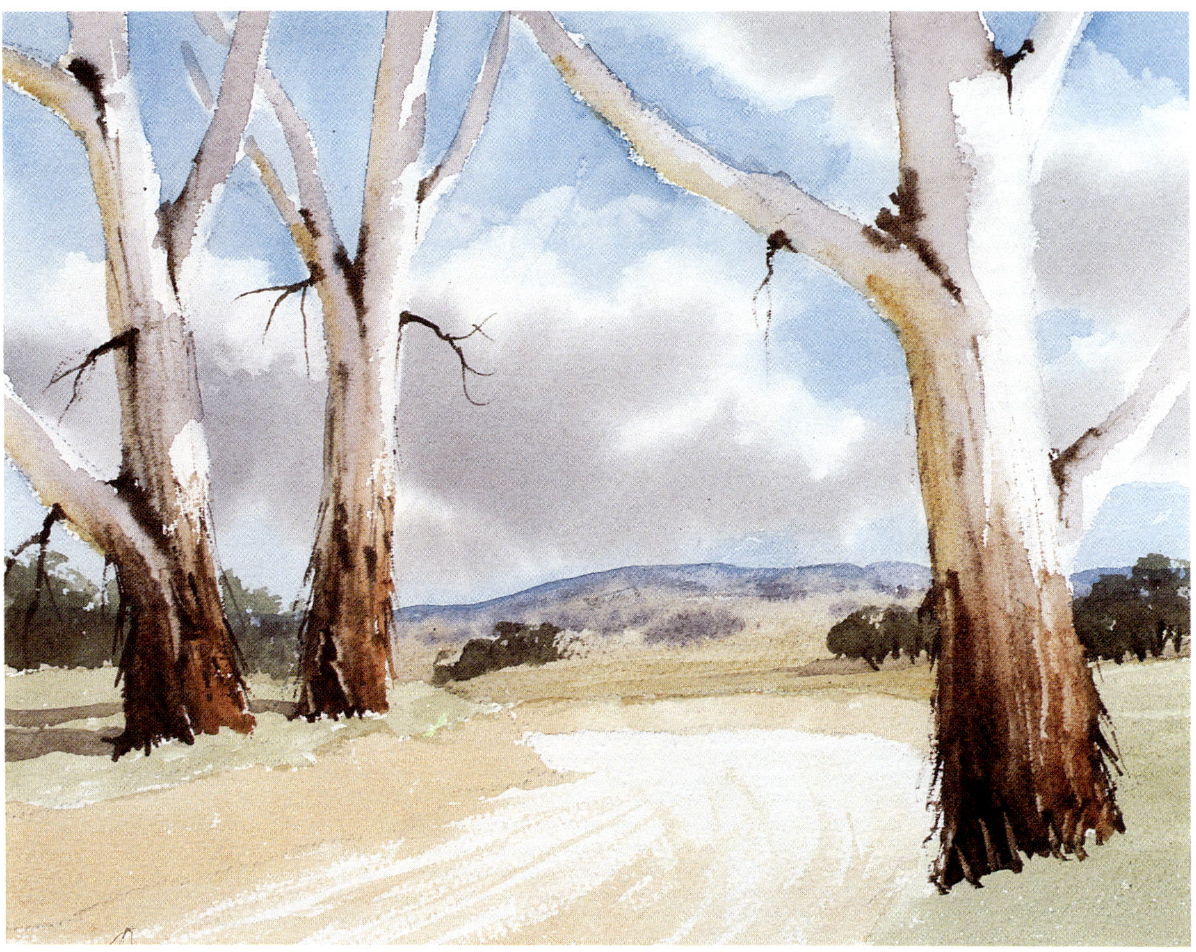

STEP 2

A Paint a weak mixture of raw sienna with a touch of antwerp blue over all foreground grass areas.
Allow to dry.

B Paint middleground trees with raw umber and a touch of antwerp blue.

C Paint gum tree trunks and limbs using the same methods as set out in 'Gum tree on the hill'.

D Paint road and banks of the road with a mixture of raw sienna and light red.

E Shade behind the gum trees on the left using a cobalt blue and light red mixture.

Gums along the road

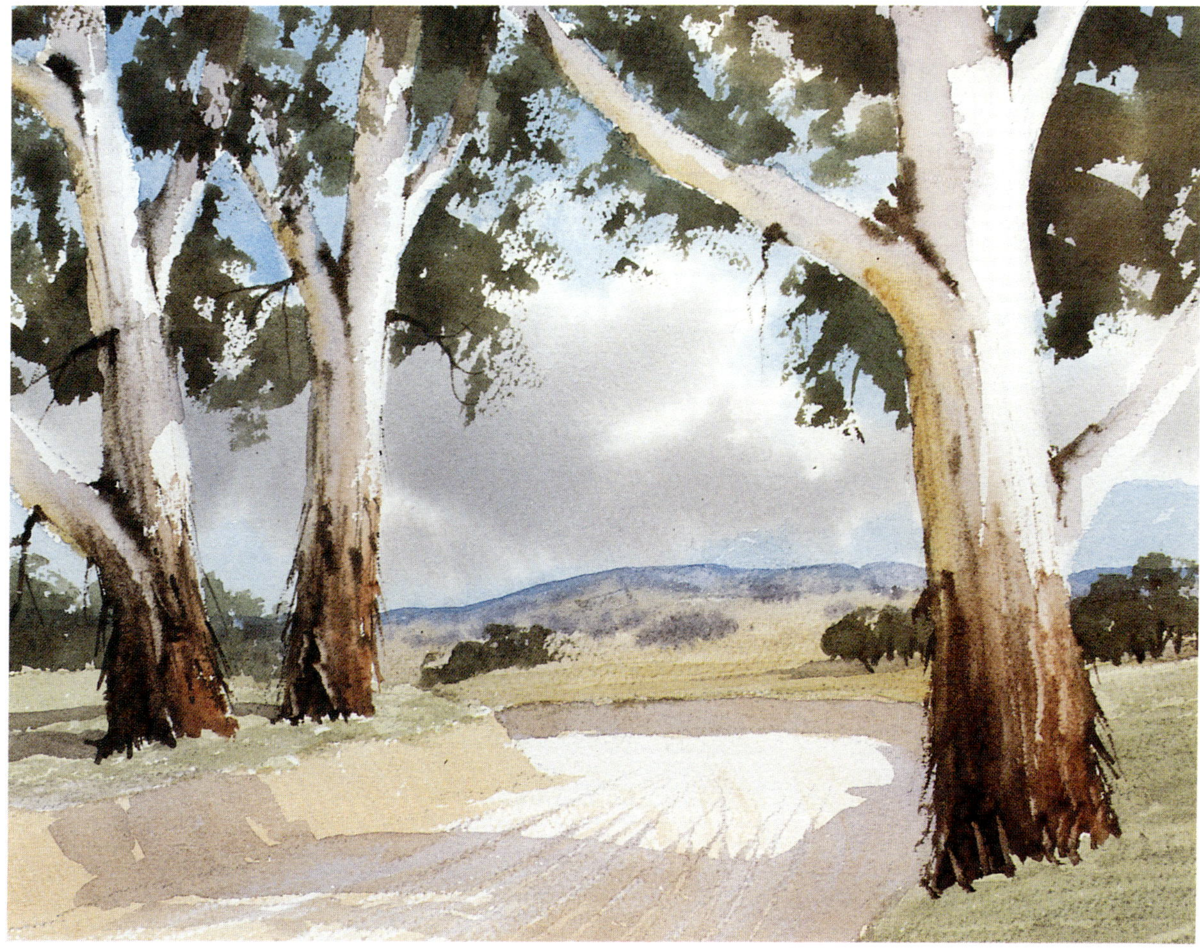

STEP 3

A Paint leaf masses using a mixture of raw umber and a touch of antwerp blue. Notice the gaps in the leaf masses.

B Add shade on the road and banks using a cobalt blue and light red mixture. Notice how the shadows follow the contours of the road and bank. Make some knife strokes in the road shadow while wet to indicate furrows in the road, and paint some small round brush strokes on the road.

C Strengthen the grass in the right hand corner with raw umber with a touch of antwerp blue. Use the same mixture for the grass on the left side foreground.
Allow to dry.

Gums along the road

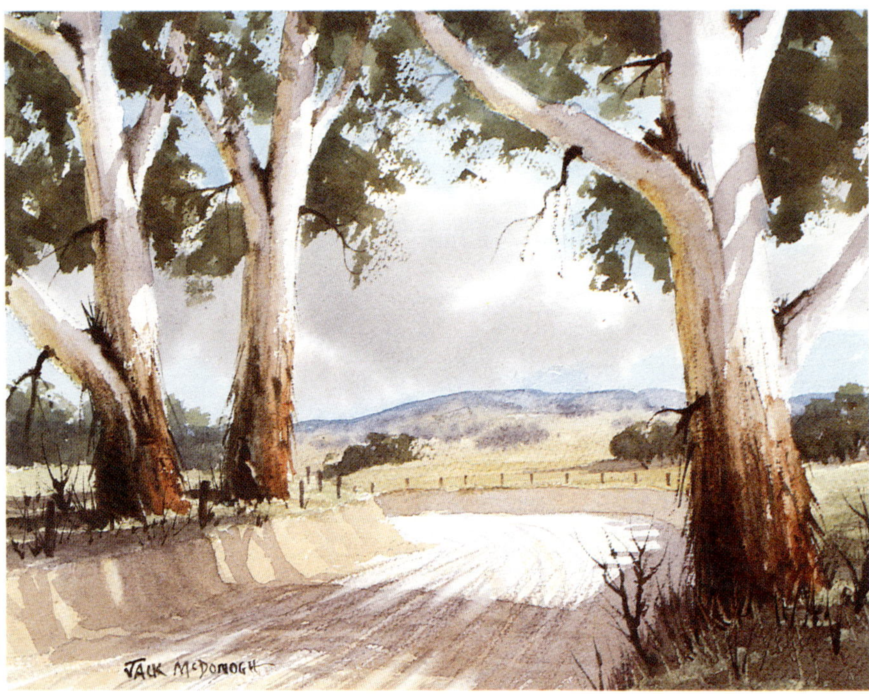

STEP 4

As is my usual custom, I now proceed to strengthen all sections of the painting where I think it is necessary.

A Paint some shade areas into the leaf masses with the same mixture of raw umber and antwerp blue you used for the first wash.

B Strengthen the shadows on the road and banks with a second wash of the same mixture of cobalt blue and light red you used in the first wash. Do not strengthen the shadow on the bank at the bend in the road. We need reflected light on this bank.

C Strengthen right hand corner grass with a mixture of raw umber and antwerp blue. Make some knife strokes and get grassy edge with the varnish brush.

D Shadow behind right hand side gum with cobalt blue and light red mixture. Varnish brush the edge of the shadow and use some knife strokes.

E Paint some shadows on the sunny side of the gum tree trunks with a cobalt blue and light red mixture.

F Using the lift-off brush soften the edge of some of the shadows on the gum trees. Also 'lift-off' at the edges of the road shadow to indicate marks or grooves in the road, and in some small areas on the left bank.

G With a small round brush add some extra strokes at the grass edges and some twiggy pieces. Use burnt umber and with the same colour add the fence posts.

Alice Springs country

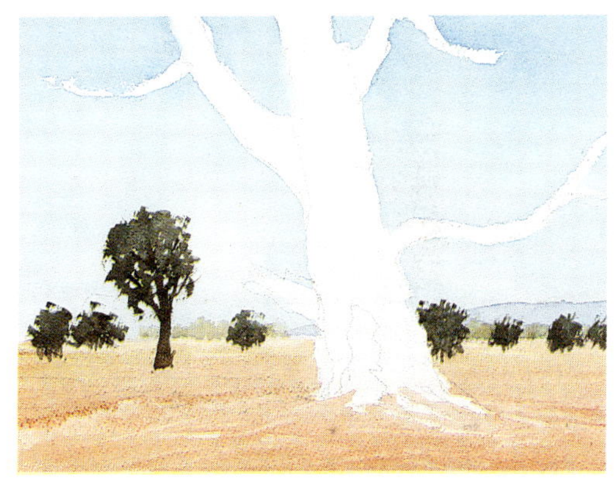

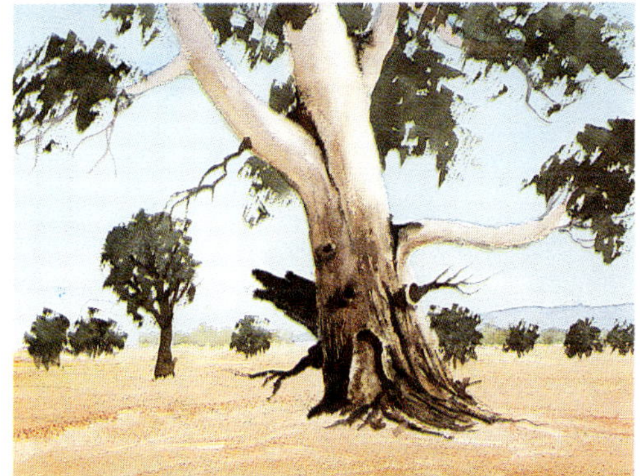

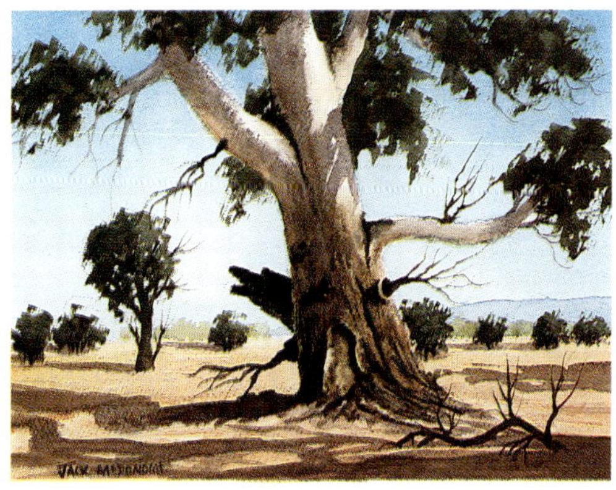

Alice Springs country

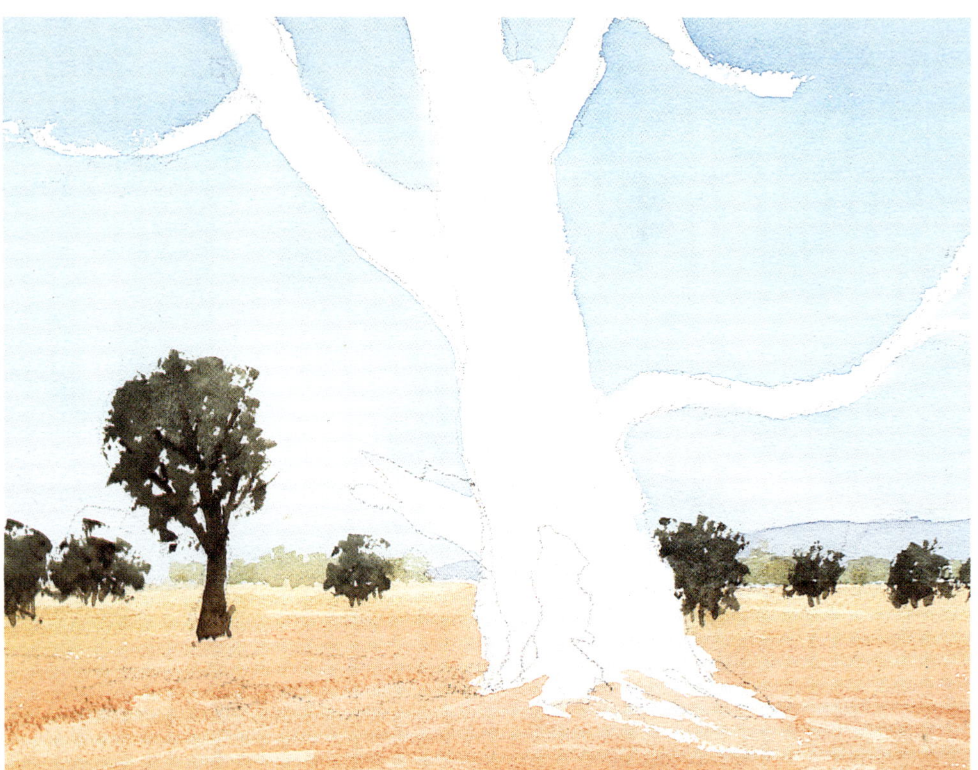

STEP 1

A Pencil outline of scene.

B Wet area of sky with clear water and paint with antwerp blue. Tilt board from the bottom edge to make colour darker at the top of the painting.
Allow to dry.

C Paint earth using a mixture of raw sienna and light red, with more raw sienna in distant earth. Use knife strokes and razor blade to give texture to the earth.
Allow to dry.

D Paint distant hill using cobalt blue.
Allow to dry.

E Paint furthest small trees with raw sienna and a touch of antwerp blue.
Allow to dry.

F Paint all other distant trees with a mixture of raw umber and a touch of antwerp blue for the leaves and burnt umber for the trunks.
Allow to dry.

Alice Springs country

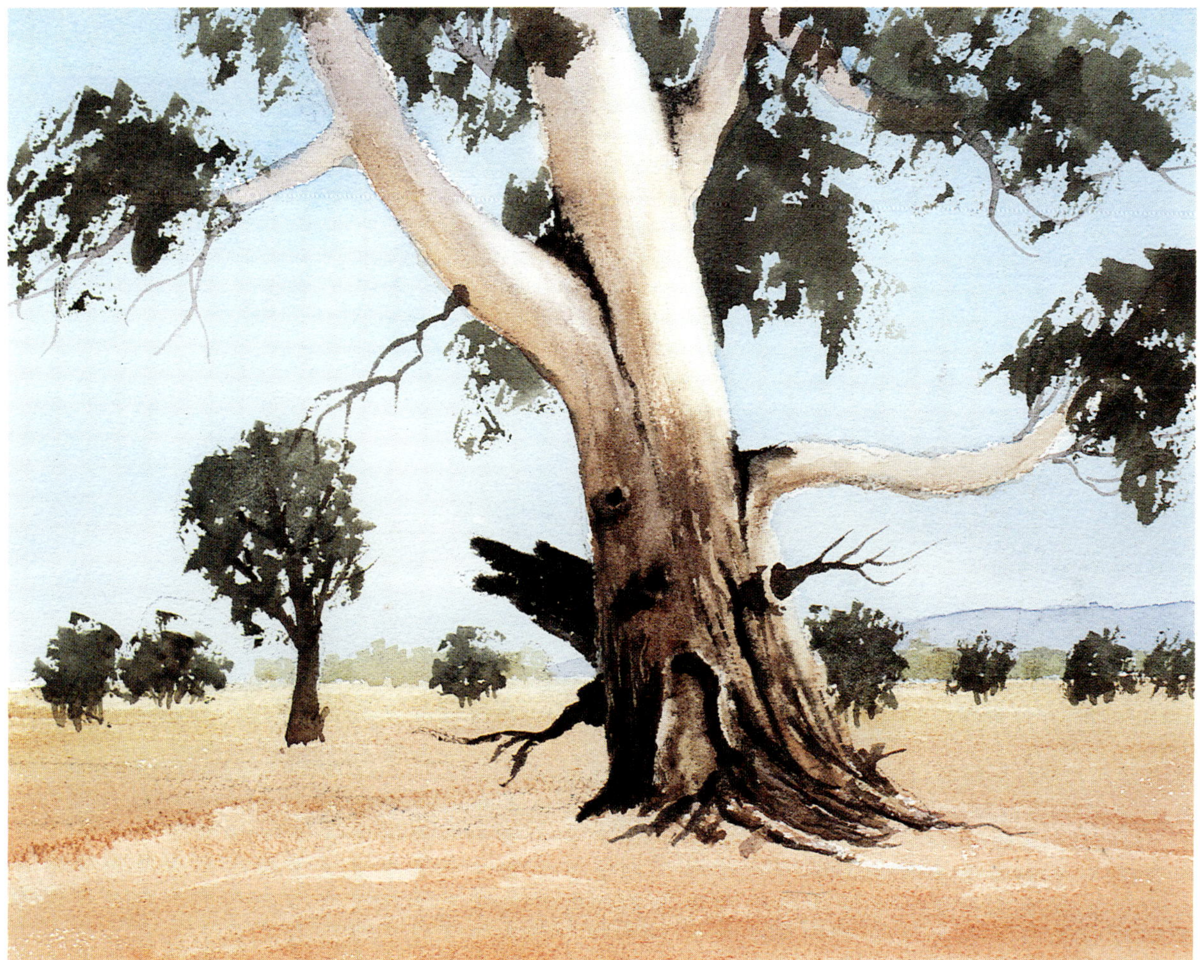

STEP 2

A Paint gum tree using a mixture of cobalt blue and light red for shaded areas, making sure to leave some white areas on the sunny side of the tree.

B Paint a mixture of raw sienna with some light red on the back edge of the tree on the shaded side to show reflected light.

C While still wet work burnt umber into the base of the trunk. In some darker parts add a touch of antwerp blue to the burnt umber. Allow to dry.

D Paint leaves using a mixture of raw umber with a touch of antwerp blue.
Allow to dry.

Alice Springs country

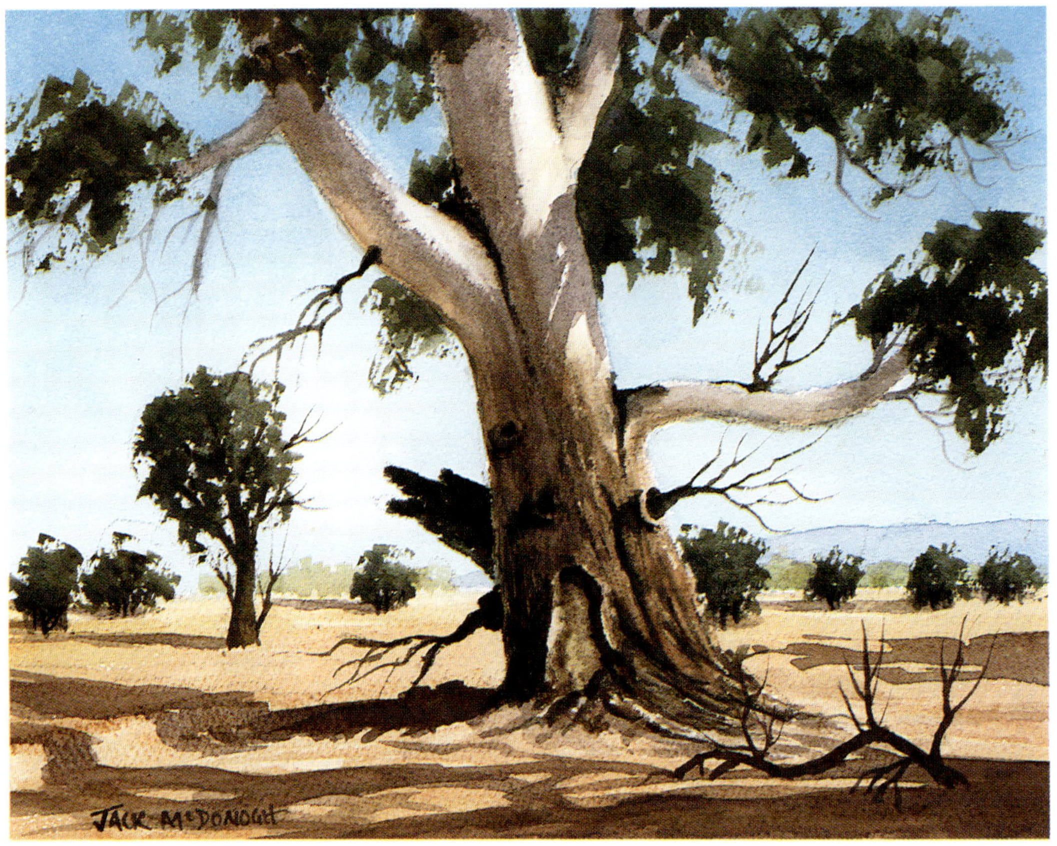

STEP 3

A With a large brush add another wash of antwerp blue to the sky, starting at the top of the picture.

Paint onto the dry surface and fade the extra colour out about half way down with the use of a tissue.

B Strengthen shadows on trunk and limbs with a cobalt blue and light red mixture.

C Work cobalt blue into the shaded areas of all distant trees.

D Paint shade on ground from all trees with a mixture of cobalt blue and light red.
Allow to dry.

E Add and strengthen dead wood on trees. Use burnt umber with some antwerp blue.

F Strengthen shaded parts of leaf masses. Use a mixture of raw umber with a touch of antwerp blue.

G Strengthen shadow colours on the ground in foreground and behind the gum tree at the base. Use a strong cobalt blue and light red mixture. With this colour paint the dead limb on the ground when shaded areas are dry.

Dusk by the creek

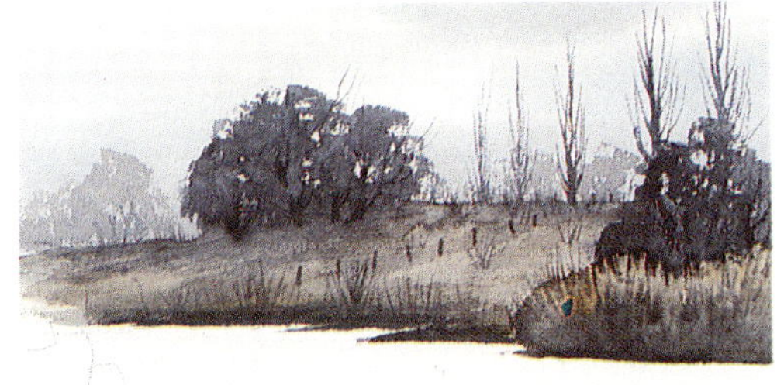

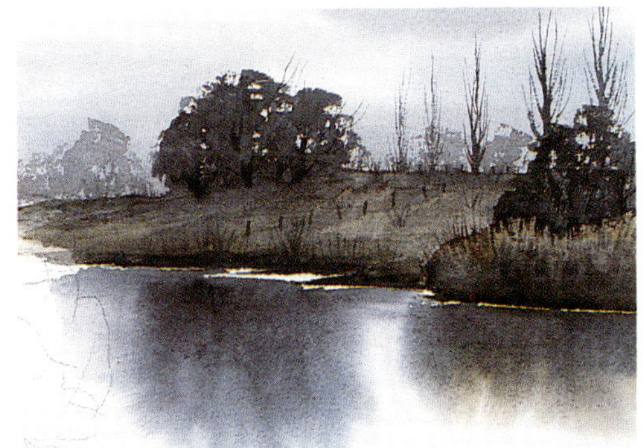

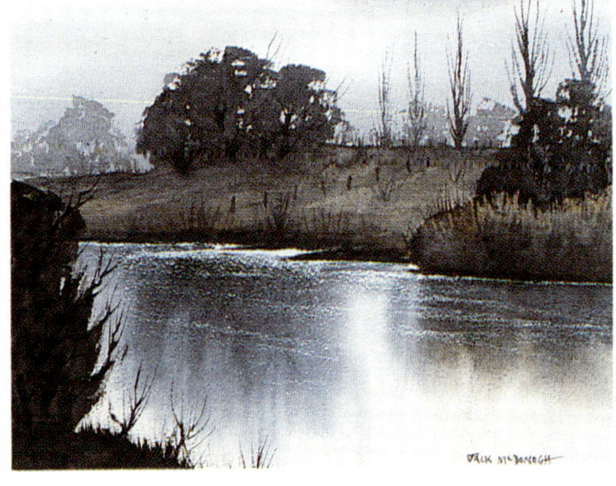

Dusk by the creek

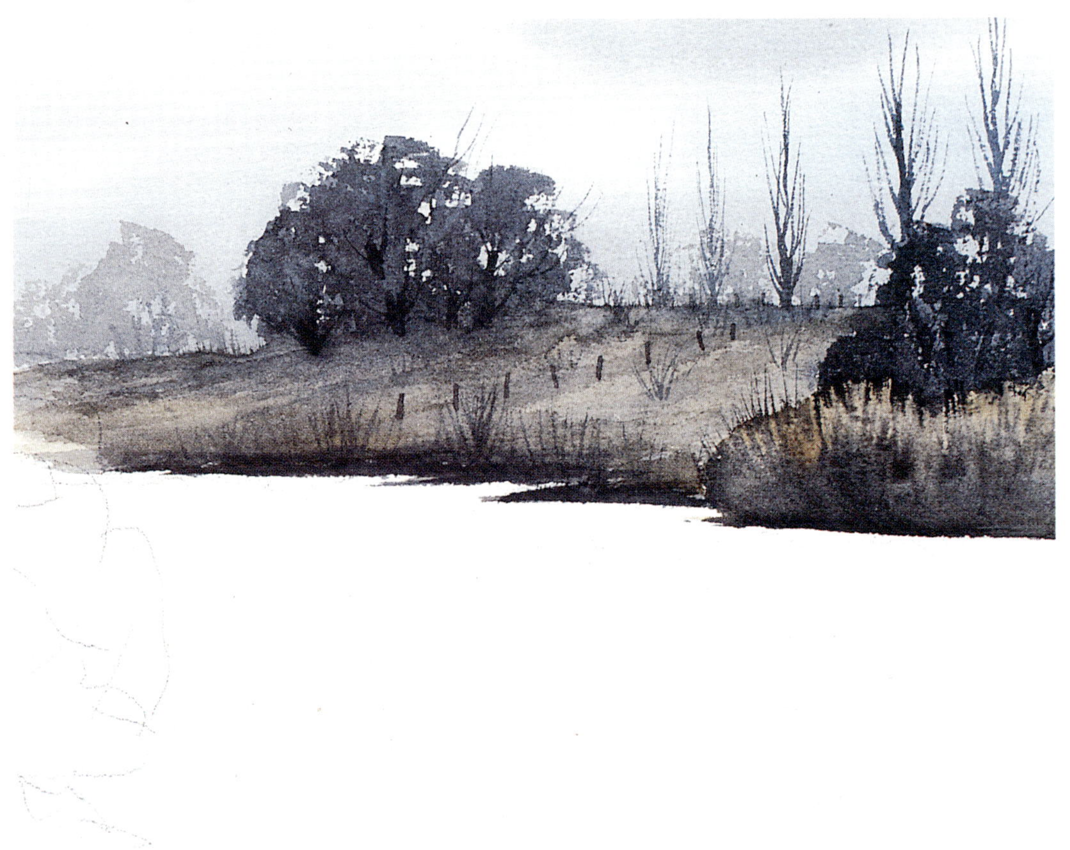

STEP 1

Most of this picture is painted with the two colours winsor blue and light red. Some raw umber is added in parts.

A Light pencil outline of the scene.

B Wet sky area with clear water and paint clouds using a winsor blue and light red mixture. Keep this to a fairly weak mixture and leaning towards the blue.
Allow to dry.

C Paint distant trees and poplars with the same mixture as used for the clouds. Some nearer poplars have a slightly stronger mixture.
Allow to dry.

D Paint the darker trees with a strong mixture of winsor blue and light red.
Allow to dry.

E Paint grassy slopes with a mixture of winsor blue and light red (about the same strength as used in the sky) with some raw umber added, and treat bushy clump on right hand side with the same mixture.
Allow to dry then paint fence posts.

Dusk by the creek

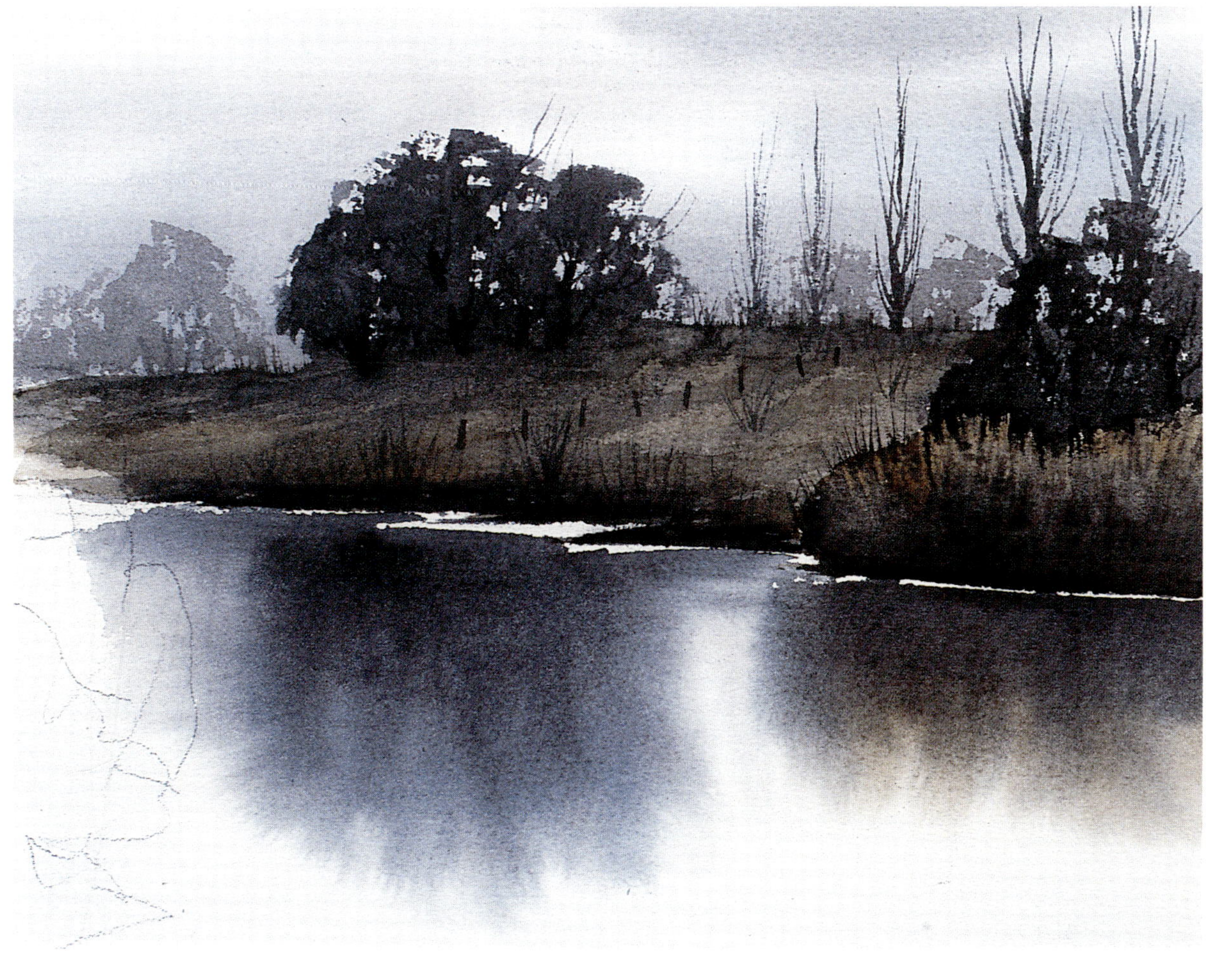

STEP 2

A Paint reflections by first covering the water area with clear water and painting a strong mixture of winsor blue and light red onto the surface.

Add some raw umber to the right hand side reflection. Then tilt the board slightly from the back to get a small run vertically downwards in the reflections.

Note the white areas left near the shore.
Allow to dry.

Dusk by the creek

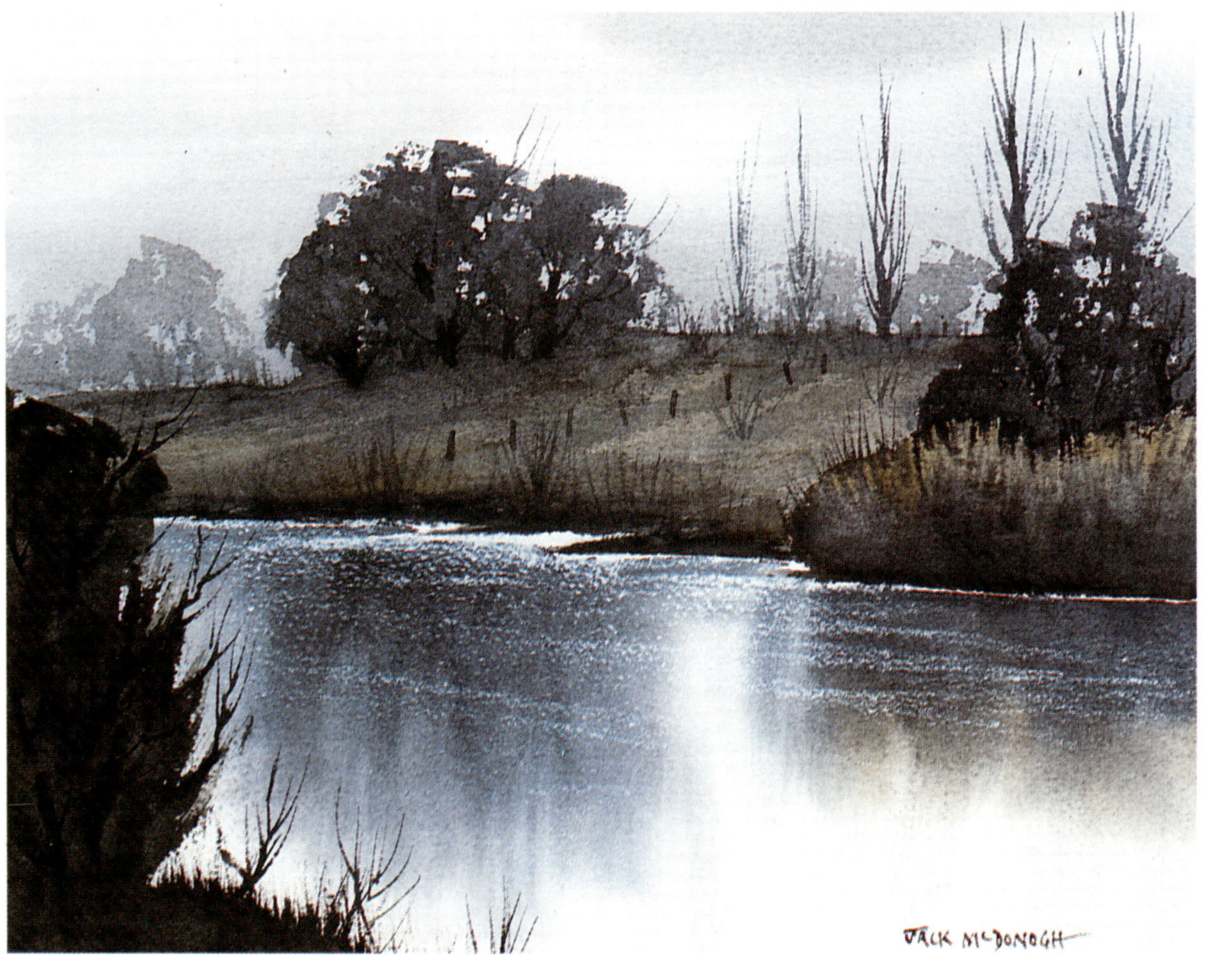

STEP 3

A On the dry surface and with a large brush, darken the reflections near the shoreline with a mixture of winsor blue and light red.

B Use a lift-off brush to give some lighter parts to the reflections. Note that they come vertically down the picture.

C Make sure the surface of the paper is dry then, with the razor blade, scratch some highlights and sparkle to the water.

D Paint left foreground using raw umber, winsor blue and light red. Use the varnish brush while the washes are wet to give the grassy edge.

Break in the blizzard

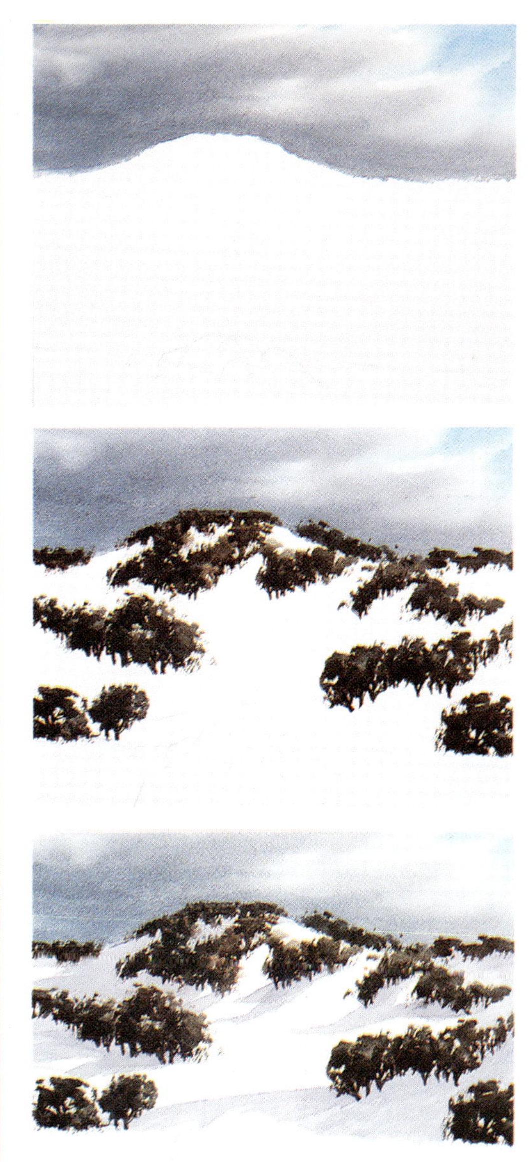

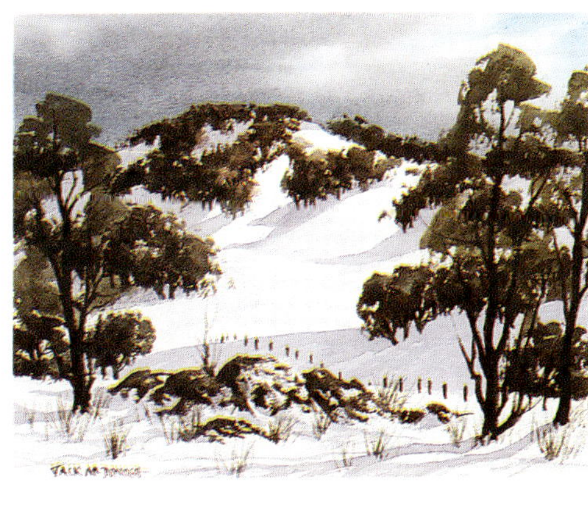

Break in the blizzard

STEP 1

An important point to keep in mind when painting snow scenes is that you are using the white of your paper to indicate snow.

A Pencil outline of scene.

B Wet sky area and paint clouds. Use a strong mixture of light red and winsor blue. Use antwerp blue for sky colour.
Allow to dry.

Break in the blizzard

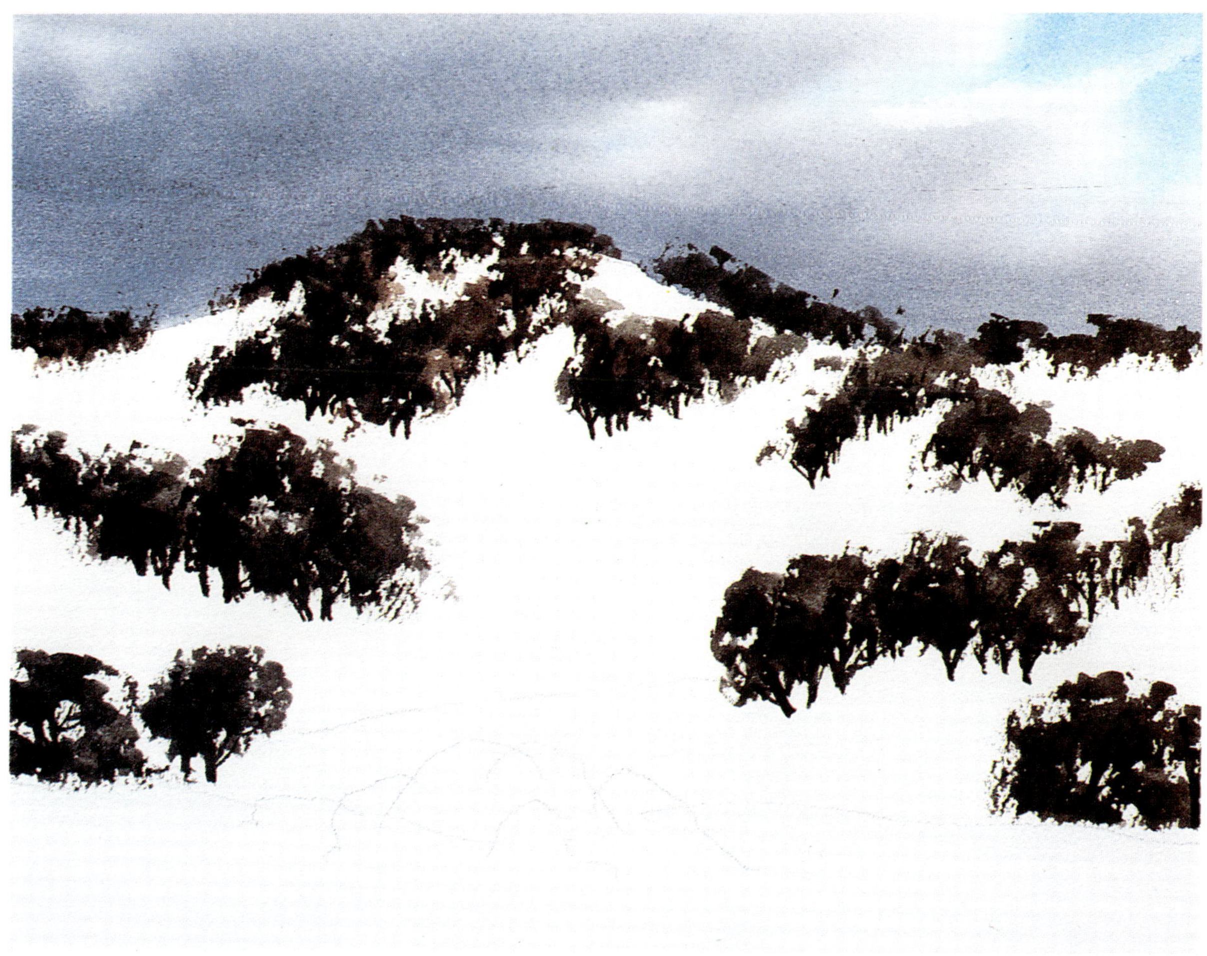

STEP 2

A Paint trees using burnt umber.

B Paint trees in shaded areas and, to indicate shade, use the burnt umber darkened with a touch of antwerp blue.
Allow to dry.

C Using a small round brush indicate trunks and limbs of trees with the same mixture as used in Step 2B.
Allow to dry.

Break in the blizzard

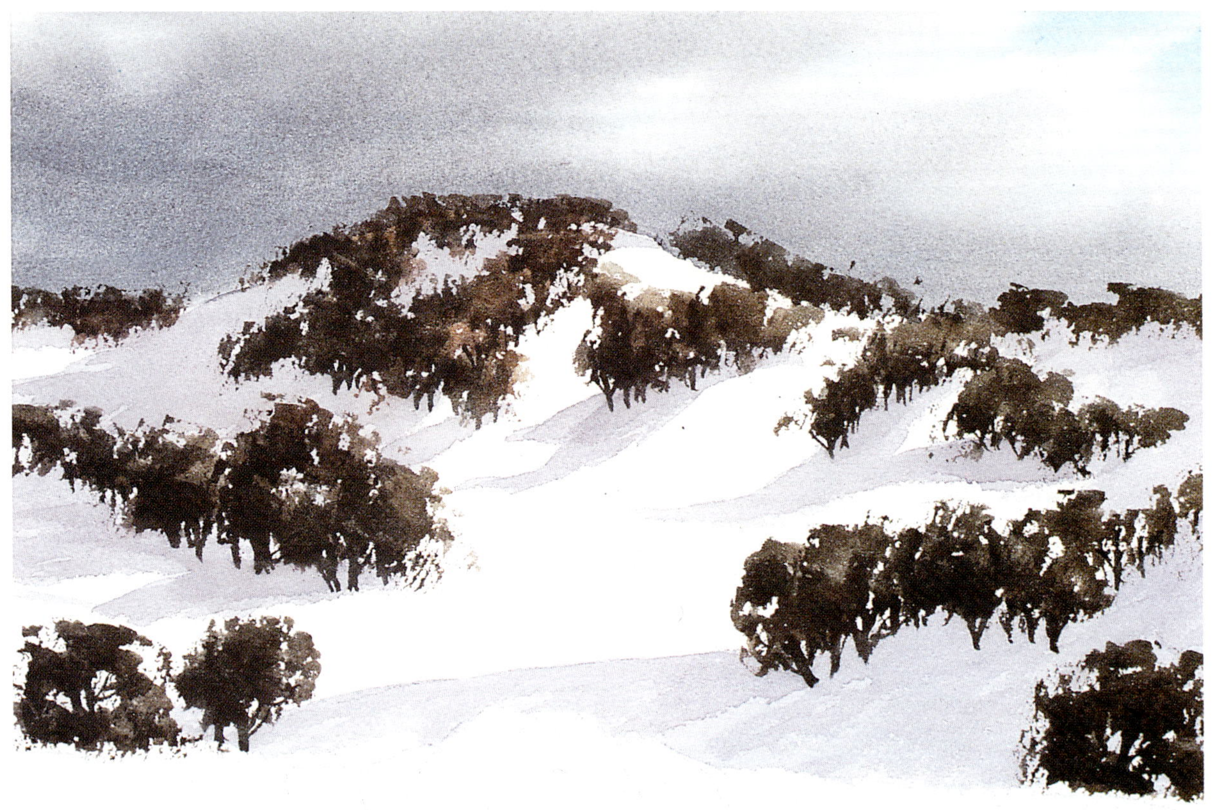

STEP 3

A Indicate snow areas in shade. Use cobalt blue with a very small touch of light red.
Allow to dry.

B Strengthen areas of snow under trees with another application of cobalt blue and light red.

Break in the blizzard

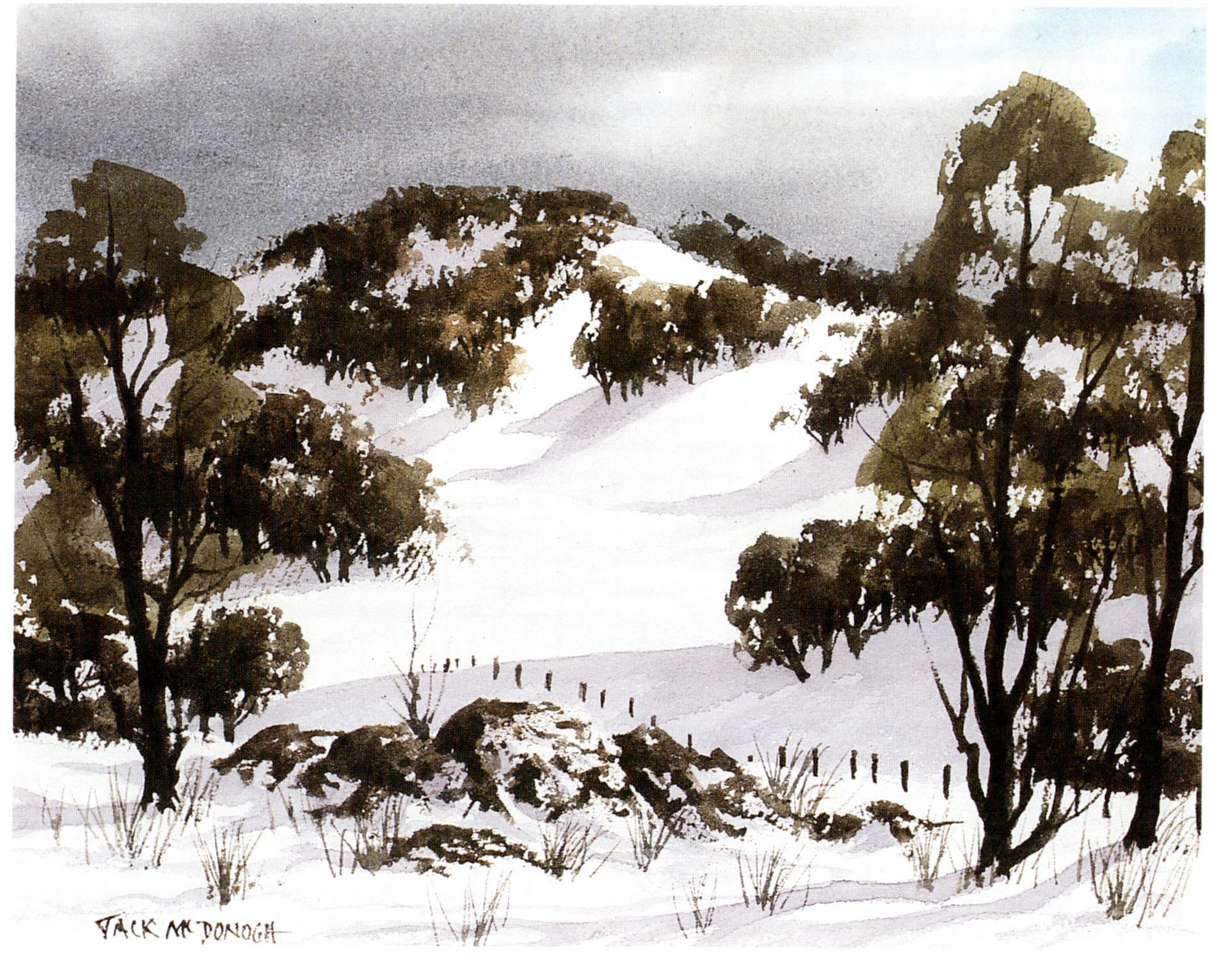

STEP 4

A Paint rocks using burnt umber. Darken shaded side of rocks with burnt umber and a touch of antwerp blue.

B Paint trees on each side of the foreground with burnt umber and antwerp blue. Paint trunks and limbs first.
Allow to dry.

C Add leaves to trees using raw umber with a touch of antwerp blue.

D Indicate shadows from trees and rocks on snow. Use cobalt blue with a touch of light red.

E Indicate grassy areas with a fine round brush.
Use raw umber.

F Add some very pale washes of cobalt blue and light red in parts.

Winter by the creek

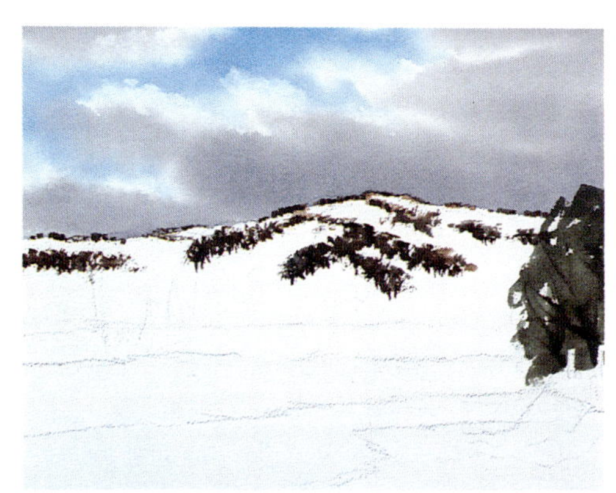

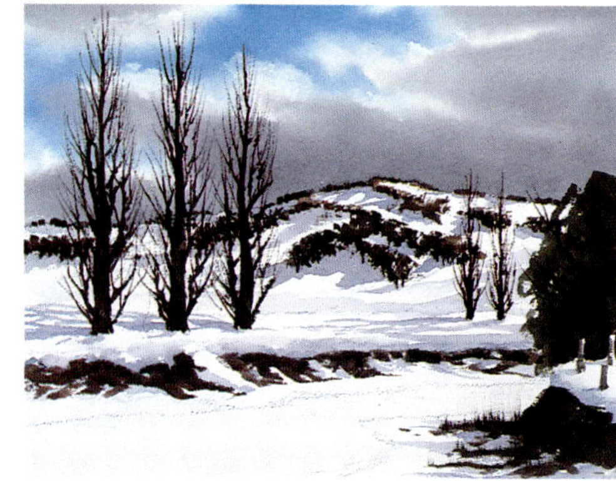

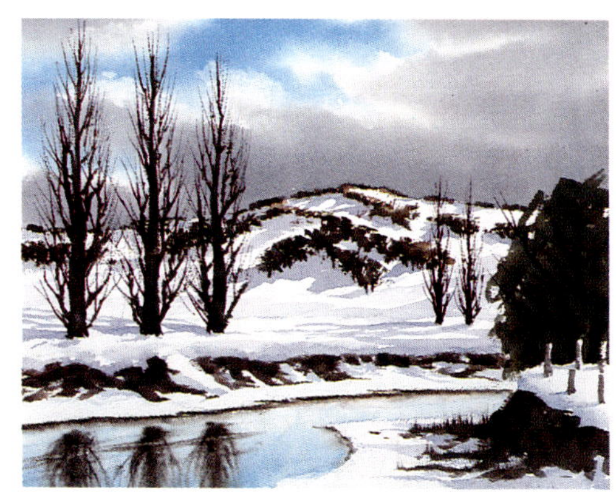

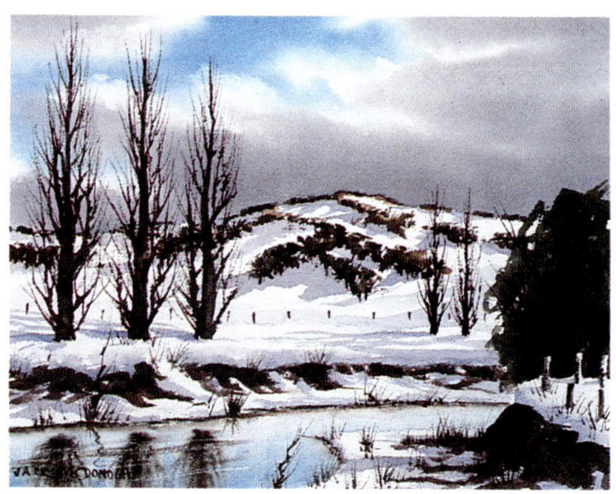

Winter by the creek

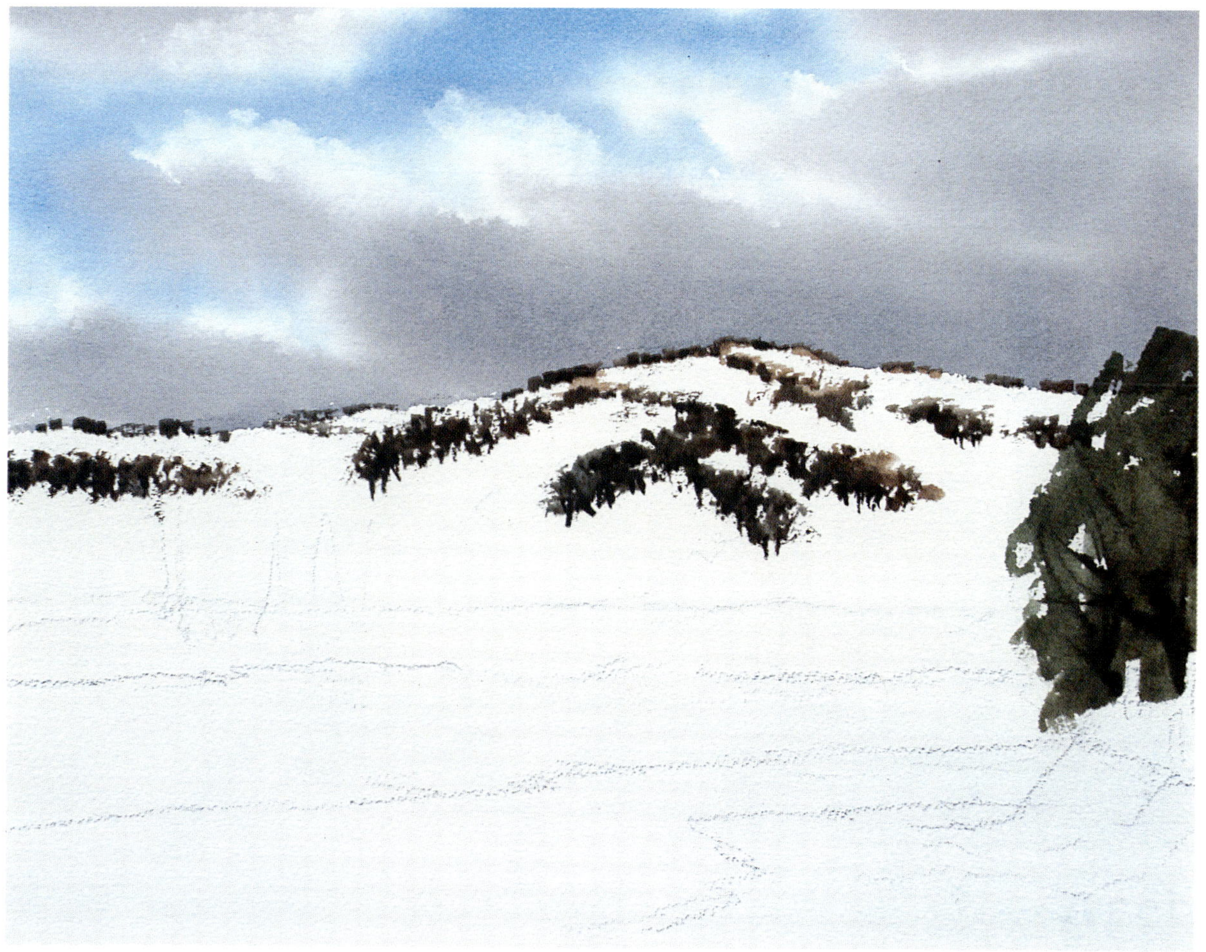

STEP 1

A Pencil outline of scene.

B Wet sky area and paint clouds with light red and winsor blue. Allow to dry.

C Paint distant trees using burnt umber. Shaded areas of trees are shown with burnt umber and a touch of antwerp blue.

D Paint trees on right hand side using a raw umber and antwerp blue mixture.

Winter by the creek

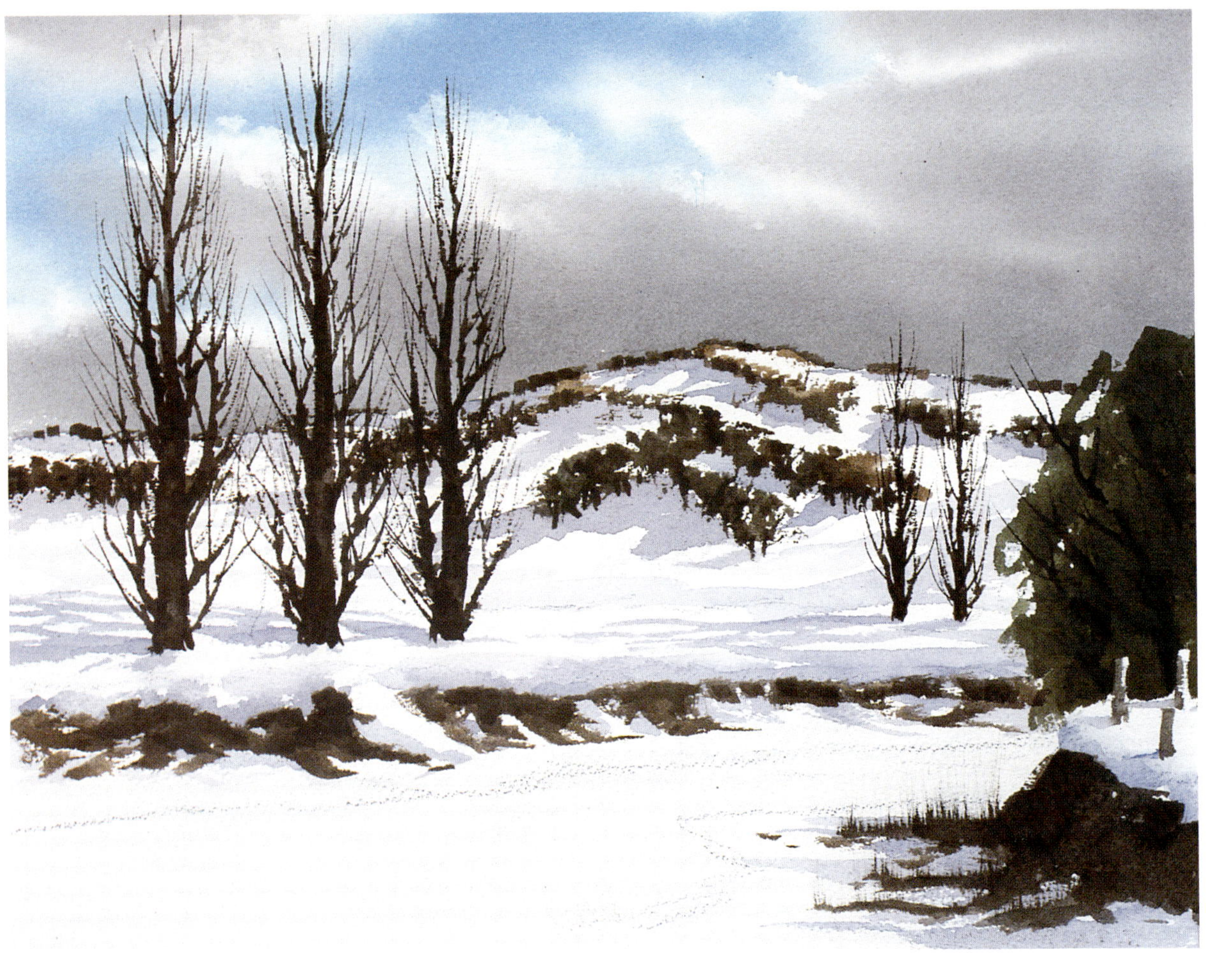

STEP 2

A Indicate shaded areas of snow on the hill with cobalt blue and a touch of light red.

B Paint poplar trees with burnt umber darkened with a touch of winsor blue.

C Indicate earth on the banks of the creek with burnt umber. Paint darker areas with some winsor blue added to the burnt umber. Allow to dry.

D Put shade on snow along the banks with cobalt blue and light red as used in Step 2A and also behind poplars.

E Strengthen trees on right with a wash of raw umber and antwerp blue.

Winter by the creek

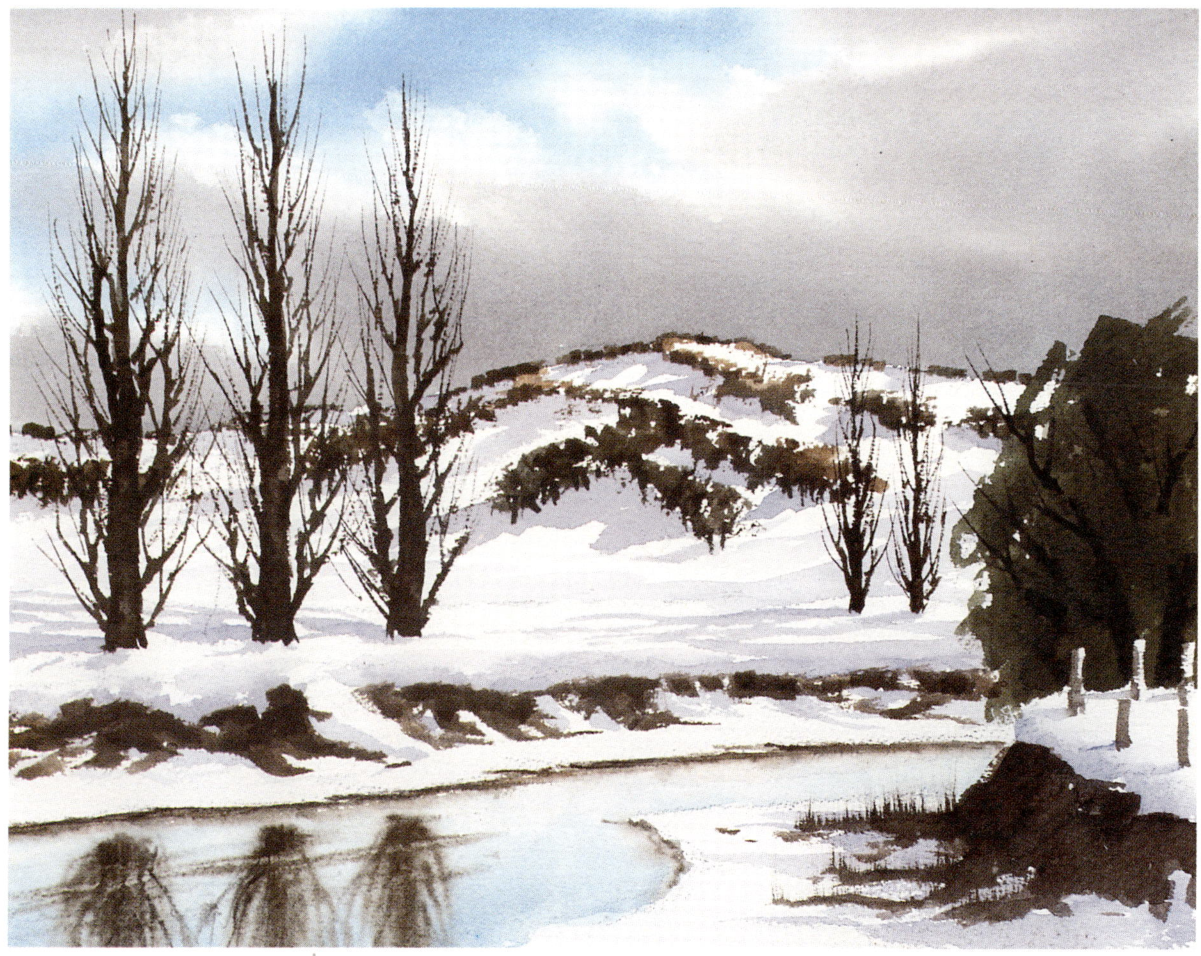

STEP 3

The main exercise in this step is to paint the reflections in the water. The surface of the water area is wet with clear water and the 'wet-in-wet' technique used.

A Wet water area with clear water.

B Add antwerp blue with the colour stronger in the foreground.

C Darken edge of water on further bank with burnt umber.

D Paint poplar reflections using burnt umber with a touch of winsor blue.

E Put some knife strokes through the poplar reflections. Allow to dry.

Winter by the creek

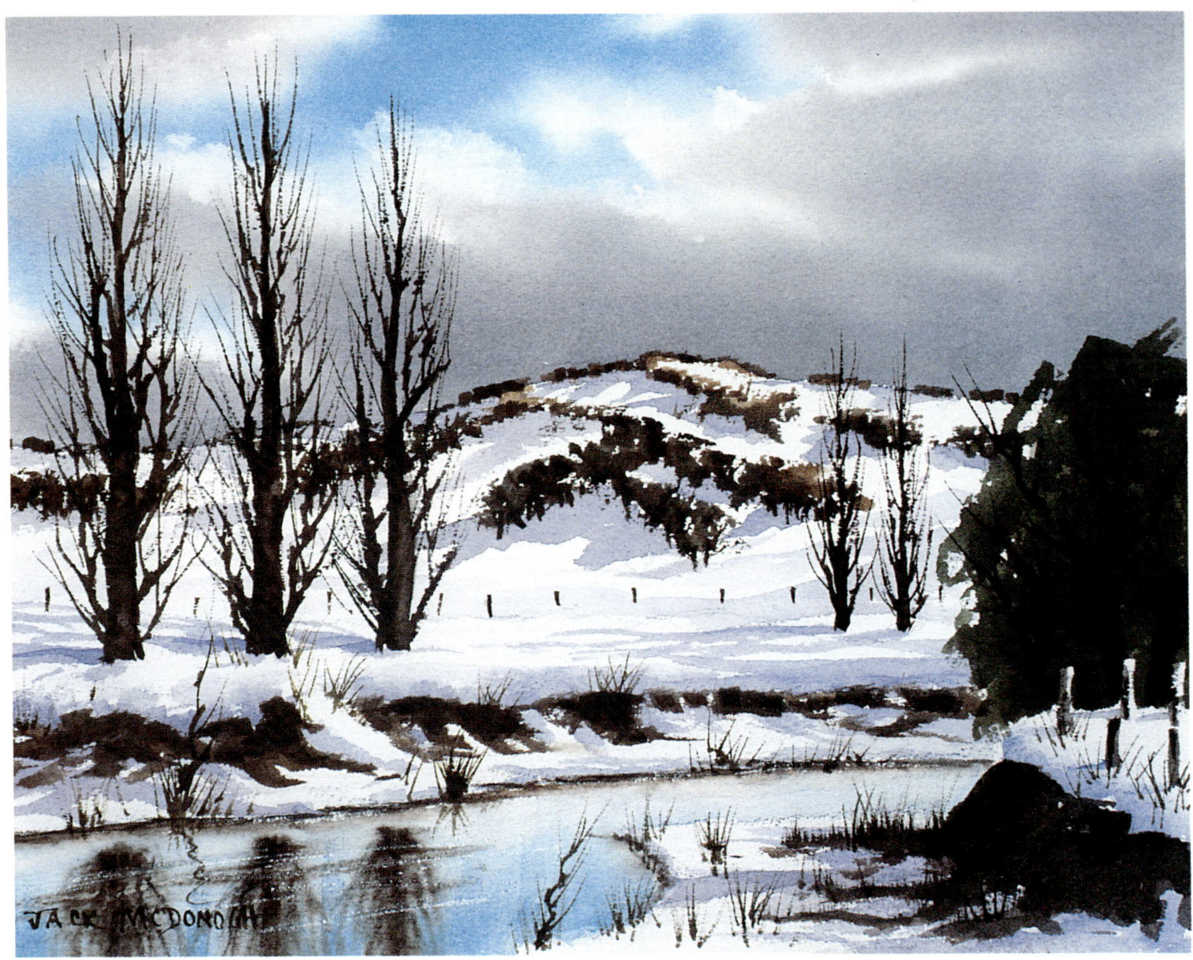

STEP 4

A Strengthen shadows on the snow along the banks and just behind the poplar trees. The shadow is strongest just behind the base of the trees. Use the same mixture of cobalt blue and a touch of light red. Allow to dry.

B Strengthen the reflections of the poplars with some burnt umber with a touch of winsor blue. Do this on the dry surface. Allow to dry.

C Scratch some highlights on the water with the razor blade.

D Add grass and twiggy pieces appearing through the snow. Use burnt umber.

Snow in the bush

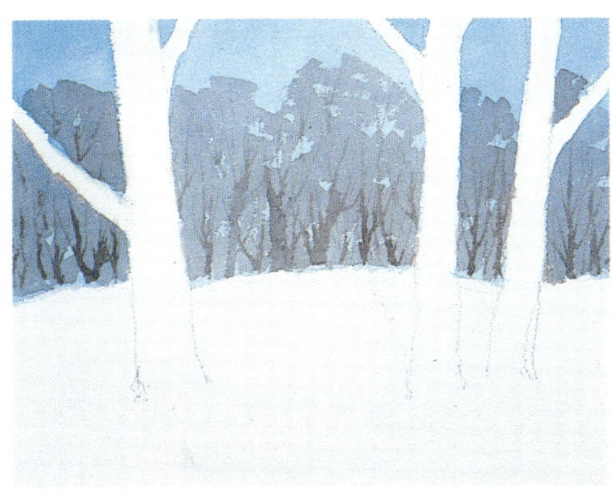

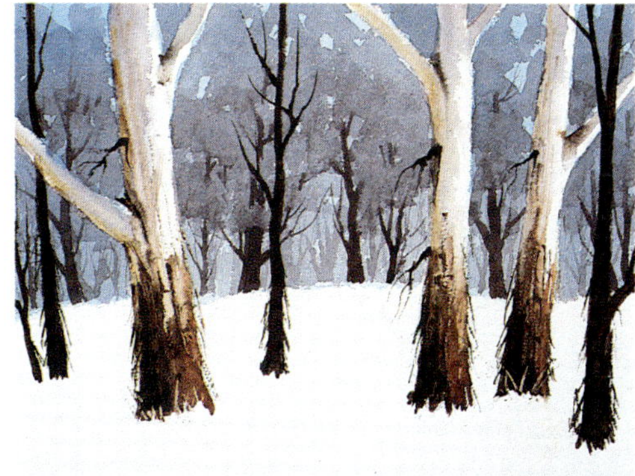

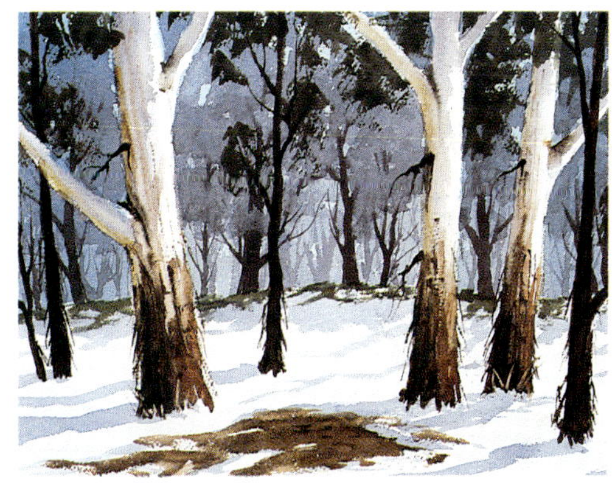

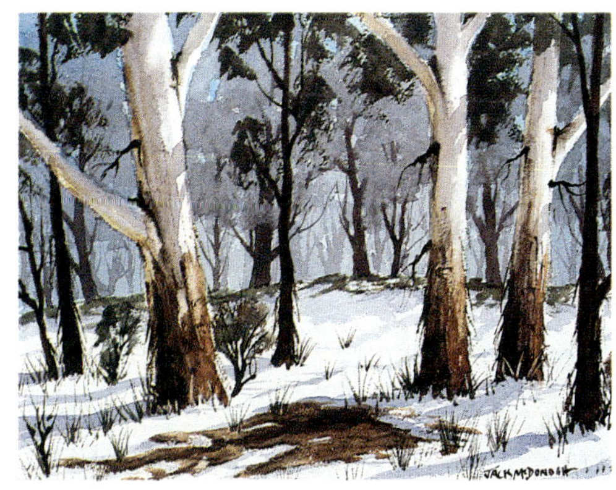

Snow in the bush

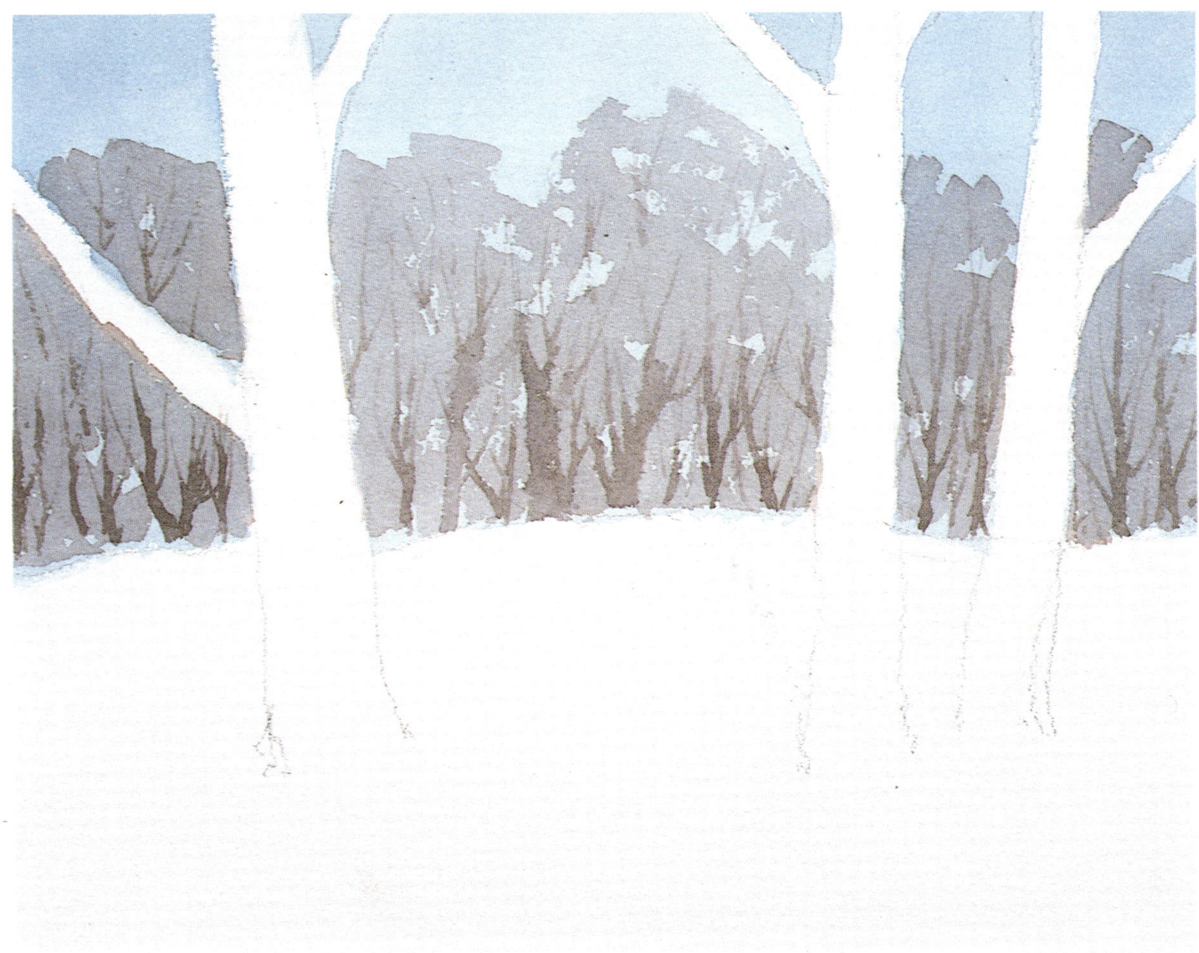

STEP 1

A Pencil outline of the scene.

B Paint clear water over sky area leaving trees dry.

C Paint a wash of antwerp blue into wet area and tilt the board up from the bottom edge to get stronger blue at top of painting.
Allow to dry.

D With a light mixture of cobalt blue and light red paint the distant trees.

Snow in the bush

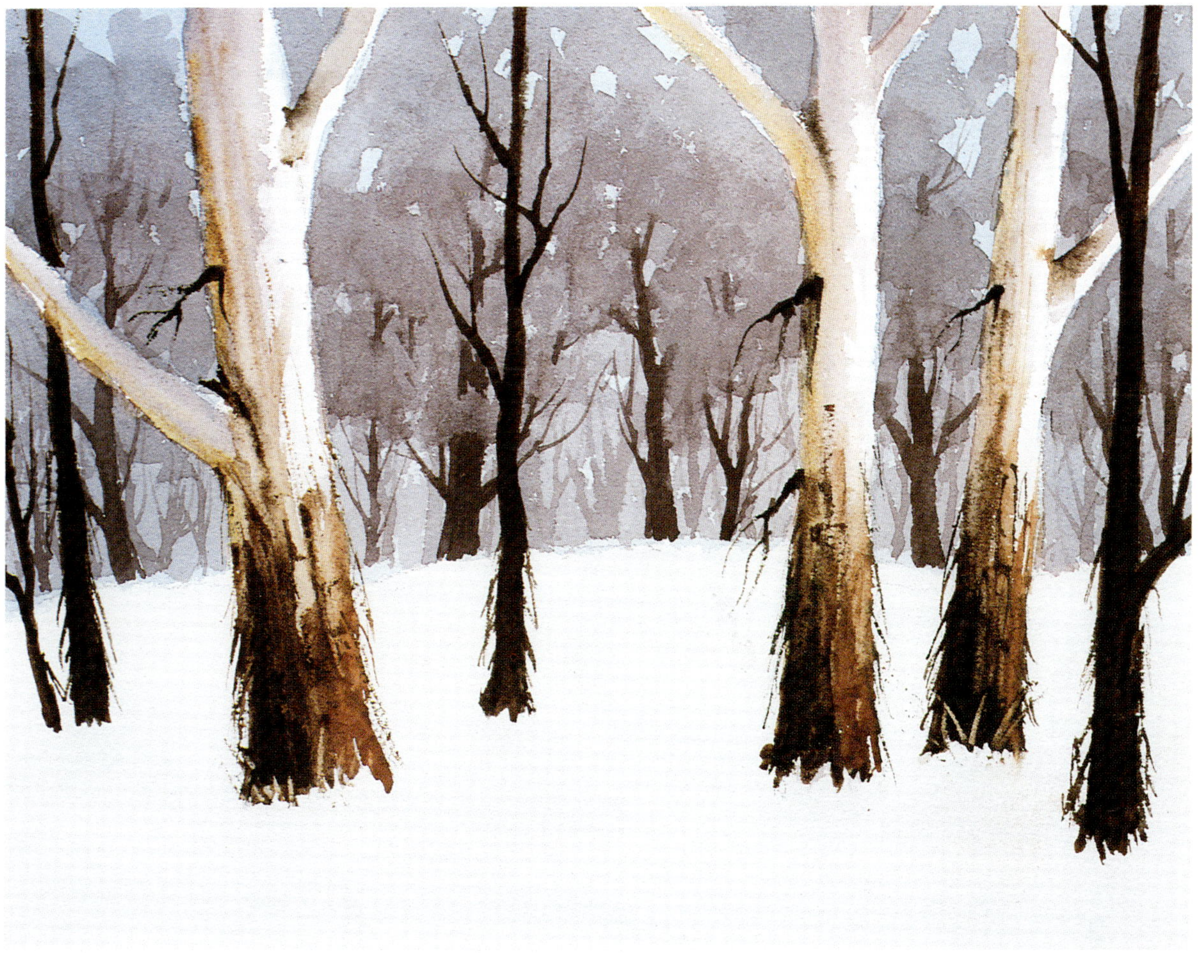

STEP 2

A With a stronger wash of cobalt blue and light red paint the nearer trees in the background. Paint trunks and limbs with a stronger mixture of cobalt blue and light red.
Allow to dry.

B Paint gums in the same manner as set out in the earlier gum tree pictures.

C Paint dark foreground trees with burnt umber.

Snow in the bush

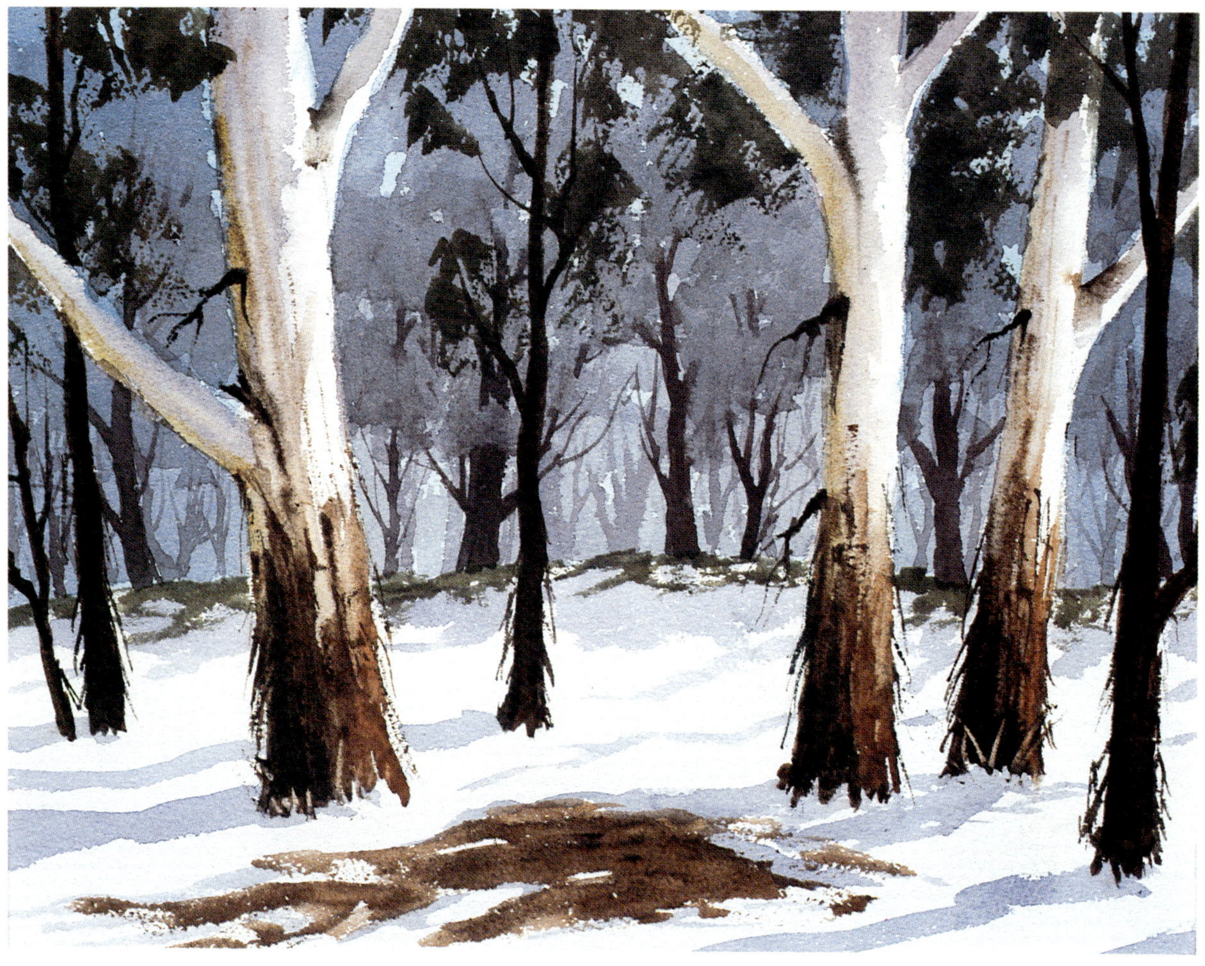

STEP 3

A Paint grassy areas near background trees with a mixture of raw umber and a touch of antwerp blue.

B Paint leaves on foreground trees with a mixture of raw umber and a touch of antwerp blue.

C Paint bare earth in foreground with a mixture of burnt umber and burnt sienna.
Allow to dry.

D Paint shadows on snow with a mixture of cobalt blue and a touch of light red.

Snow in the bush

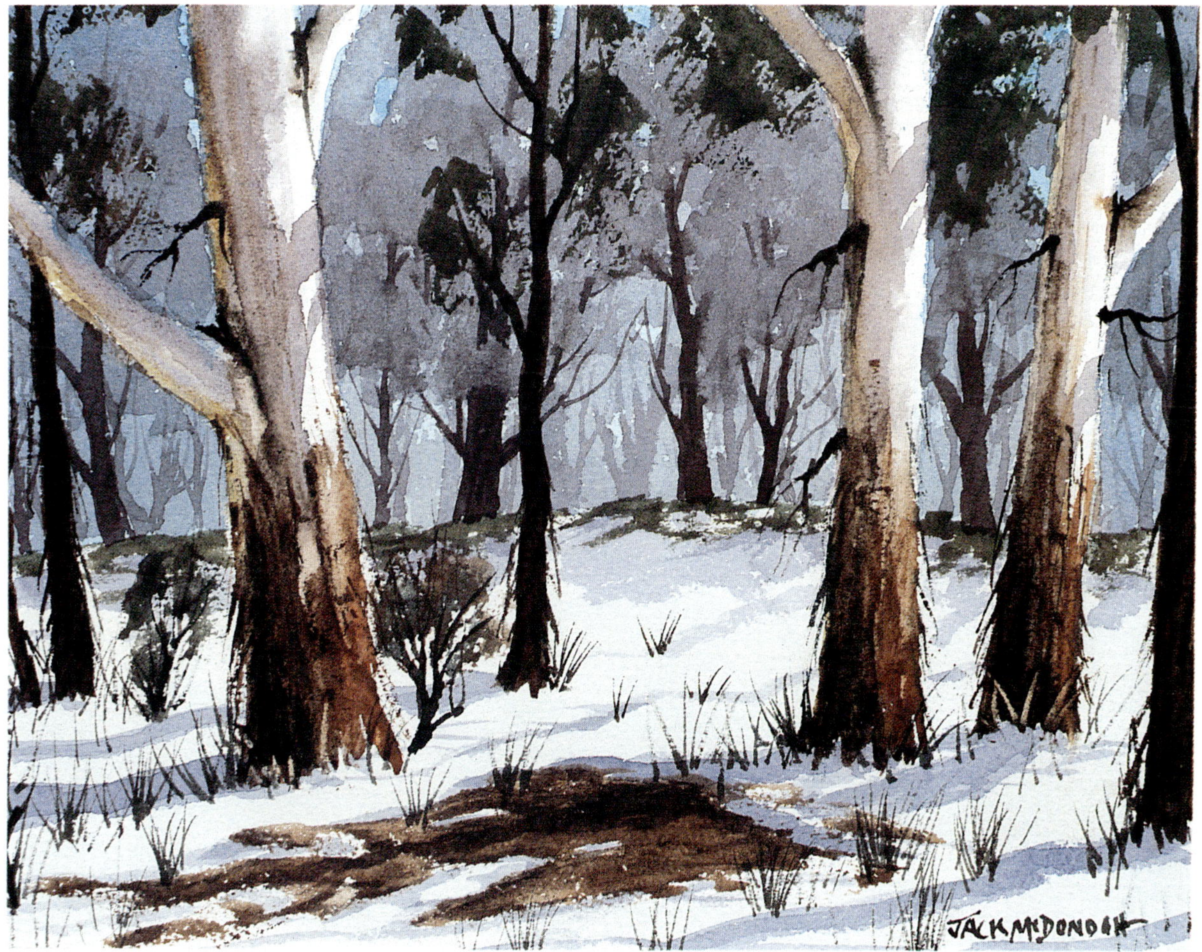

STEP 4

A Strengthen small areas of blue sky near top of picture with a touch of antwerp blue.

B Paint shadows on trunks of gum trees with a mixture of cobalt blue and light red.

C Strengthen snow shadows with a mixture of cobalt blue and a touch of light red. Make shadows darkest near the object throwing the shade.

D Paint grass and small bushes with burnt umber.

Abandoned diggings

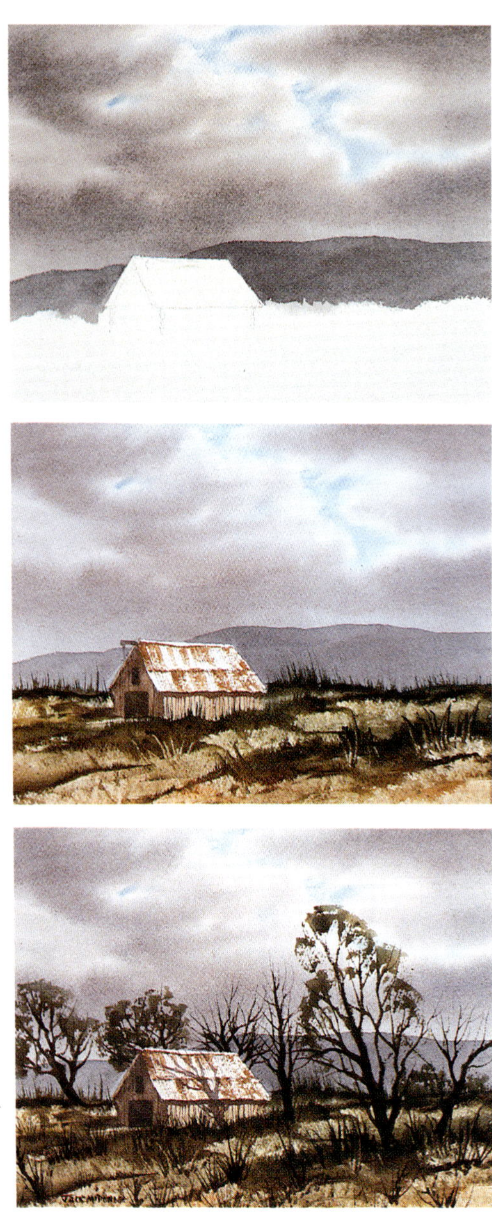

Abandoned diggings

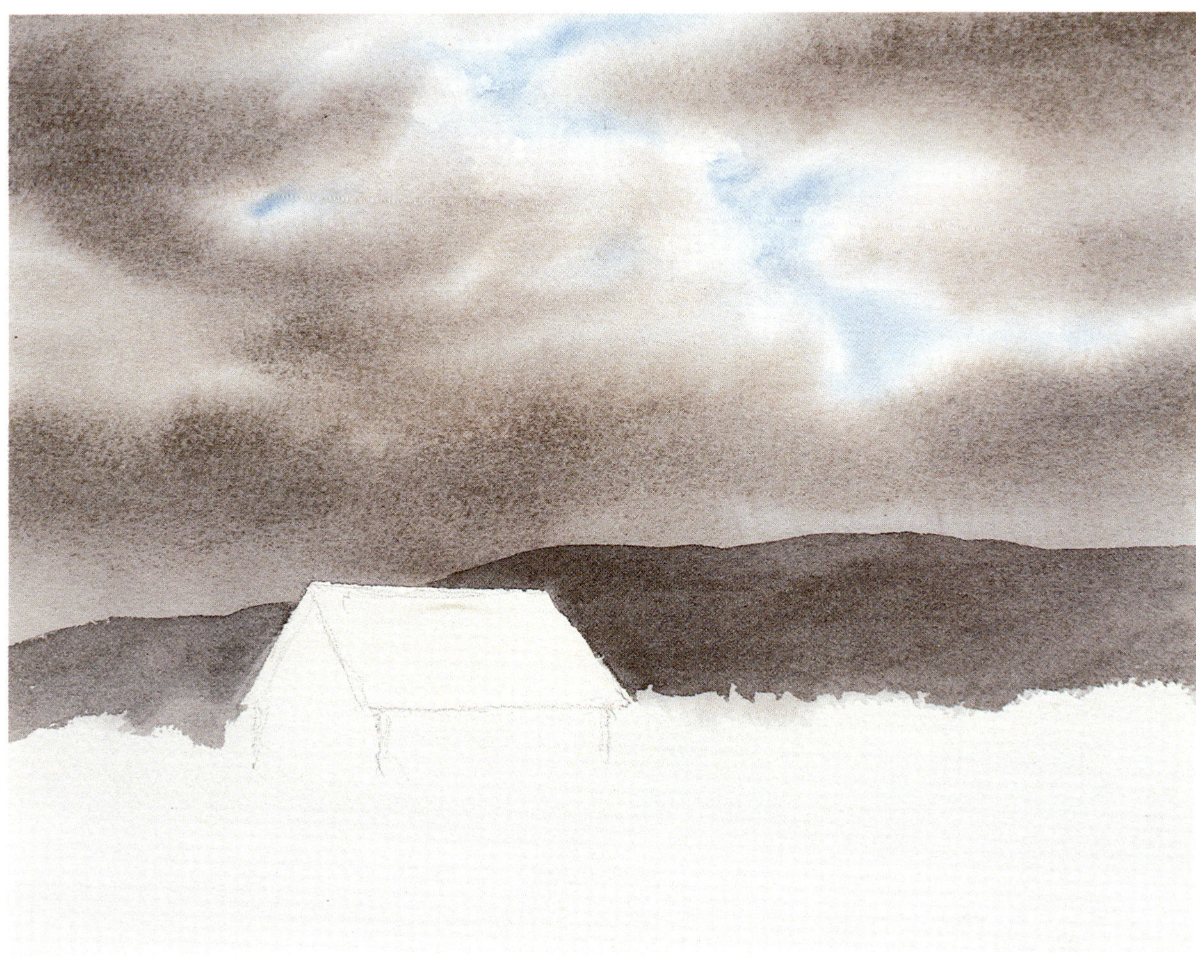

STEP 1

A Pencil outline of scene.

B Wet sky area and paint clouds using a light red and winsor blue mixture, with antwerp blue for sky areas.
Allow to dry.

C Paint distant hill using the same mixture as used for the clouds.

Abandoned diggings

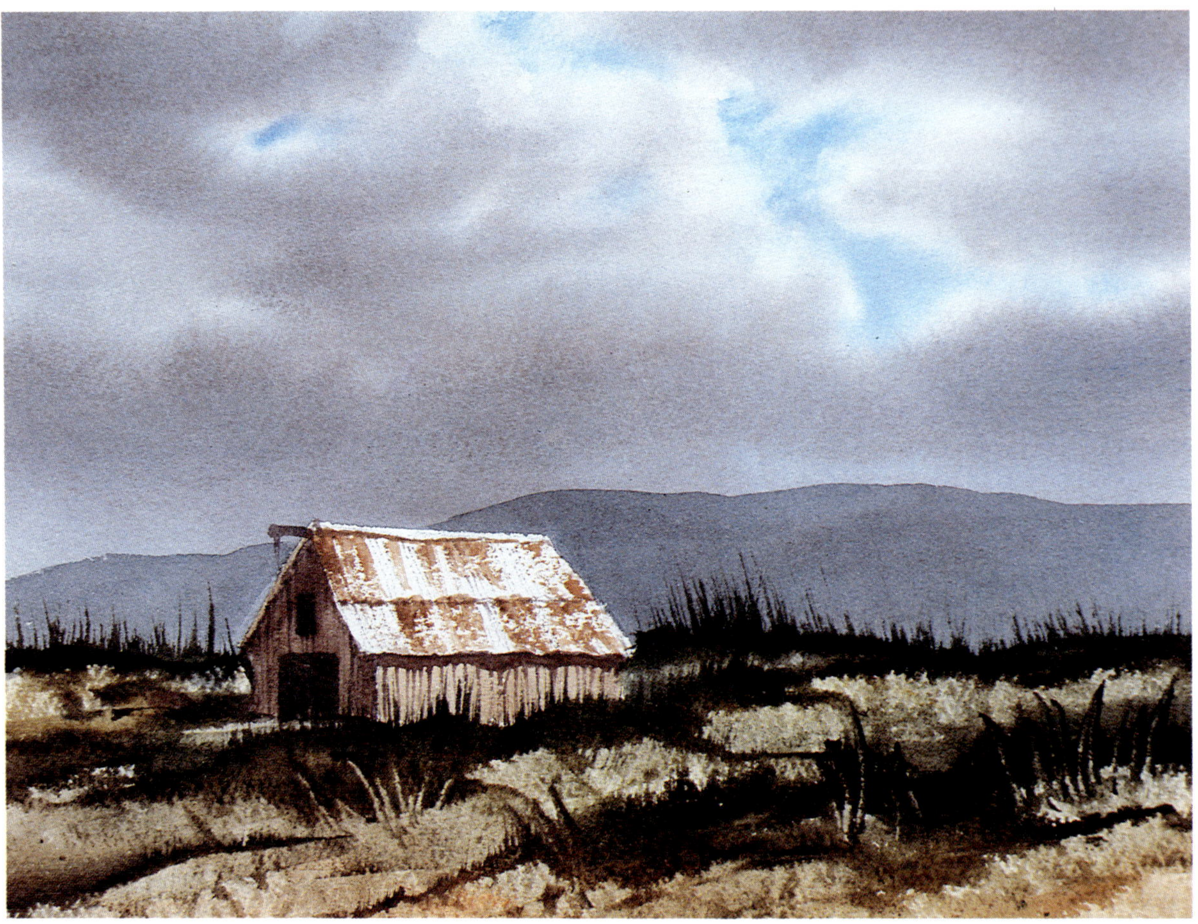

STEP 2

A Paint a strong wash of raw umber over whole earth area, with some burnt umber darkened with a touch of antwerp blue worked into the wet surface. Then use the razor blade to indicate the broken ground of the surface diggings. While still wet use the varnish brush to indicate grassy edges and add some knife strokes. Work some burnt sienna into the foreground earth.
Allow to dry.

B Paint shaded areas on shed with a mixture of cobalt blue and light red. Allow to dry and indicate wooden structure of walls with the same shade colour.
Allow to dry.

C Paint openings into shed with a strong mixture of cobalt blue and light red.

D Paint rust on roof with burnt sienna with a touch of cobalt blue.
Allow to dry.

Abandoned diggings

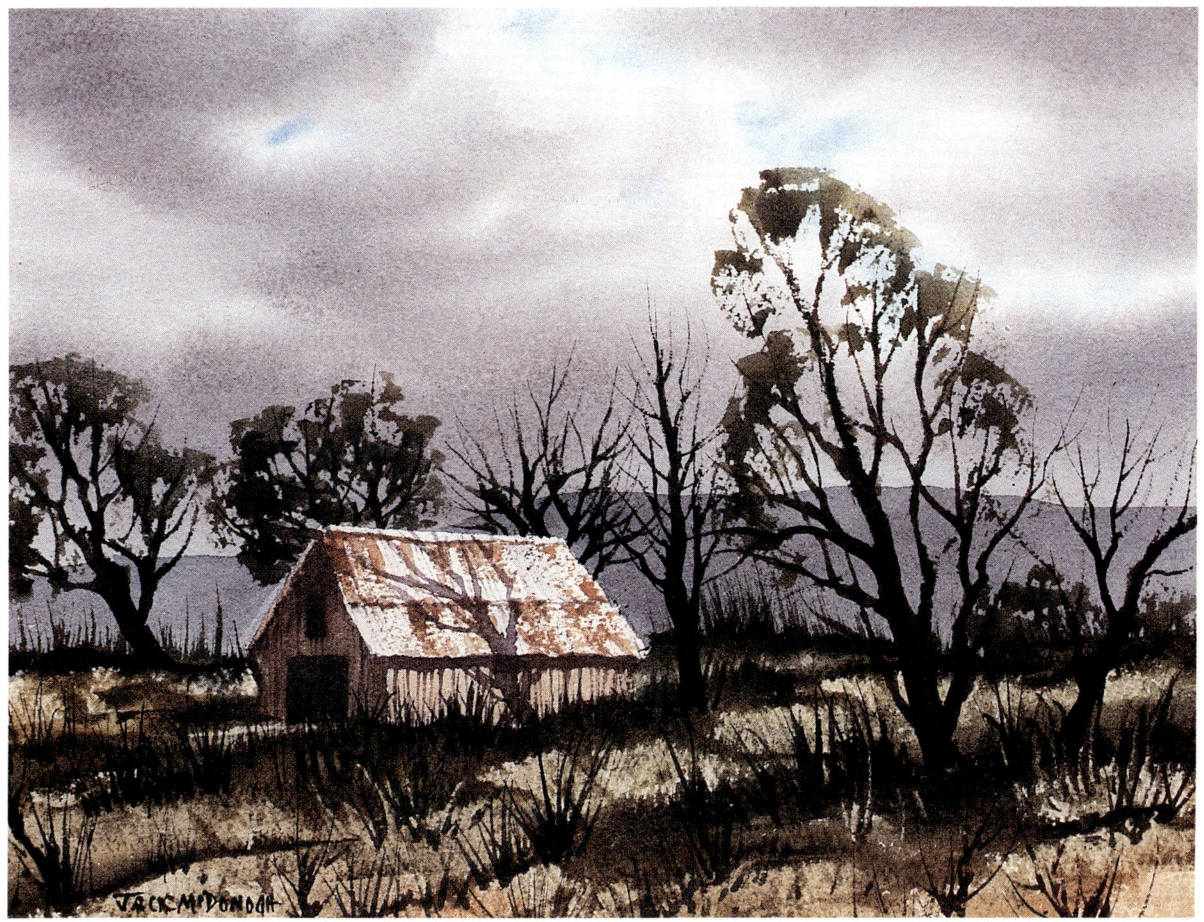

STEP 3

A Using a fine round brush paint extra grass and twiggy pieces.

B Paint all tree trunks using a mixture of burnt umber with a touch of antwerp blue.
Allow to dry.

C Paint leaves on trees with raw umber and a touch of antwerp blue.

D Paint shadow from a nearby tree on the shed roof with a mixture of cobalt blue and light red.

Poplars by the river

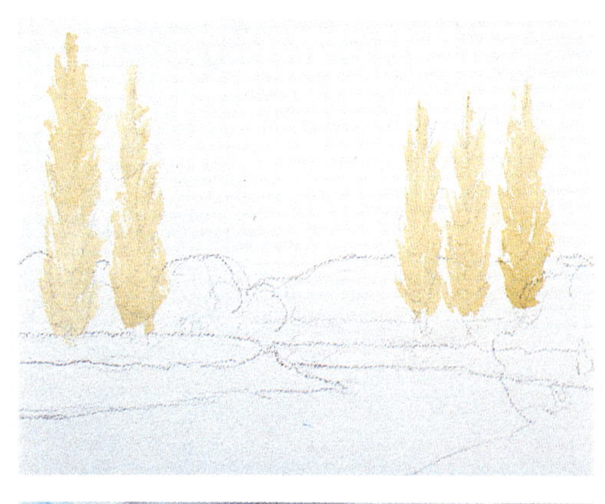

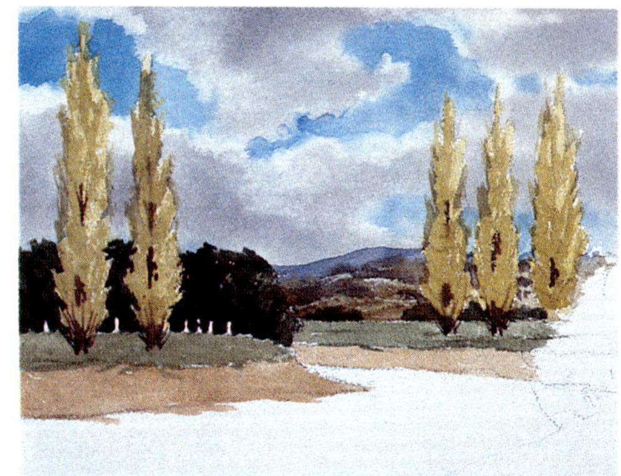

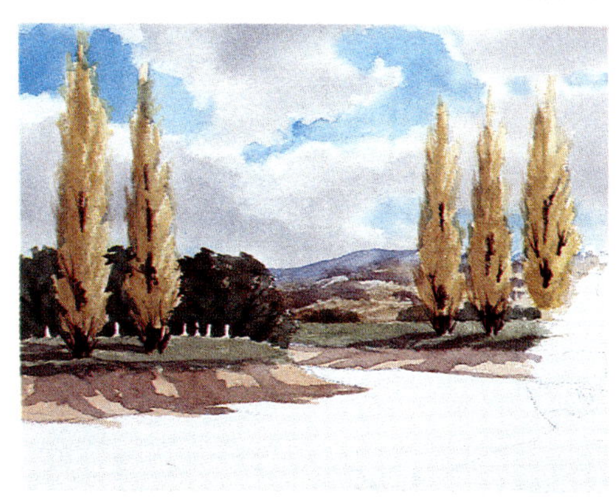

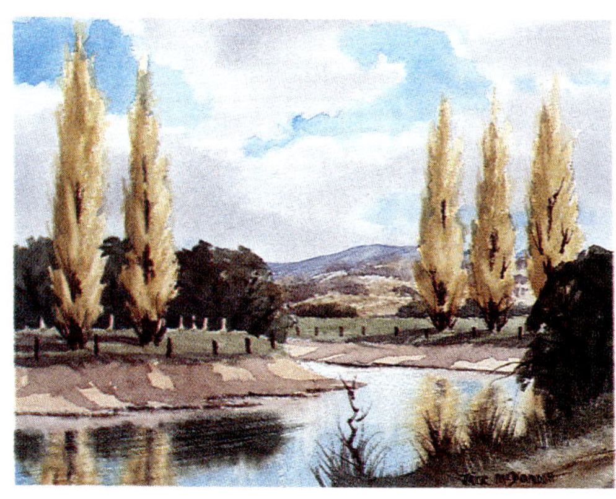

Poplars by the river

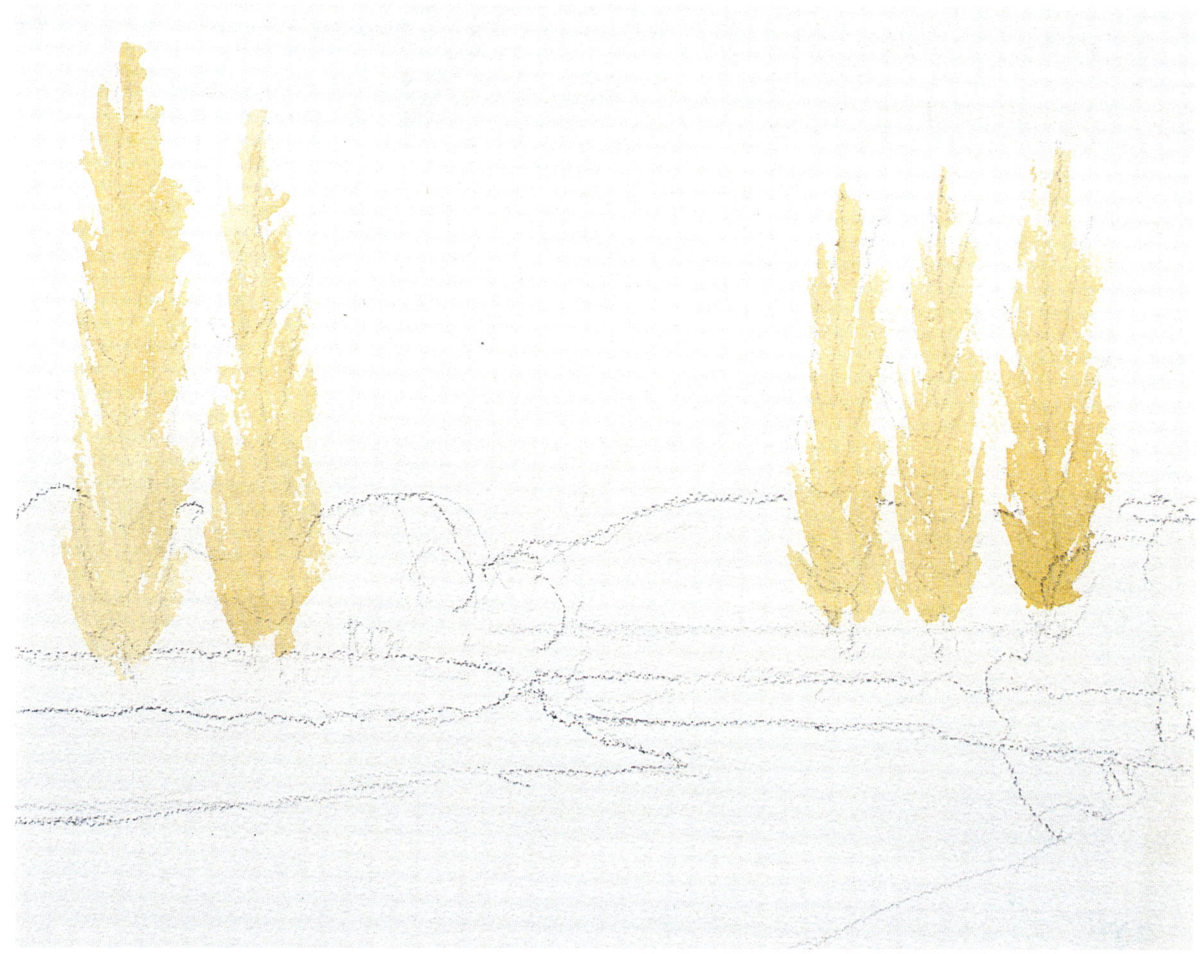

STEP 1

A Pencil outline of scene.

B Paint poplars using a weak mixture of indian yellow and cadmium yellow pale.
Allow to dry.

Poplars by the river

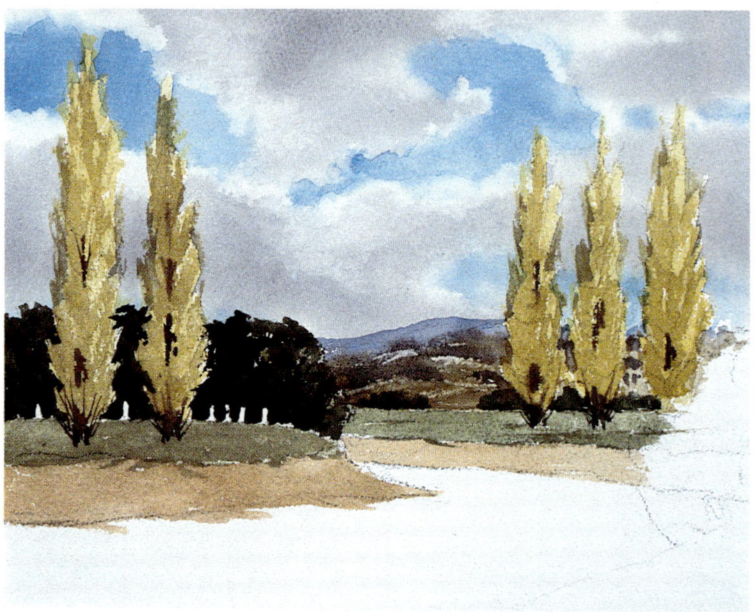

STEP 2

A Wet sky area. Avoid wetting the poplar trees. Paint clouds into wet area with a mixture of light red and winsor blue, using antwerp blue for sky areas.
Allow to dry.

B Paint distant hill with cobalt blue and work slopes into the blue with raw umber. Paint small distant trees onto wet surface with a strong mixture of cobalt blue and light red.
Allow to dry.

C Paint grassy areas with a mixture of raw sienna and a touch of antwerp blue. Dry and paint river banks with a mixture of raw sienna and light red.
Allow to dry.

D Paint trees at further side of the right hand paddock using raw umber with a touch of antwerp blue.

E Use the same mixture with a little more antwerp blue to paint trees behind poplars on the left hand side. Leave white areas for posts. Paint tree trunks with burnt umber darkened with a touch of antwerp blue.
Allow to dry.

F Give poplars a second wash with a weak mixture of indian yellow with a touch of raw umber. Leave some parts of original wash, particularly on the sunny side of the trees, in this case the right side.

G Paint poplar trunks with burnt umber.
Allow to dry.

Poplars by the river

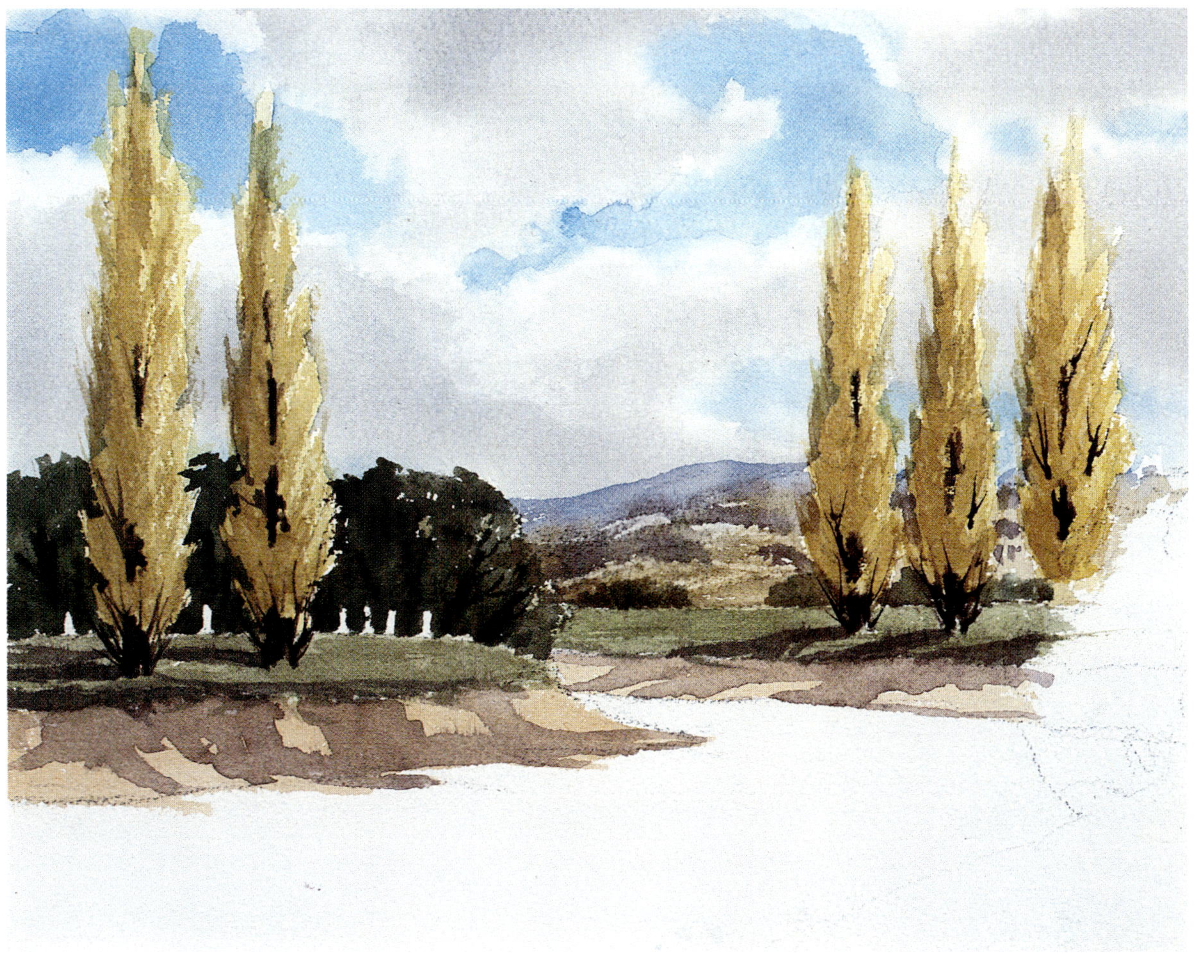

STEP 3

A Apply a third wash to the poplar trees. A mixture of indian yellow with a little more raw umber than in Step 2 should be used to strengthen the shaded sides of the poplar trees.

B Darken trunks of poplars on shaded side with burnt umber and a touch of antwerp blue.

C Paint shadows behind poplar trees and on river banks with a mixture of cobalt blue and light red. Make shadows darker by the base of the trees.
Allow to dry.

Poplars by the river

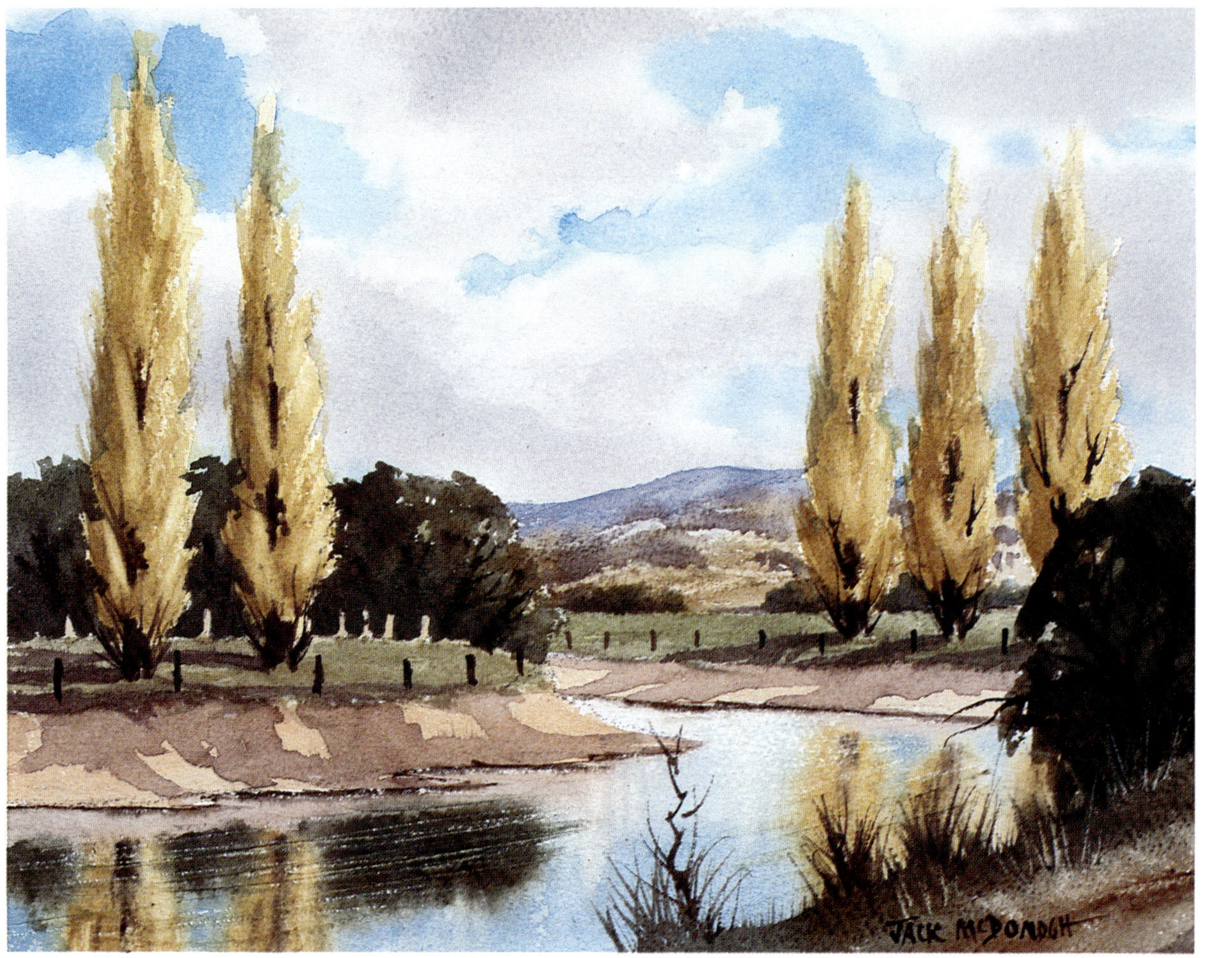

STEP 4

A With the same indian yellow and raw umber mixture as used in Step 3, apply another wash to the poplar trees, darkening all the time on the shaded side.

B The water and reflections are now painted and the 'wet-in-wet' technique is used.

Wet the area of the river with clear water.

Show reflection of the bank first with a cobalt blue and light red mixture. Add strokes of burnt umber with a fine brush at edge of water.

Now paint the reflection of the poplar trees with indian yellow and a touch of raw umber.

Brush antwerp blue in, lightening the colour towards the further bank. Do not paint the blue over the poplar tree reflections—work around them.

With a strong raw umber and antwerp blue mixture paint reflections of trees on left hand side. Work some cobalt blue into the reflection of these trees. Use some knife strokes on water surface.
Allow to dry.

C Work cobalt blue into shaded areas of trees on the left side behind the poplars.

D Paint foreground tree on right hand side with a mixture of raw umber and a touch of antwerp blue. Paint trunks using burnt umber and a touch of antwerp blue.

E Paint grassy area in right hand foreground using raw umber. Use knife strokes and razor blade to get textures. Use varnish brush to get grassy edge.
Allow to dry.

F Strengthen tree in right foreground with a mixture of raw umber and a touch of antwerp blue.

G Scratch some highlights on the water with the razor blade.

H Do some vertical 'lifting-off' of highlights on the water with the lift-off brush.

I With a fine round brush add strokes to grassy edge of foreground and some twiggy pieces.

J Do some 'lifting-off' on the sunny side of the poplar trees.

K Add fence posts using burnt umber. Soften the white of the posts on the left with thinned raw umber.

Poplars by the road

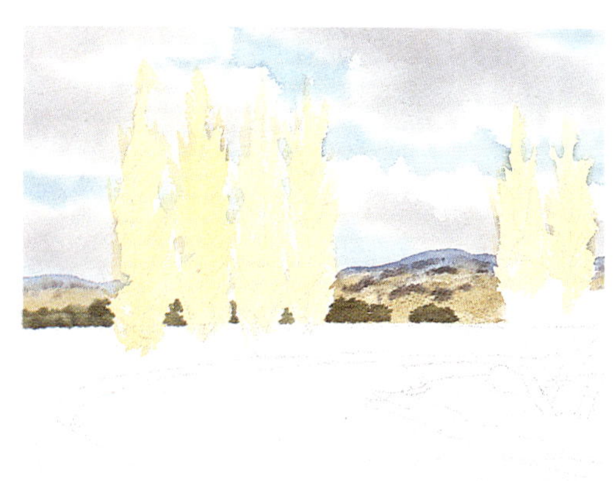

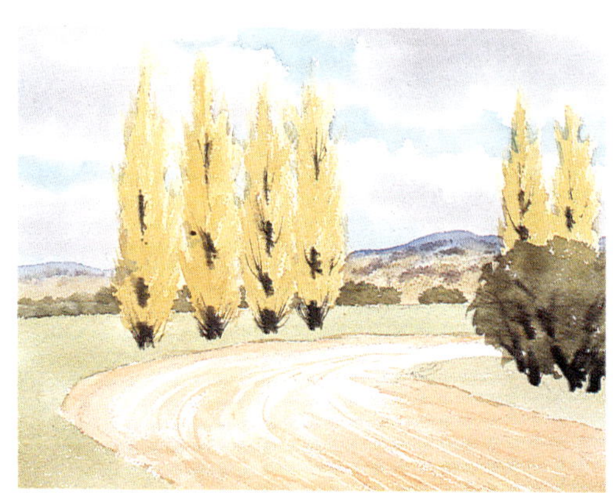

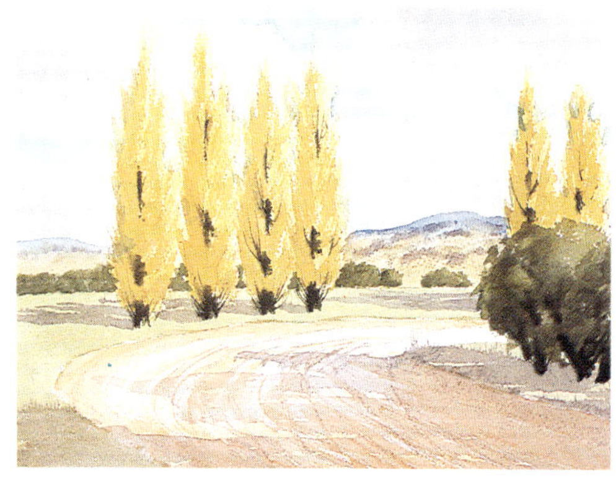

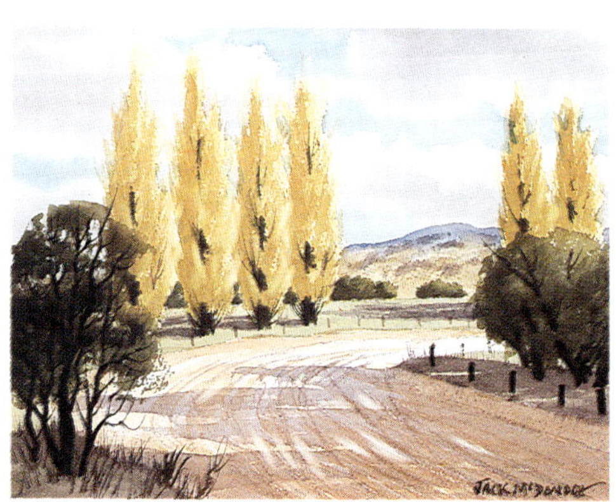

Poplars by the road

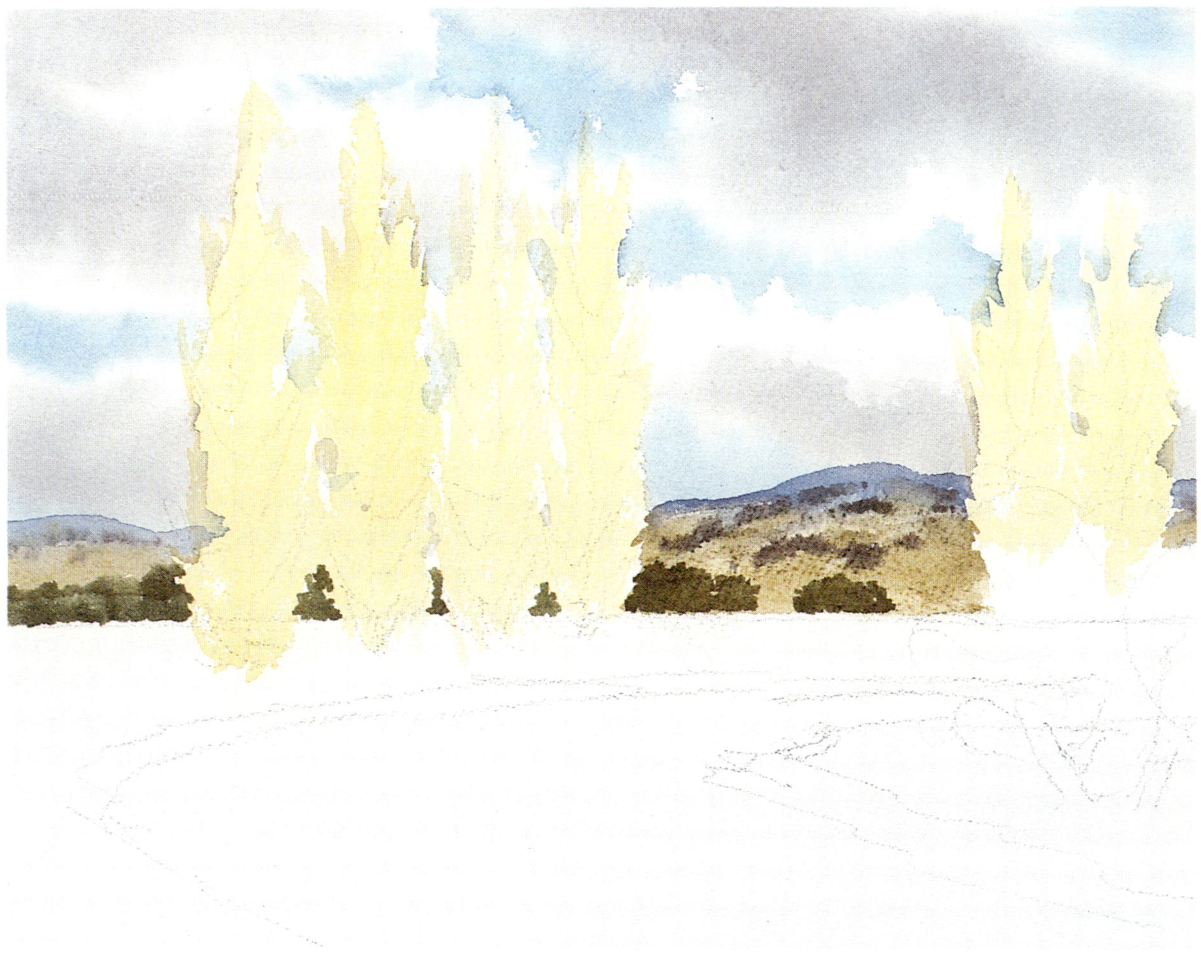

STEP 1

A Pencil outline of the scene.

B Use a pale wash of indian yellow and cadmium yellow pale mixture to indicate the poplar trees.
Allow to dry.

C Wet the entire sky area with clear water and paint clouds with a mixture of light red and winsor blue. Paint blue sky area with antwerp blue.
Allow to dry.

D Paint distant hill with cobalt blue. Work raw umber into the cobalt bluc to indicate grassy slopes. With a strong mixture of cobalt blue and light red indicate trees on distant slopes while the paper is still wet.
Allow to dry.

E Paint middle distance row of trees with a mixture of raw umber and a touch of antwerp blue.
Allow to dry.

Poplars by the road

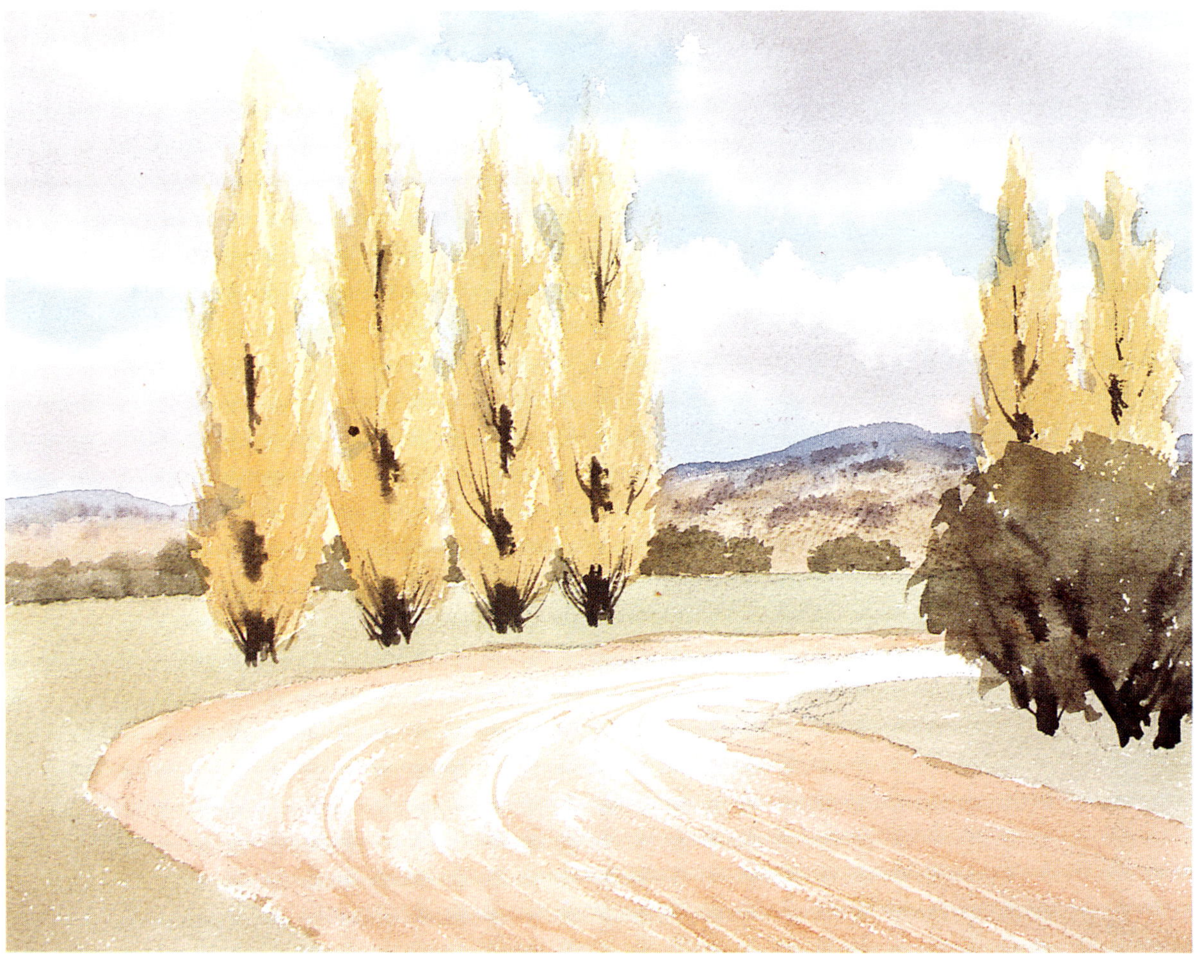

STEP 2

A Paint a pale mixture of raw sienna and a touch of antwerp blue over all grassy areas.
Allow to dry.

B Put a second wash over the poplar trees using a mixture of indian yellow and a touch of raw umber. Leave some parts of the original wash showing on the sunny sides of the trees.
Allow to dry.

C Indicate trunks of the poplar trees with burnt umber.

D Paint trees on right using a mixture of raw umber and a touch of antwerp blue. Paint the trunks with burnt umber.

E Paint road and edges with a mixture of raw sienna and light red. Note the white area left untouched. Use some knife strokes while wet to indicate road marks and paint some fine lines towards the white areas.
Allow to dry.

Poplars by the road

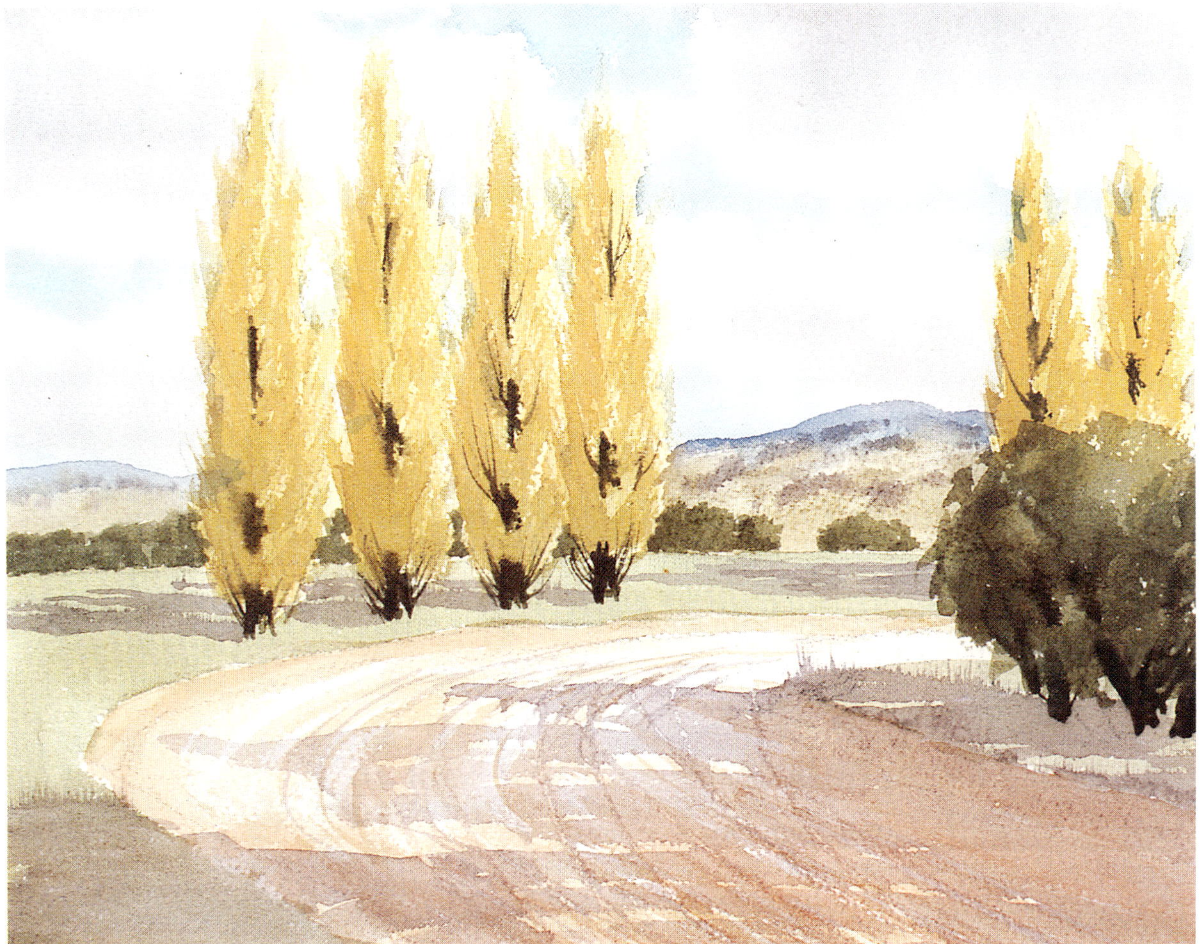

STEP 3

A Paint another wash over the poplar trees using a mixture of indian yellow and raw umber. This time add more raw umber to darken the colour and again indicate the shaded side of the trees with this mixture.

B Strengthen the middle distance row of trees with a wash of raw umber and a touch of antwerp blue.

C Strengthen the shaded side of the trees on the right hand side with a mixture of raw umber and a touch of antwerp blue.

D Paint shadows on the road with a mixture of cobalt blue and light red. Use the same colour to indicate shadows behind poplars, trees on right and left foreground grass.
Allow to dry.

Poplars by the road

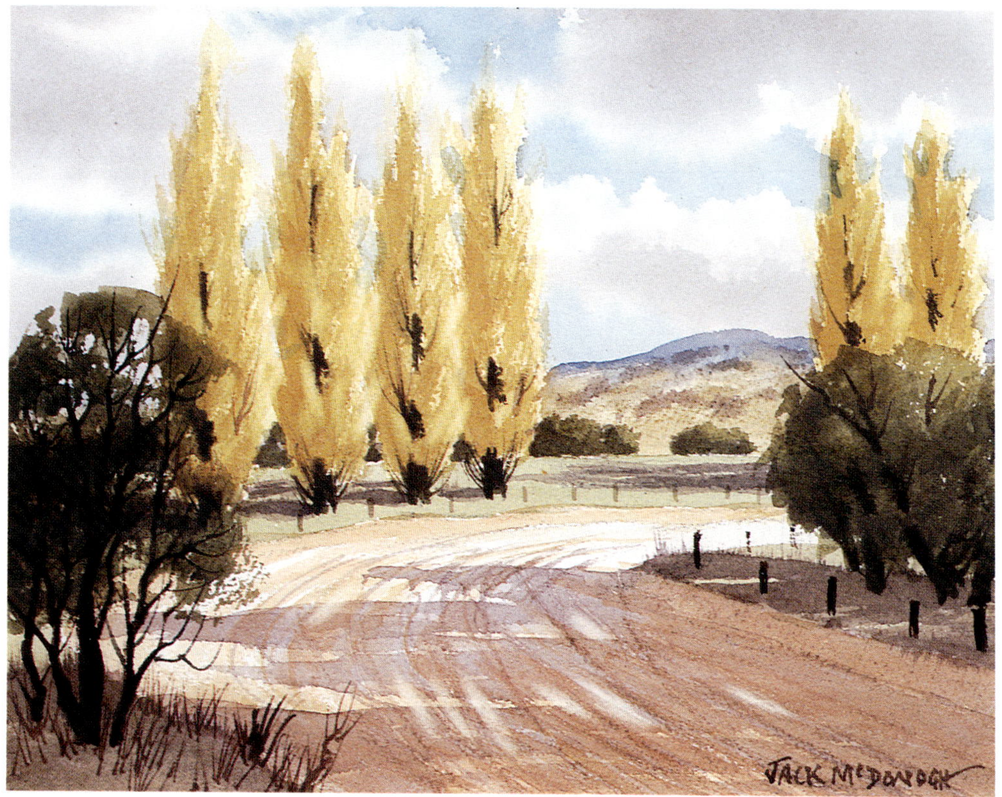

STEP 4

A With the same indian yellow and raw umber mixture as used in Step 3 apply another wash to the poplar trees, darkening all the time on the shaded side.

B Work cobalt blue into shadow areas of middle distance trees.

C Strengthen shaded areas under right hand trees, left foreground and behind poplars with a mixture of cobalt blue and light red. Use varnish brush to indicate grassy edge to shadows.

D Strengthen shadow on road with another wash of cobalt blue and light red. Use some knife strokes while wet.

E Strengthen shaded side of right hand trees with a mixture of raw umber and a touch of antwerp blue.

F Paint tree trunks in left foreground using burnt umber. When dry add leaves with a mixture of raw umber and a touch of antwerp blue. When dry, strengthen these leaves in parts with the same mixture.

G With a fine round brush add some strokes to the grassy edges and add some twiggy pieces using burnt umber. Add fence posts with the same colour.

H With the lift-off brush do some 'lifting-off' on the sunny side of the poplar trees and some parts of the shadow on the road.

Breaking wave

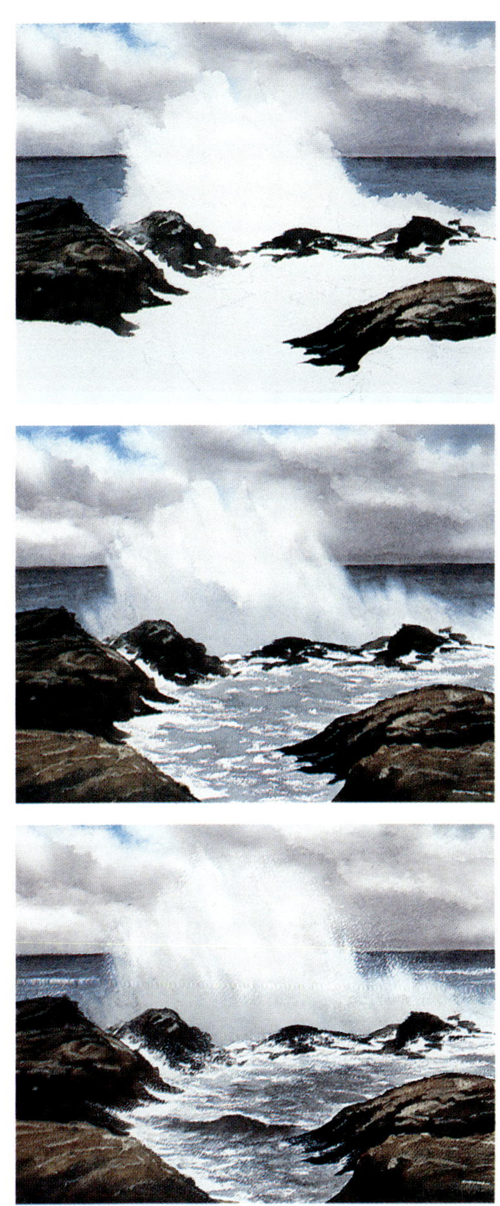

Breaking wave

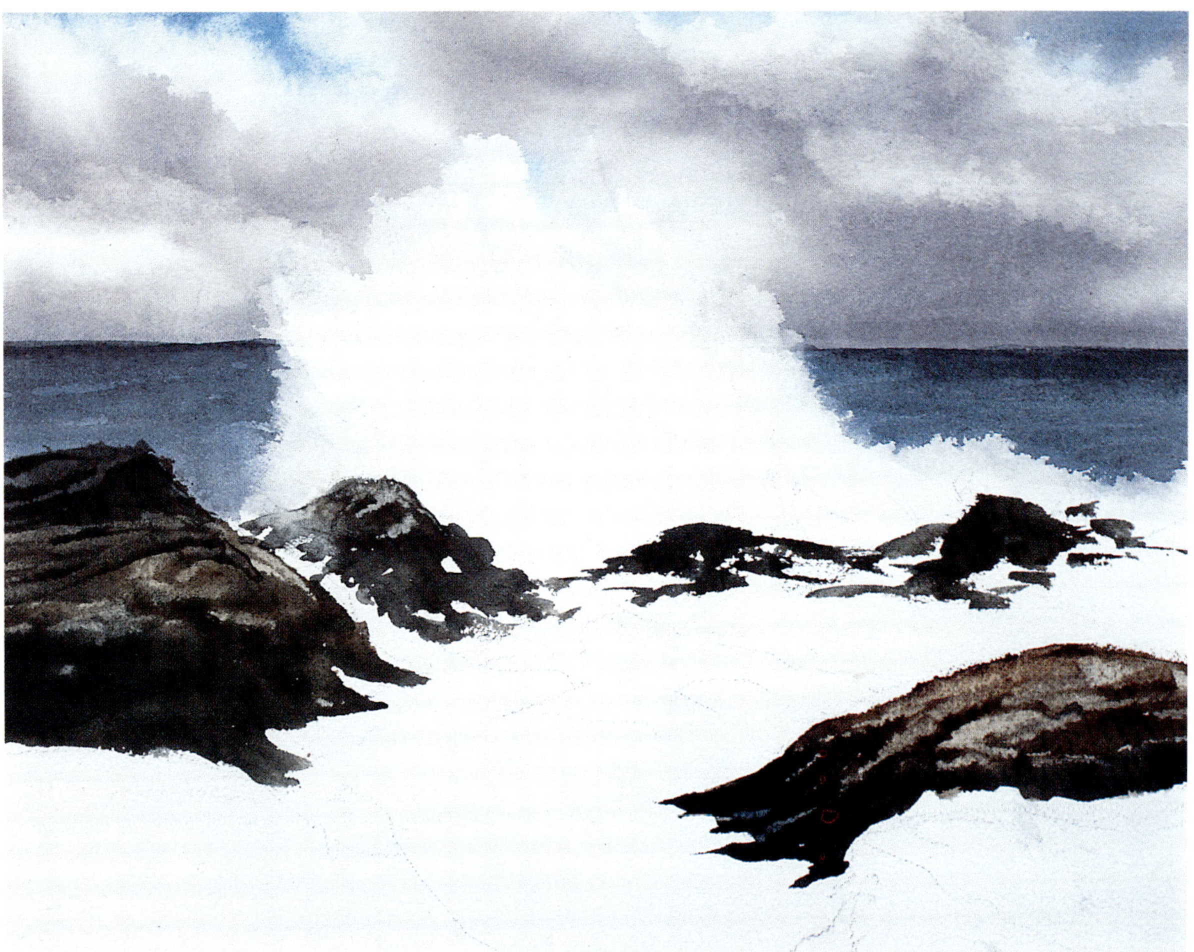

STEP 1

In the seascape pictures I often ask you to use a dry brush stroke. This is not as it seems. The brush is certainly not dry. It is fully charged with colour and moved over the paper quickly so the brush leaves broken areas of white paper.

A Pencil outline of scene.

B Wet the sky around the wave and paint the clouds with a mixture of light red and winsor blue, with antwerp blue for sky areas. Lift clouds at top edge of wave with a tissue.
Allow to dry.

C Paint sea with a mixture of winsor blue and raw umber.
Allow to dry.

D Paint rocks using raw umber, then work some payne's gray into the surface of the rocks where darks are required. This applies particularly to the rocks at the water's edge. While rock surfaces are wet use the knife to give textures.
Allow to dry.

Breaking wave

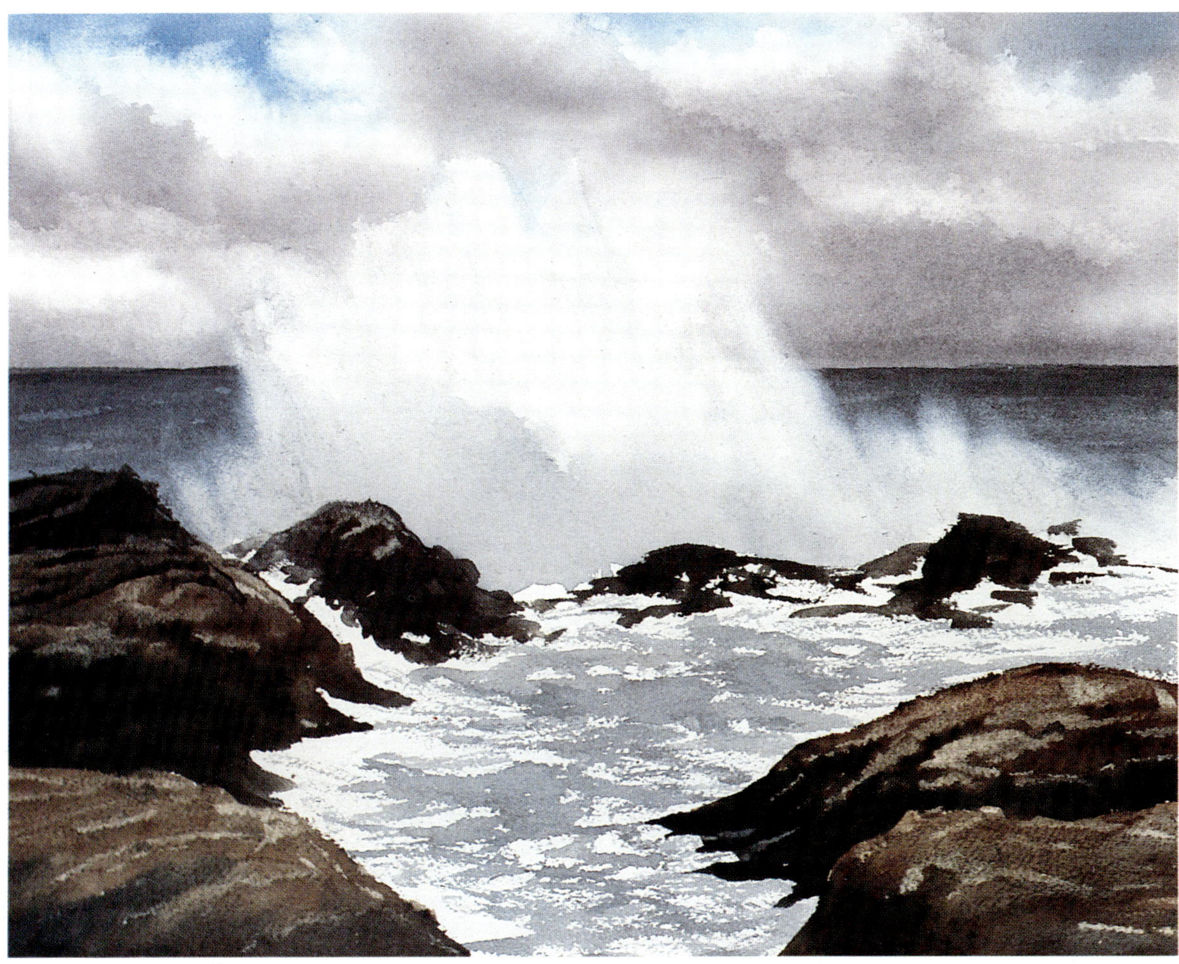

STEP 2

A Paint front rocks with raw umber adding payne's gray where darks are needed. Use some knife strokes to give textures to the rocks.

B Paint broken water in foreground with a winsor blue and raw umber mixture. Use dry brush strokes and leave plenty of white paper patches.

C With the lift-off brush soften the top edge of the wave.

D Make a weak mixture of winsor blue and raw umber and paint this over the wave and lift for highlights with a tissue.
Allow to dry.

Breaking wave

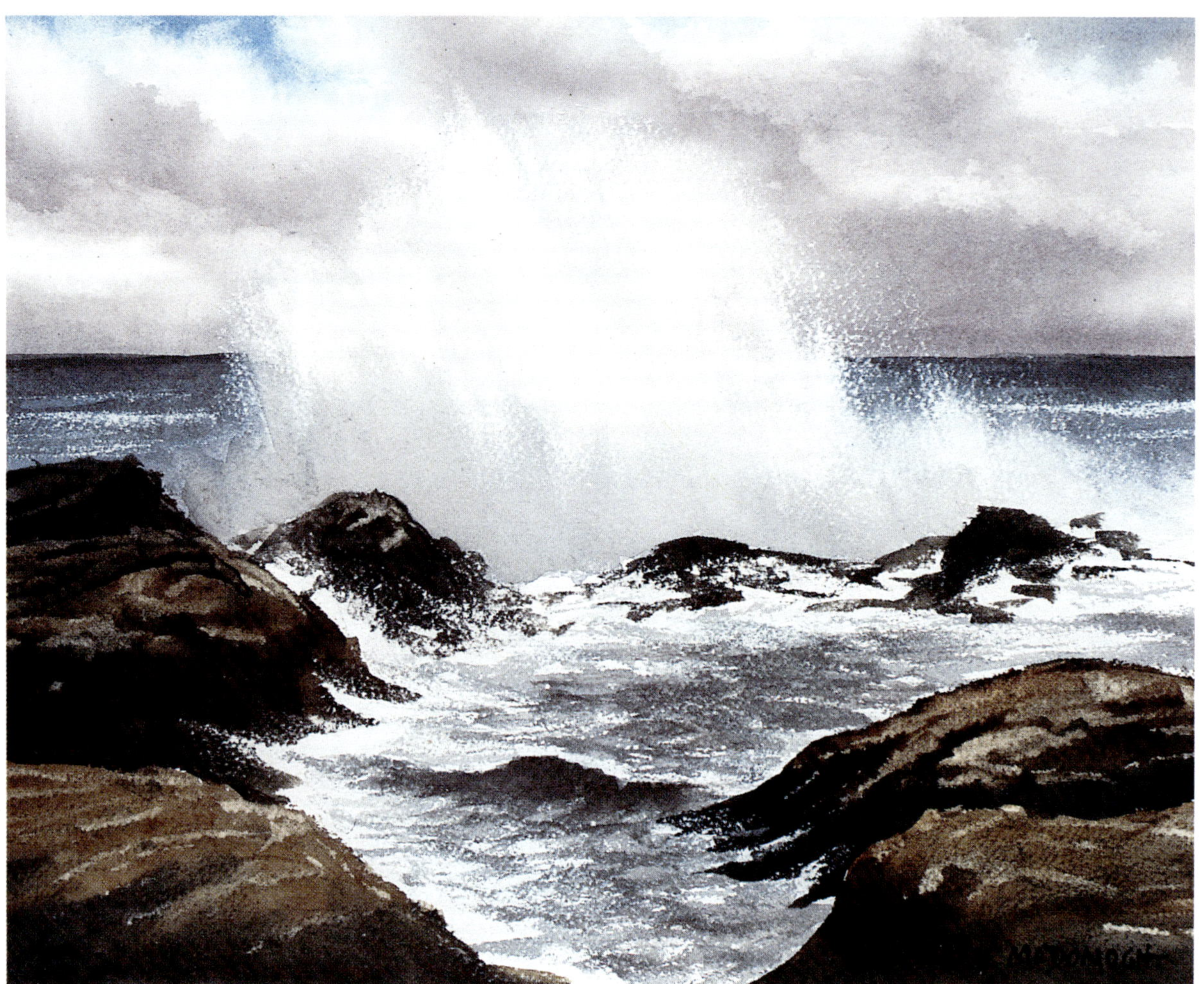

STEP 3

A Strengthen the light and shade parts of the wave with another wash with the same mixture as used in Step 2.

B With a mixture of winsor blue and raw umber strengthen the water in foreground. Use dry brush strokes.
Allow to dry.

C With the razor blade scrape along the edge of the wave to give a spray effect. Also scratch for broken water at edge of rocks. This applies particularly to the small rocks at the base of the wave.

D Use the razor blade to scrape small waves on the sea behind the breaking wave.

Rolling surf

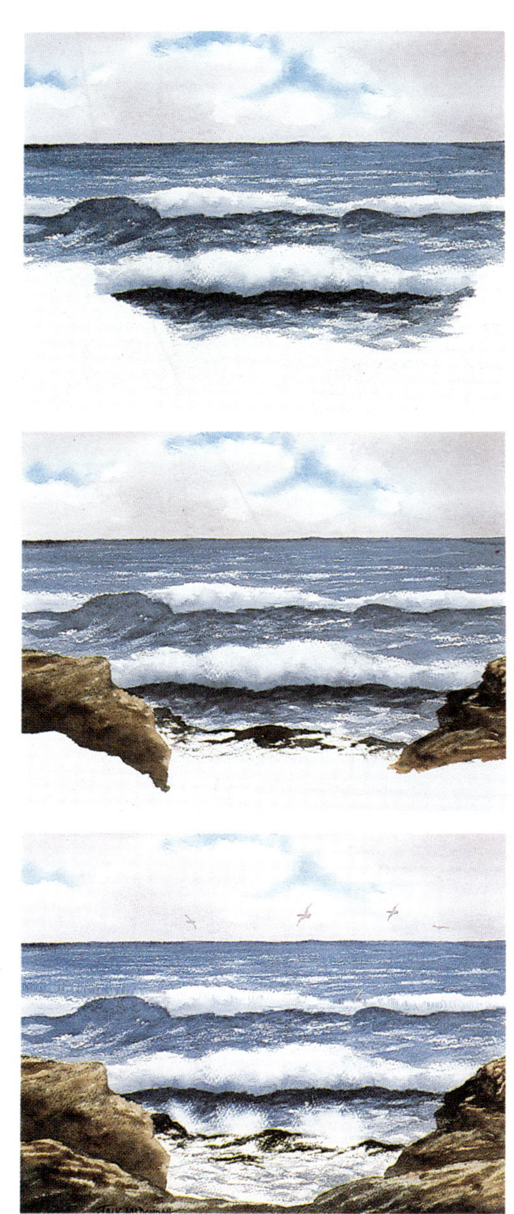

Rolling surf

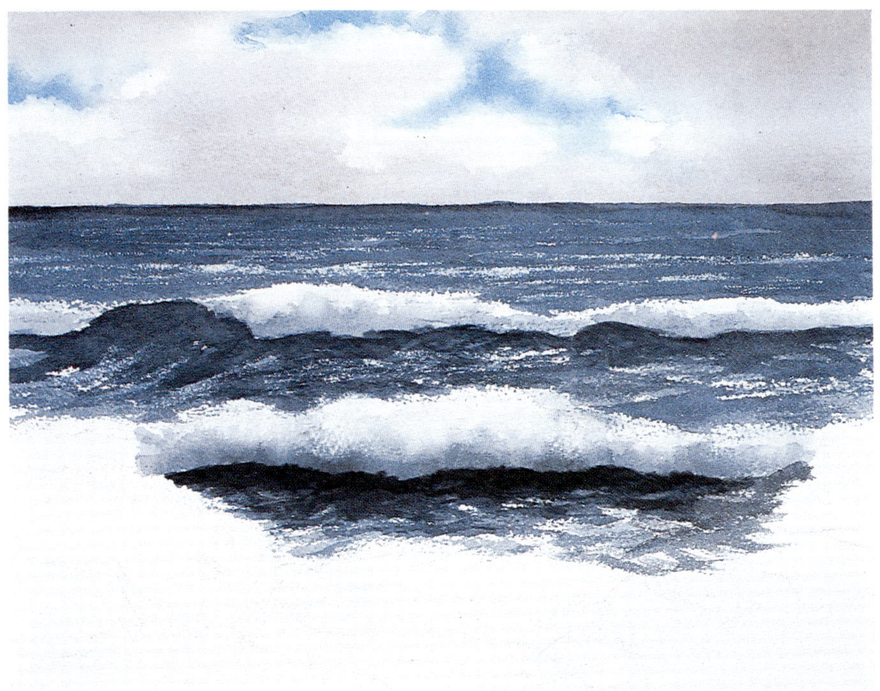

STEP 1

A Pencil outline of scene.

B Wet sky area with clear water and paint clouds with a light red and winsor blue mixture. Paint sky areas with antwerp blue.
Allow to dry.

C With a weak mixture of winsor blue and raw umber paint a wash over the sea area. Bring this to the rocks, making sure to leave white areas of the paper for the rolling parts of the waves. Use dry brush strokes for all areas of the water.
Allow to dry.

D Add another wash to the sea area beyond the waves with the same mixture as used in Step 1C but made a little stronger.
Allow to dry.

E Areas that were left as white paper for the rolling parts of the waves are now dampened with clear water. Paint a weak mixture of winsor blue and raw umber into the dampened areas and give form to the rolling waves. Lift at the top of the areas with a tissue to keep whiteness at top of waves.
Allow to dry.

F With the same mixture as used in Step 1D strengthen the colour under the rolling parts of the waves.
Allow to dry.

G Do some scratching with the razor blade on the sea surface beyond the waves to indicate small distant waves.

Rolling surf

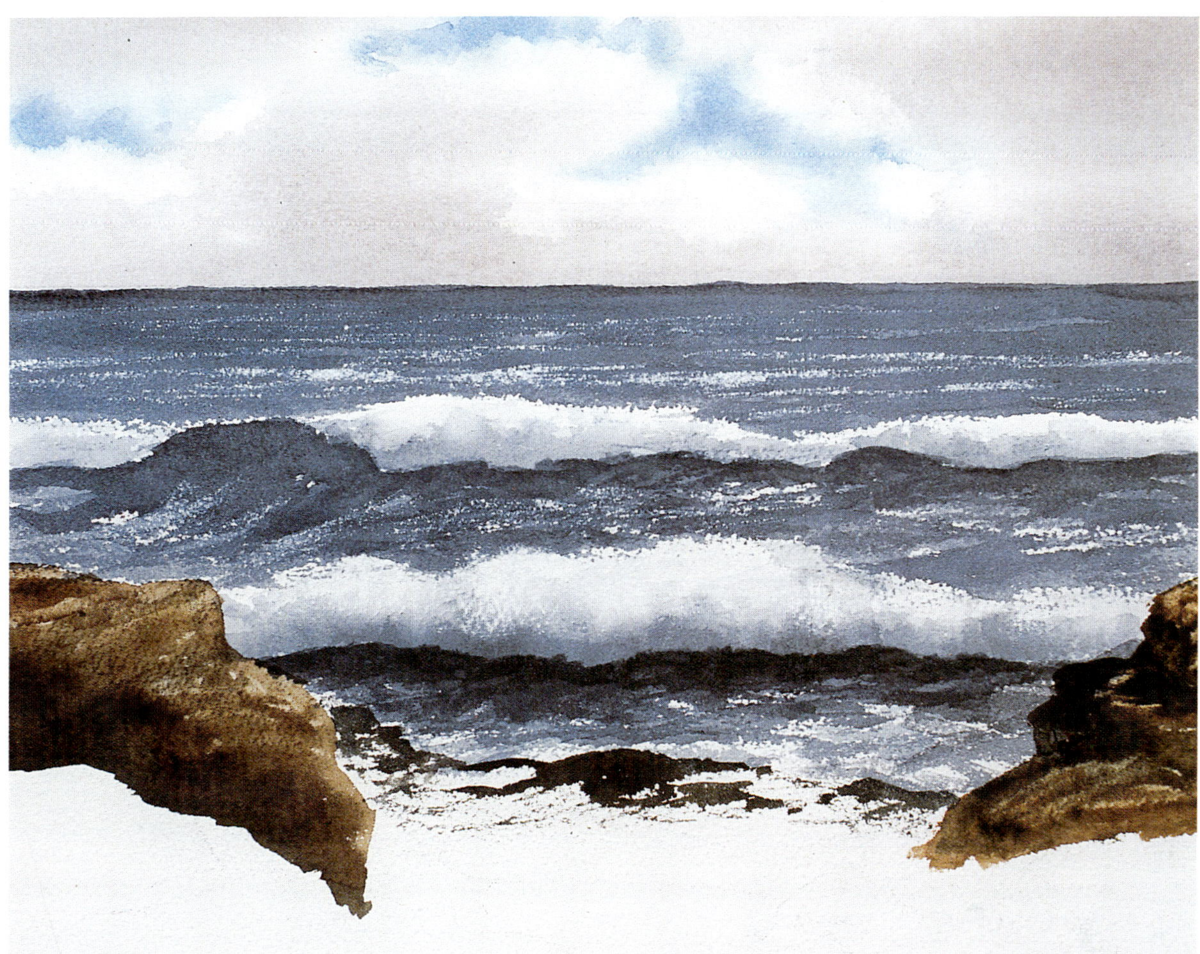

STEP 2

A Paint foreground rocks with raw umber. Use payne's gray to indicate darker parts of rocks, and knife strokes to give textures to the surface of the rocks.

B Paint rocks near the water's edge with payne's gray. Paint lighter parts of these rocks with raw umber then darken with payne's gray. Use dry brush strokes for areas of these rocks as they enter the water. Allow to dry.

Rolling surf

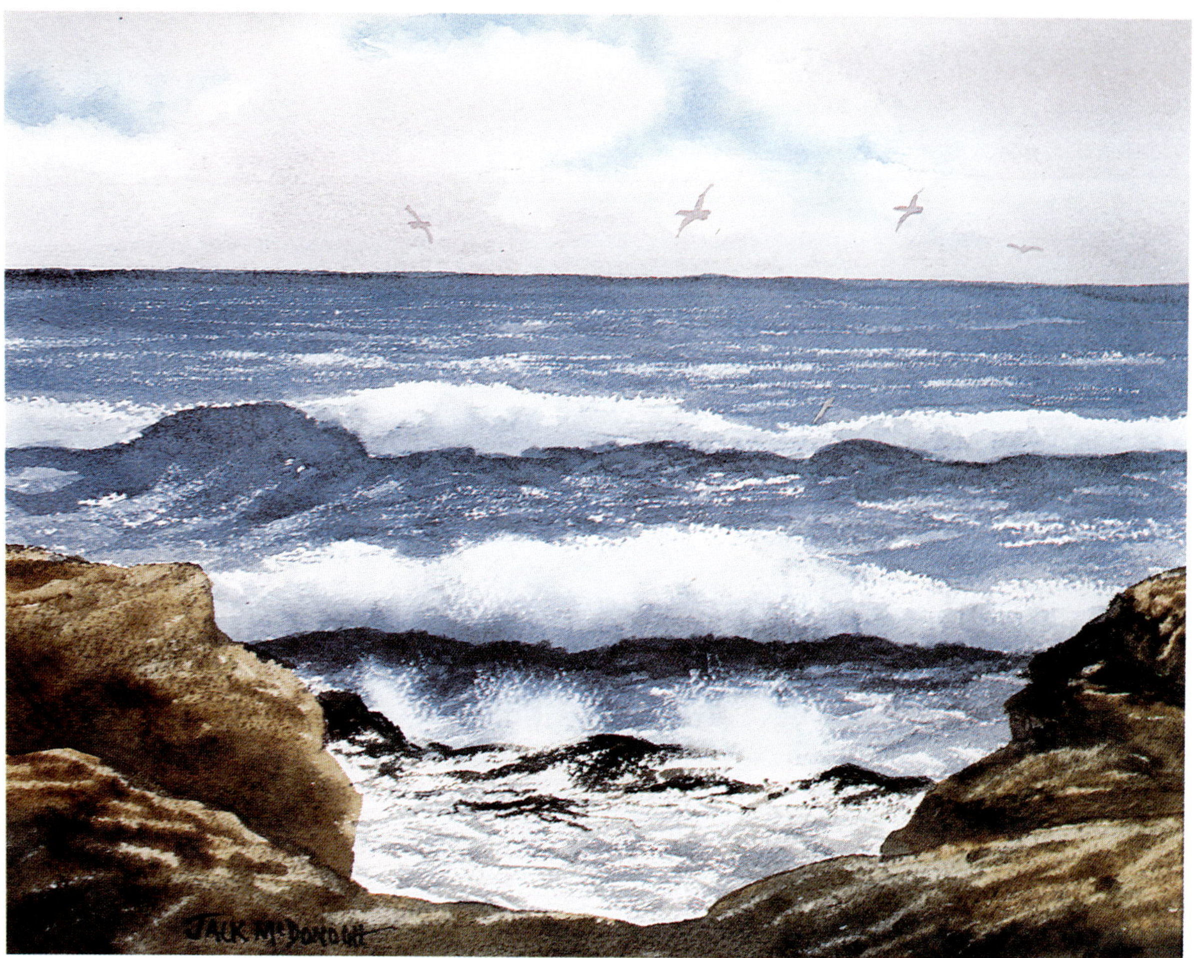

STEP 3

A Paint broken water in foreground with a mixture of winsor blue and raw umber. Use dry brush strokes.
Allow to dry.

B Rocks can be completed with raw umber with payne's gray added for darker parts. Use knife for textures on rock surfaces.
Allow to dry.

C 'Lift-off' small waves breaking at the water's edge in the foreground.
Allow to dry.

D Scrape the edges of these small waves with the razor blade to show spray.

E Add gulls with a cobalt blue and light red mixture.

The light on the rock

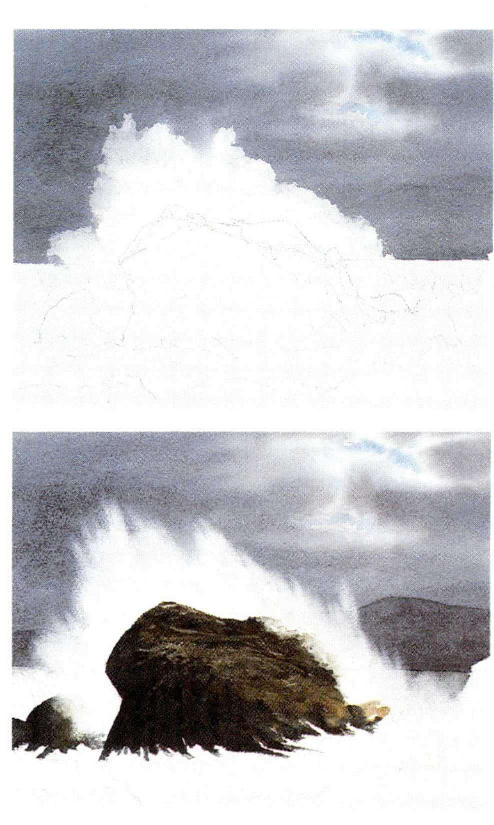

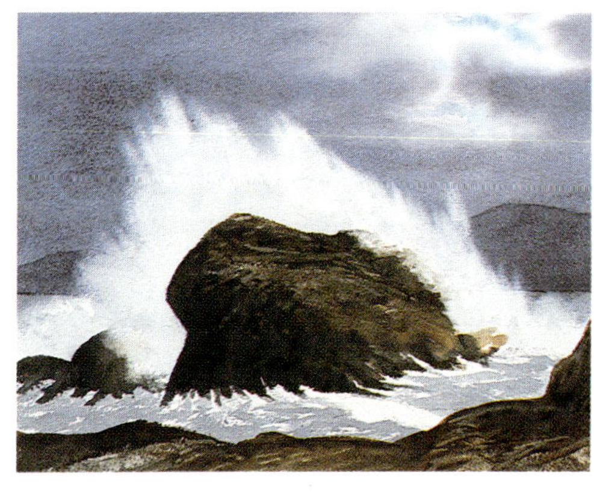

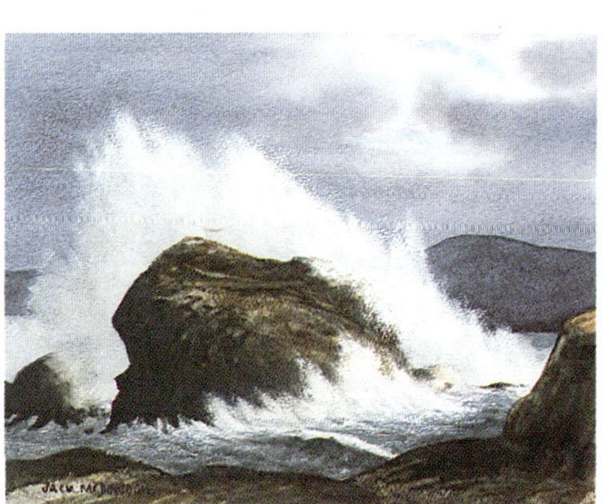

The light on the rock

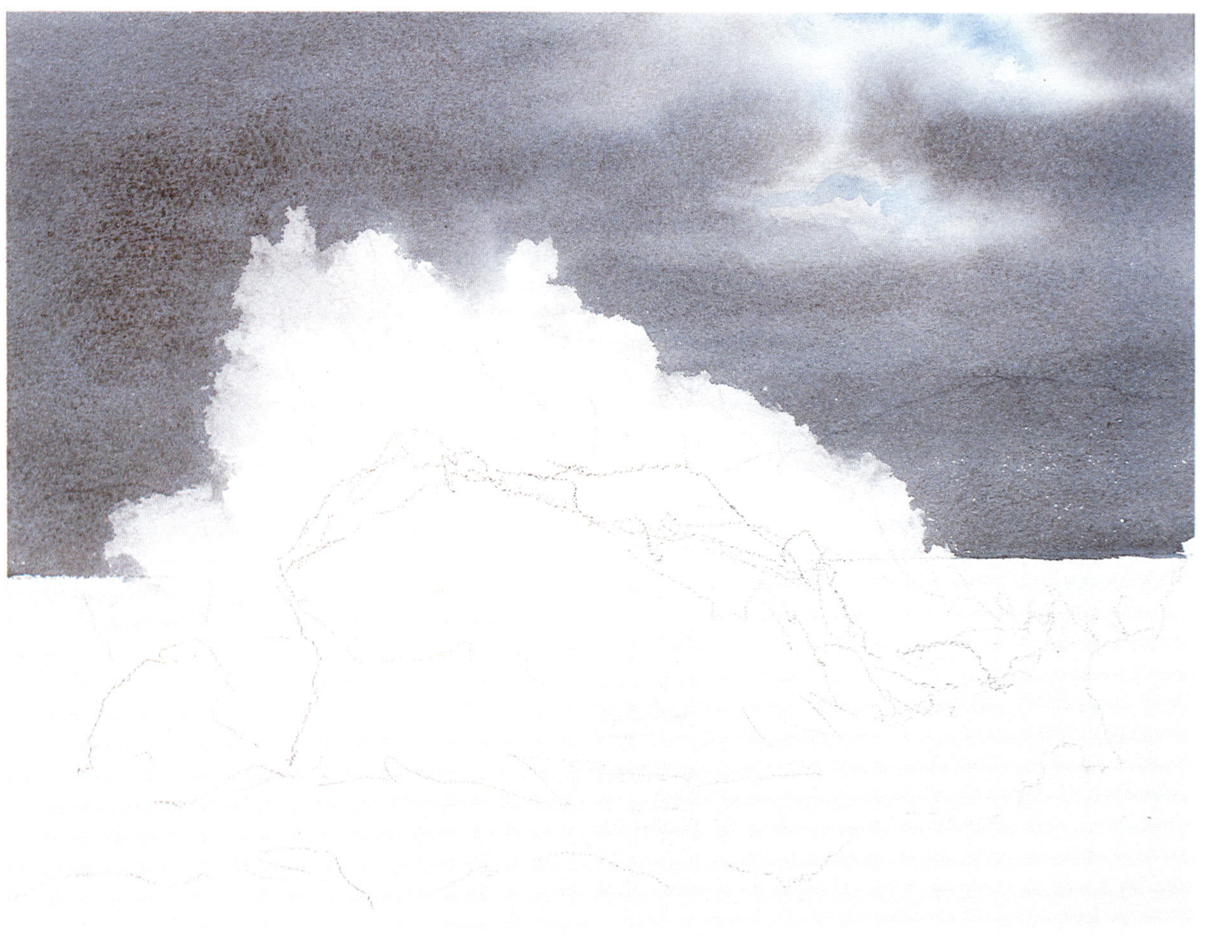

STEP 1

A Pencil outline of the scene.

B Wet sky area around the wave and paint clouds with a strong mixture of winsor blue and light red. The mixture should lean towards the winsor blue. Use antwerp blue for sky areas.
Allow to dry.

The light on the rock

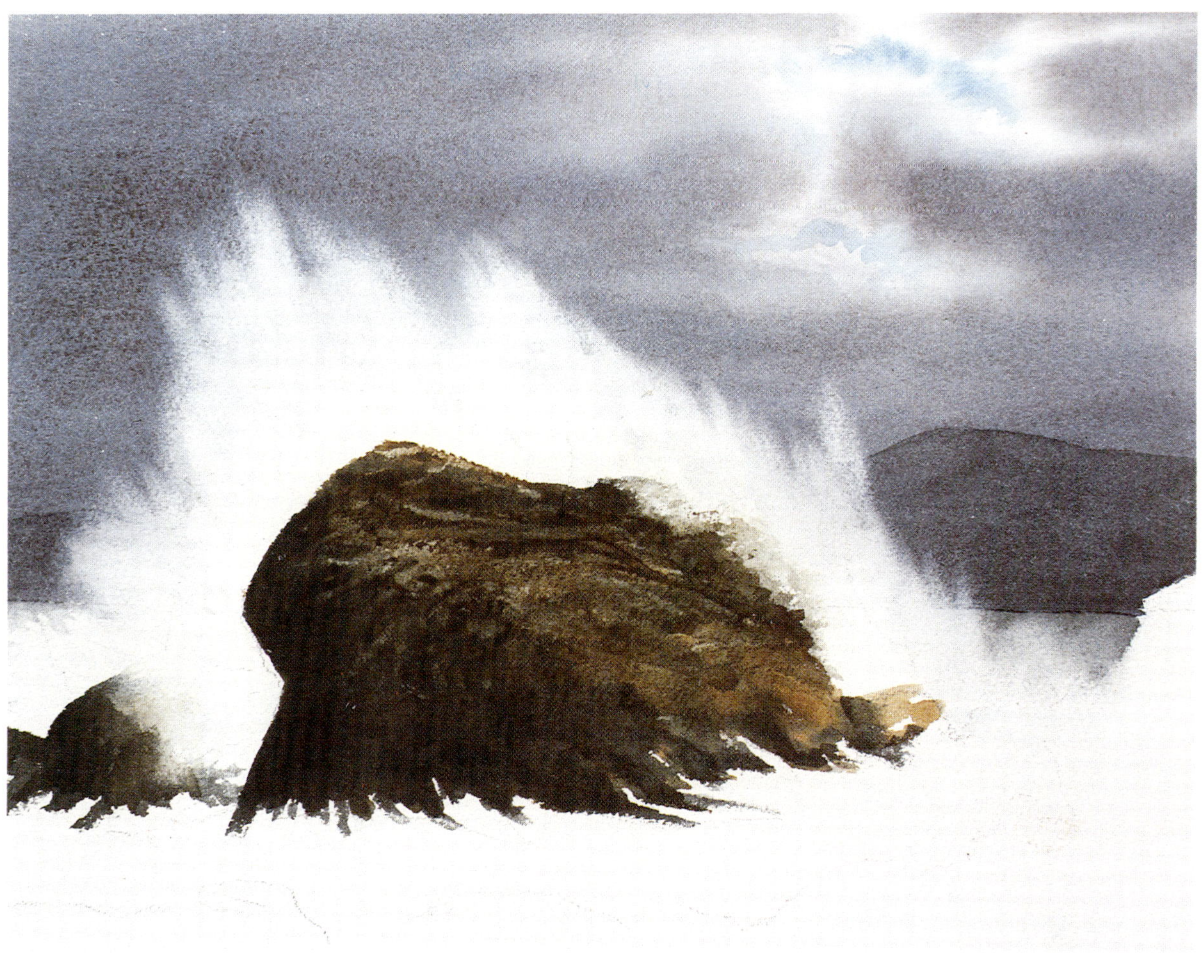

STEP 2

A Paint distant hill with the cloud mixture.

B Paint sea areas with a mixture of winsor blue and raw umber. Allow to dry.

C Paint rocks using raw umber strengthened in shaded parts with payne's gray. Use some knife strokes to give textures. Allow to dry.

D Soften top edge of wave with the lift-off brush. Allow to dry.

The light on the rock

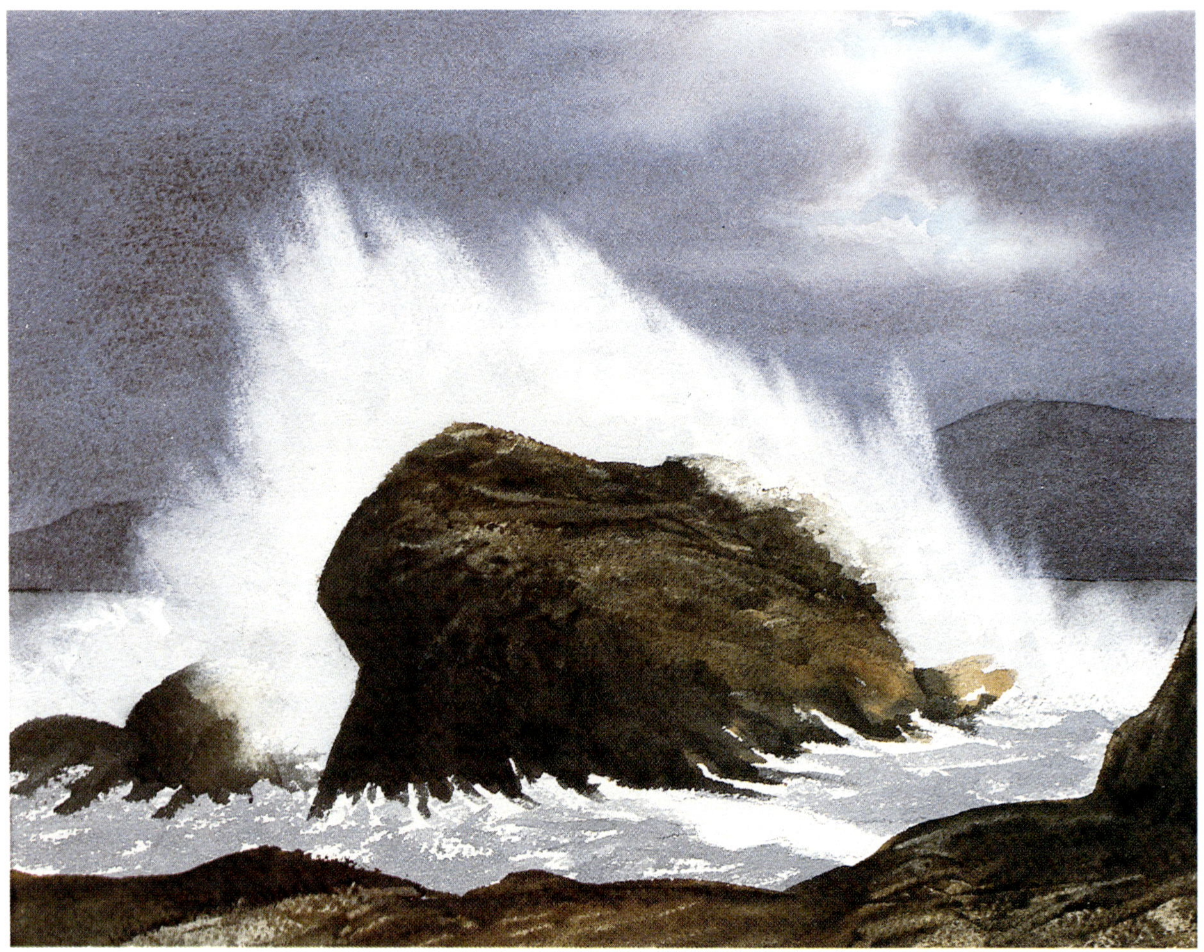

STEP 3

A Paint broken water in foreground with a mixture of winsor blue and raw umber. Use dry brush strokes.
Allow to dry.

B Paint rocks in foreground with raw umber and dark areas with payne's gray. Use the knife and razor blade to get textures.
Allow to dry.

C Mix a thin wash of winsor blue and raw umber and paint a wash over the breaking wave. Lift in spots with a tissue to keep highlights.
Allow to dry.

The light on the rock

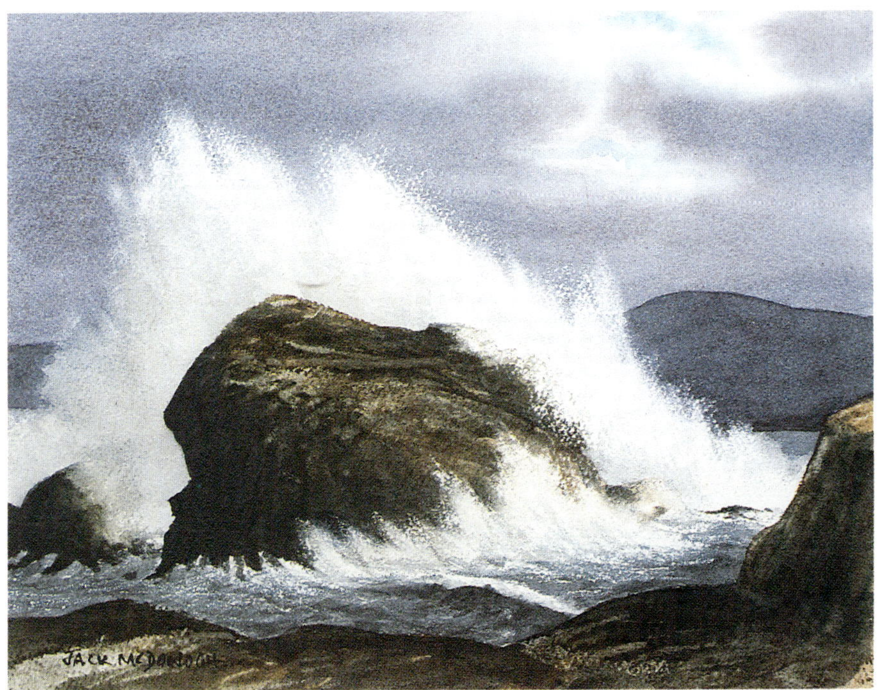

STEP 4

The main aim in this step is to strengthen all areas of the painting.

A Darken hills in background with a strengthening wash of winsor blue and light red.
Allow to dry.

B Darken water in background with a wash of winsor blue and raw umber.
Allow to dry.

C Put more shade in the breaking wave with a thin mixture of winsor blue and raw umber.

D Strengthen the foreground water with a mixture of winsor blue and raw umber.
Allow to dry.

E With a lift-off brush 'lift-off' at the rock base to make the small splashes up the face of the rock.

F I took the straightness out of the lower part at the back of the rock with raw umber and payne's gray mixed. The straightness there worried me.

G Strengthen foreground rocks with raw umber and payne's gray.

H Use razor blade to indicate spray at edge of breaking wave and edge of splashes on the sides of the rock.

Early morning mists

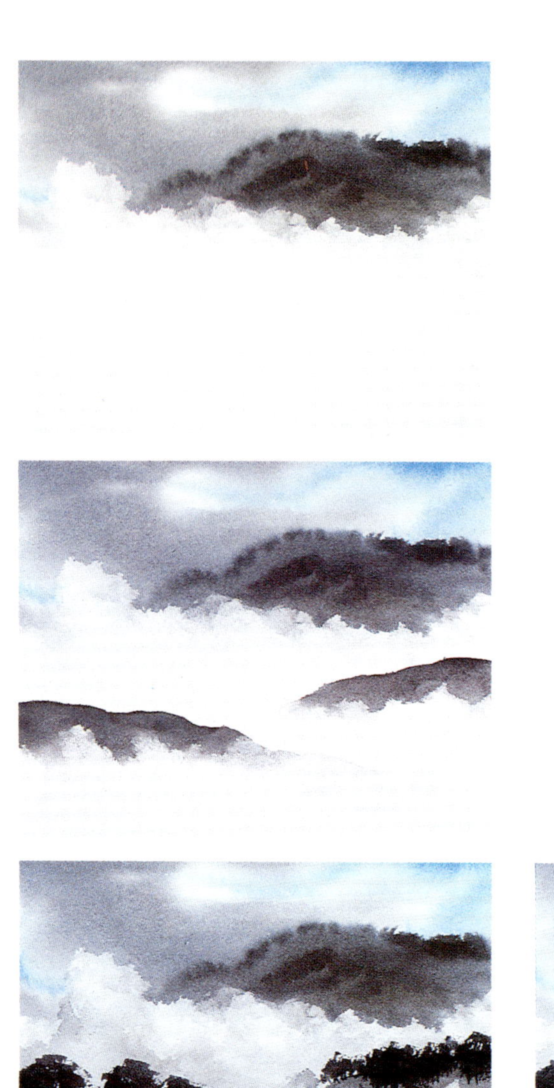

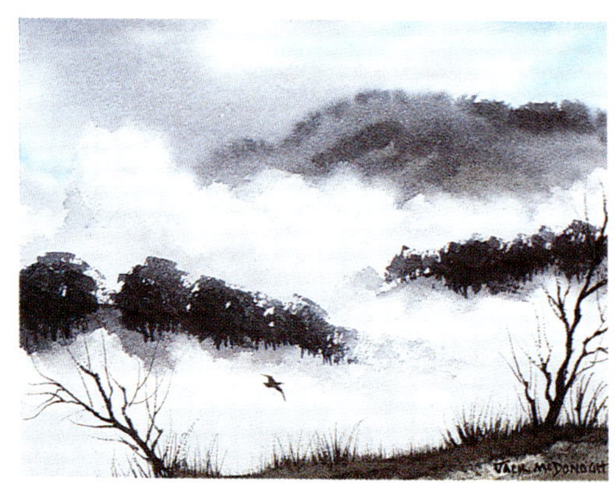

Early morning mists

STEP 1

Although it is not necessary to hurry unduly while painting some of the parts of this picture, remember that the tops of the mists in each case are lifted before the paper dries.

A Wet top half of painting surface with clear water.

B Paint clouds using a mixture of light red and winsor blue. Add antwerp blue for sky area.

C While still wet paint distant hill using a stronger mixture (than used for the clouds) of light red and winsor blue. Add trees on hill with strong mixture of light red and winsor blue.

D Using tissues lift colour and water from the surface to make the top of the mist.
Allow to dry.

Early morning mists

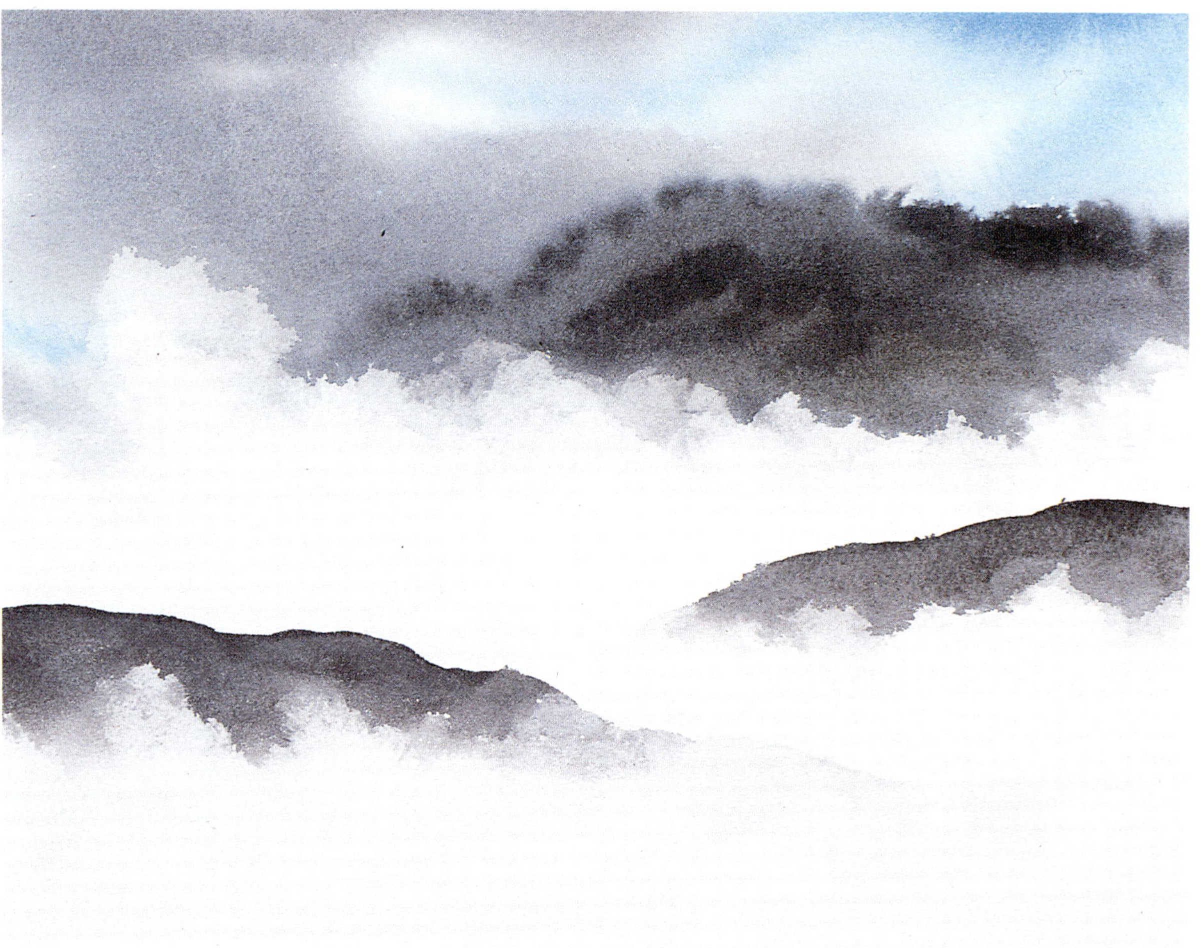

STEP 2

A On the dry surface of the paper paint the firm top of the right hand hill with a strong mixture of light red and winsor blue. Then immediately apply a wash of clear water to the lower part of this colour while still wet and lift the top of the mist with a tissue. Allow to dry.

B Repeat the same step with the left side hill. Allow to dry.

Early morning mists

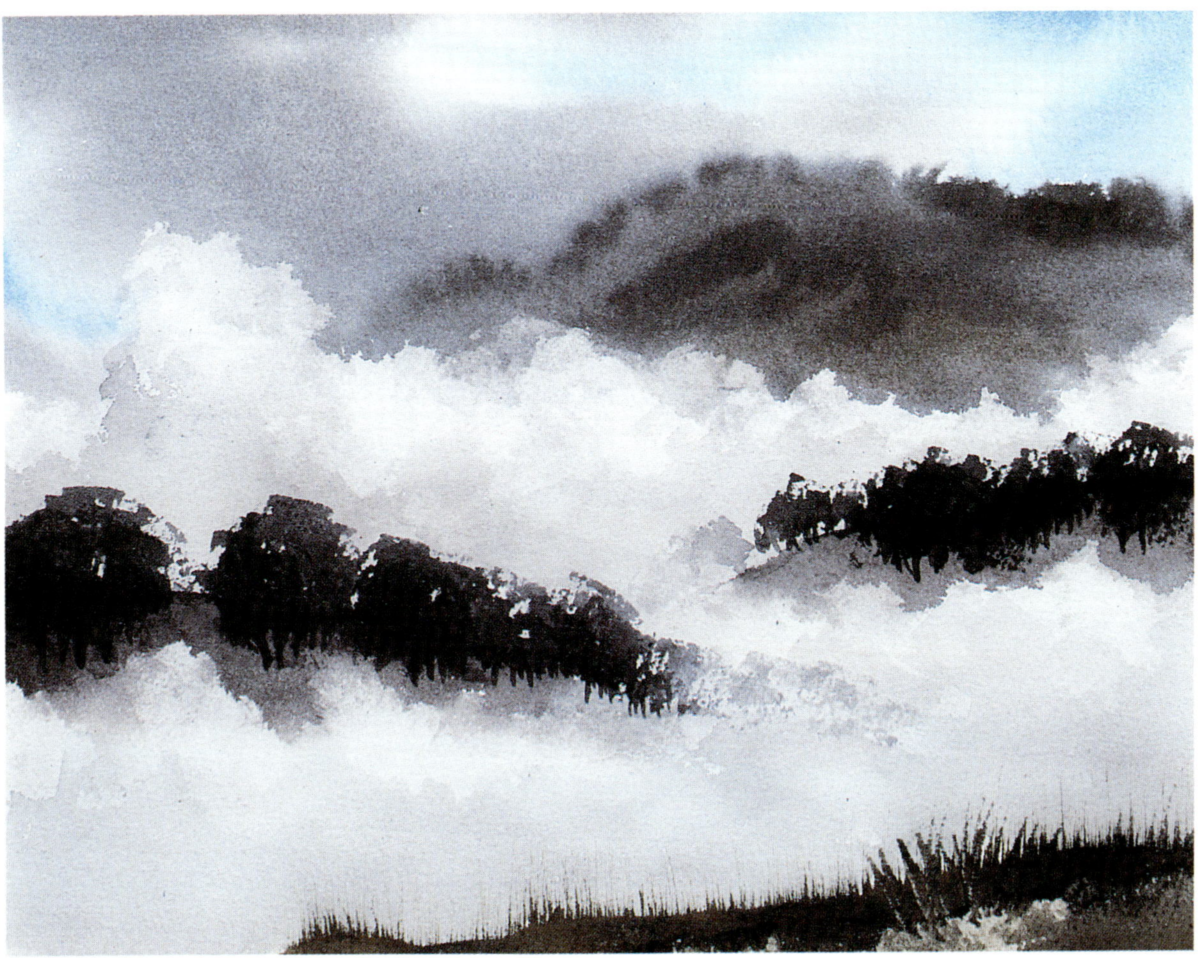

STEP 3

I see mists in the valleys as clouds on the ground. So with this in mind we now have to give form to the mists.

A Mix a colour just a bit paler than the colour you used for the clouds in Step 1, that is a mixture of light red and winsor blue.

B Cover mist areas with a thin coat of clear water. Paint the cloud colours into the mists and while still wet lift areas with a tissue to indicate highlights.
Allow to dry.

C Add trees on dry surface with a strong mixture of light red and winsor blue.

D Paint foreground with raw umber with a mixture of light red and winsor blue added. Use varnish brush to give grassy edge while wet and razor blade to give earth textures.
Allow to dry.

Early morning mists

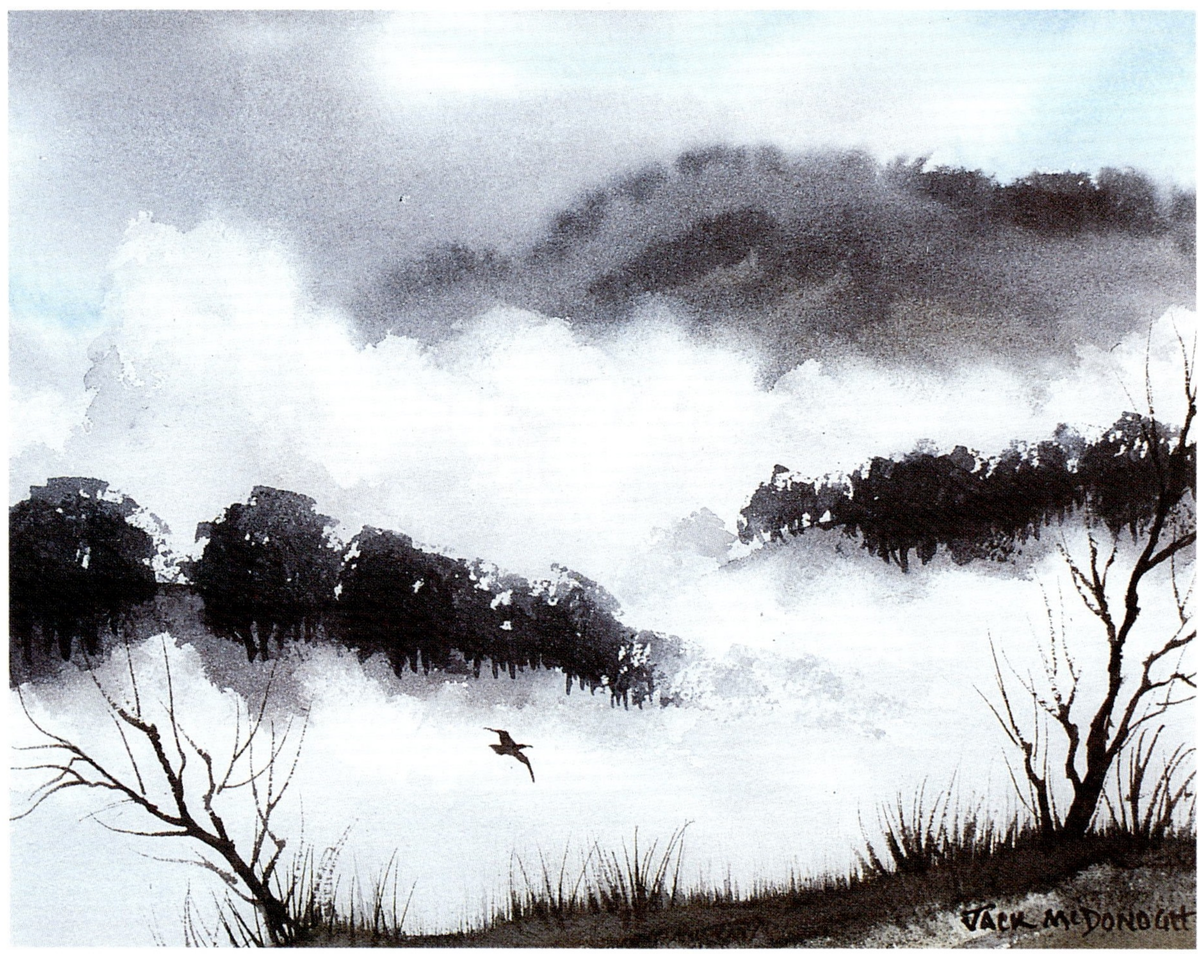

STEP 4

A With the lift-off brush 'lift' some areas at the top edges of the mists.

B Strengthen foreground earth in parts with a light red and winsor blue mixture.
Allow to dry.

C Paint foreground trees with a strong mixture of light red and winsor blue.

Using a fine round brush add some extra strokes to the grassy edges. Use burnt umber.

D Paint bird with a light red and winsor blue mixture.

Fog moving in

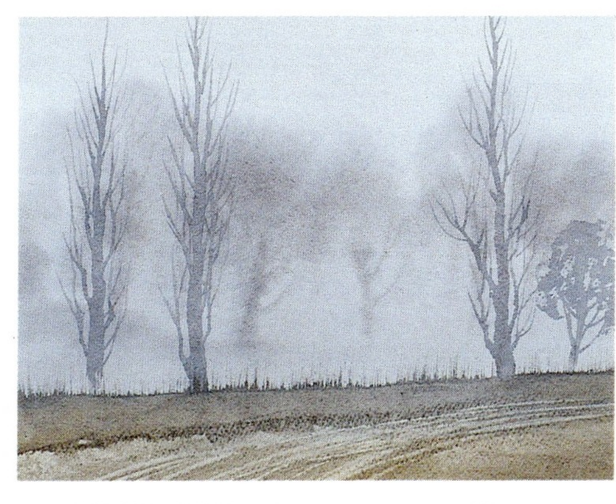

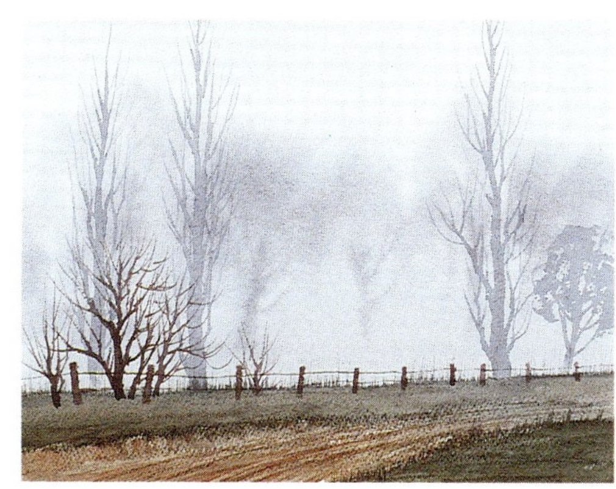

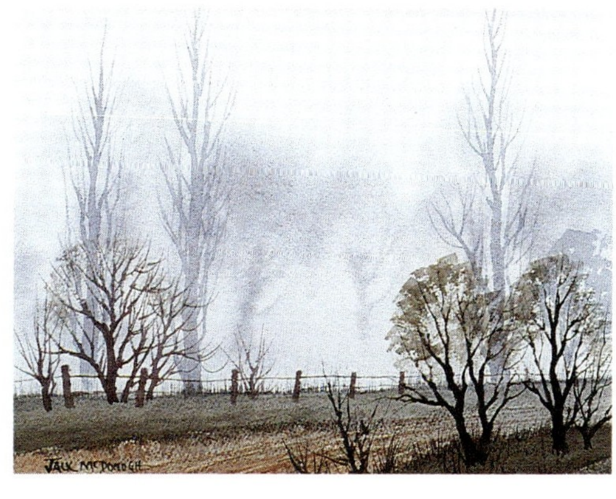

Fog moving in

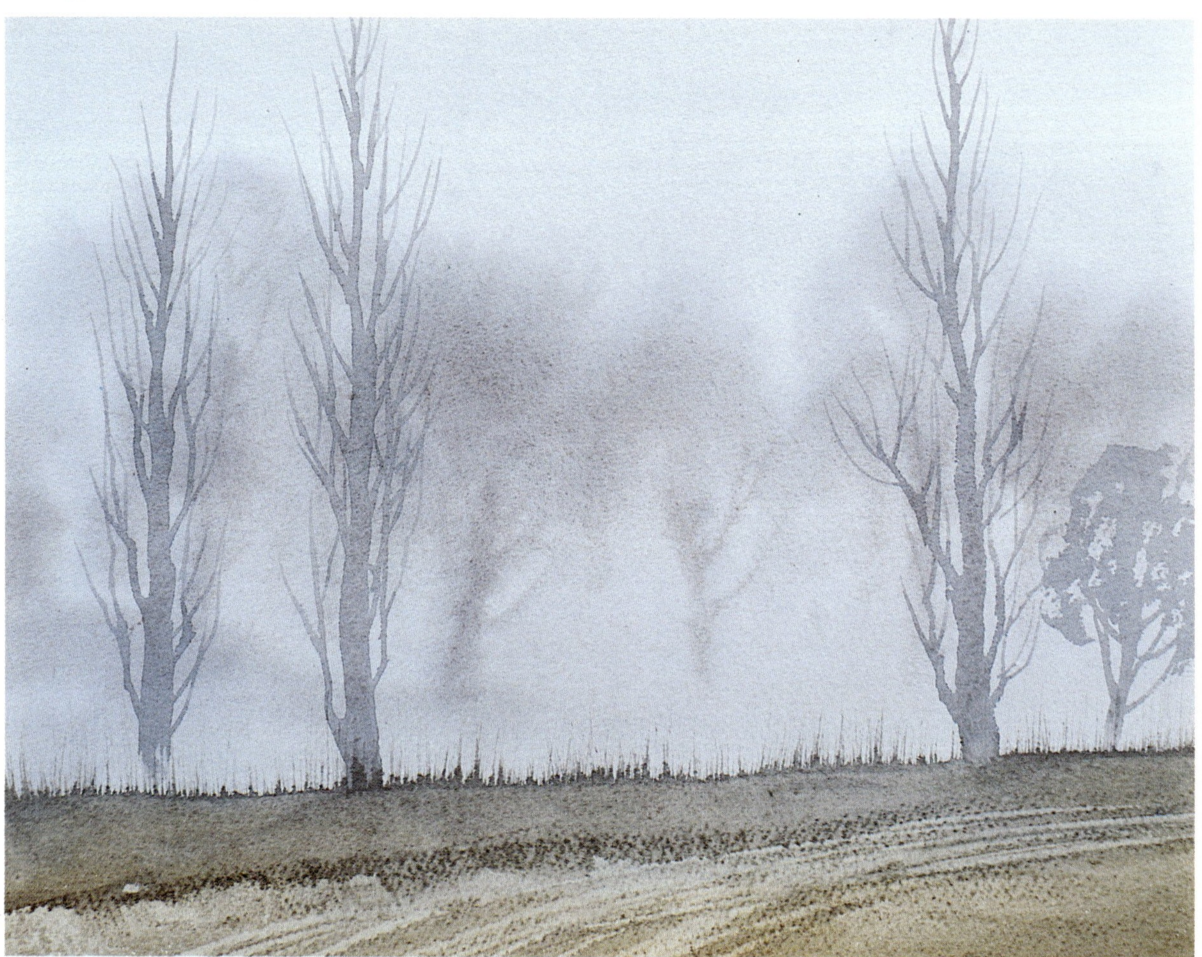

STEP 1

A Make a mixture of light red and winsor blue.

Wet entire surface of the paper with clear water and work the above mixture over the paper. Tilt board from the top to make the mixture darker at the bottom of the paper.

B While still wet, strengthen the above mixture, and paint the distant trees.
Allow to dry.

C Strengthen the mixture used in Step 1B and paint the poplar trees and the tree on the right.
Allow to dry.

D Add some raw umber to the mixture used in Step 1C and paint the foreground grass areas. Use the varnish brush to indicate grassy edges.

Indicate road area with a wash of raw umber. Razor blade the edge of the road. Add some knife strokes to the road.
Allow to dry.

Fog moving in

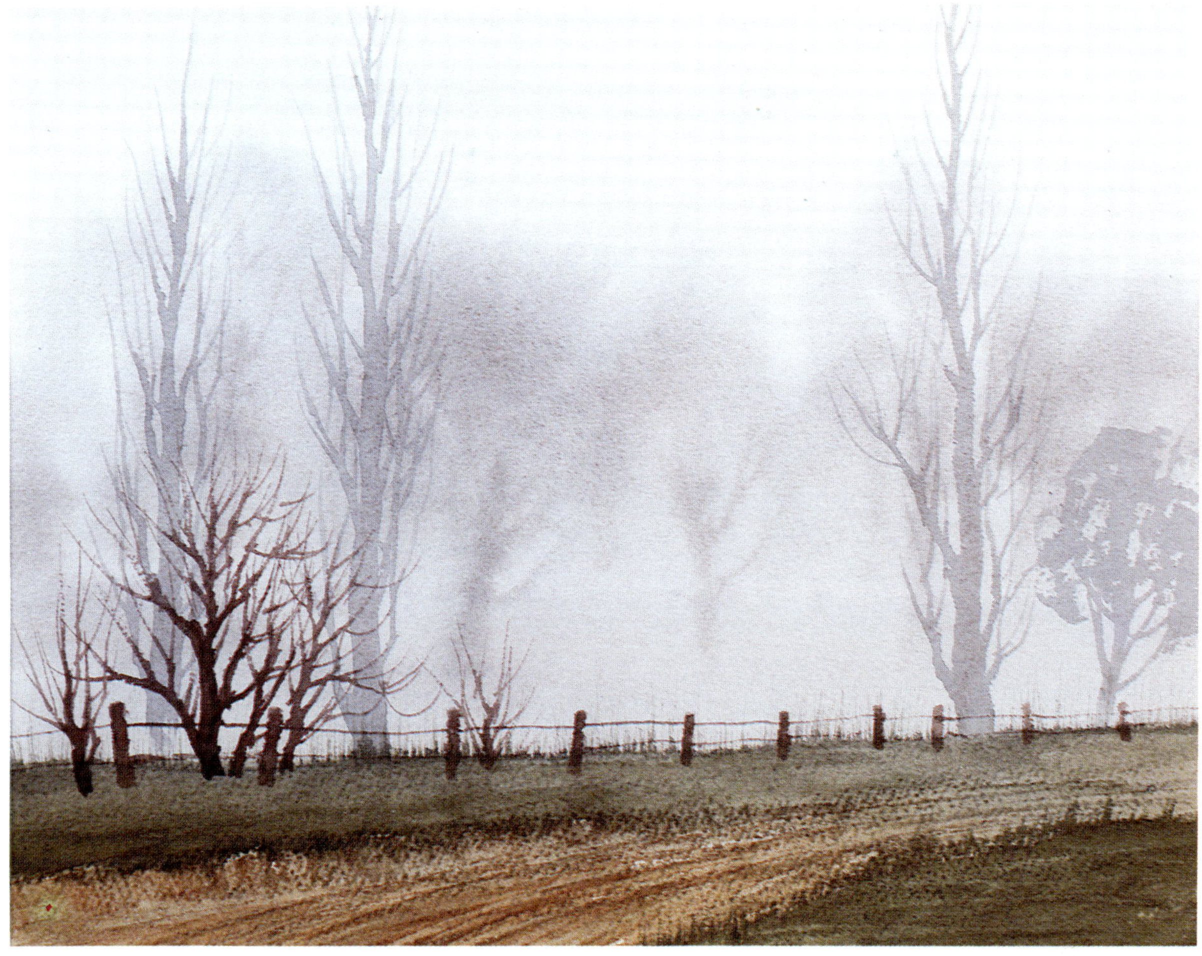

STEP 2

A Paint a wash of raw sienna and light red over the road. Use knife strokes while wet.

B Paint a pale wash of a mixture of raw umber and a touch of antwerp blue over grassy areas.
Allow to dry.

C Paint fence posts and wire with a mixture of cobalt blue and light red. Paint trees in left foreground with the same mixture.
Allow to dry.

Fog moving in

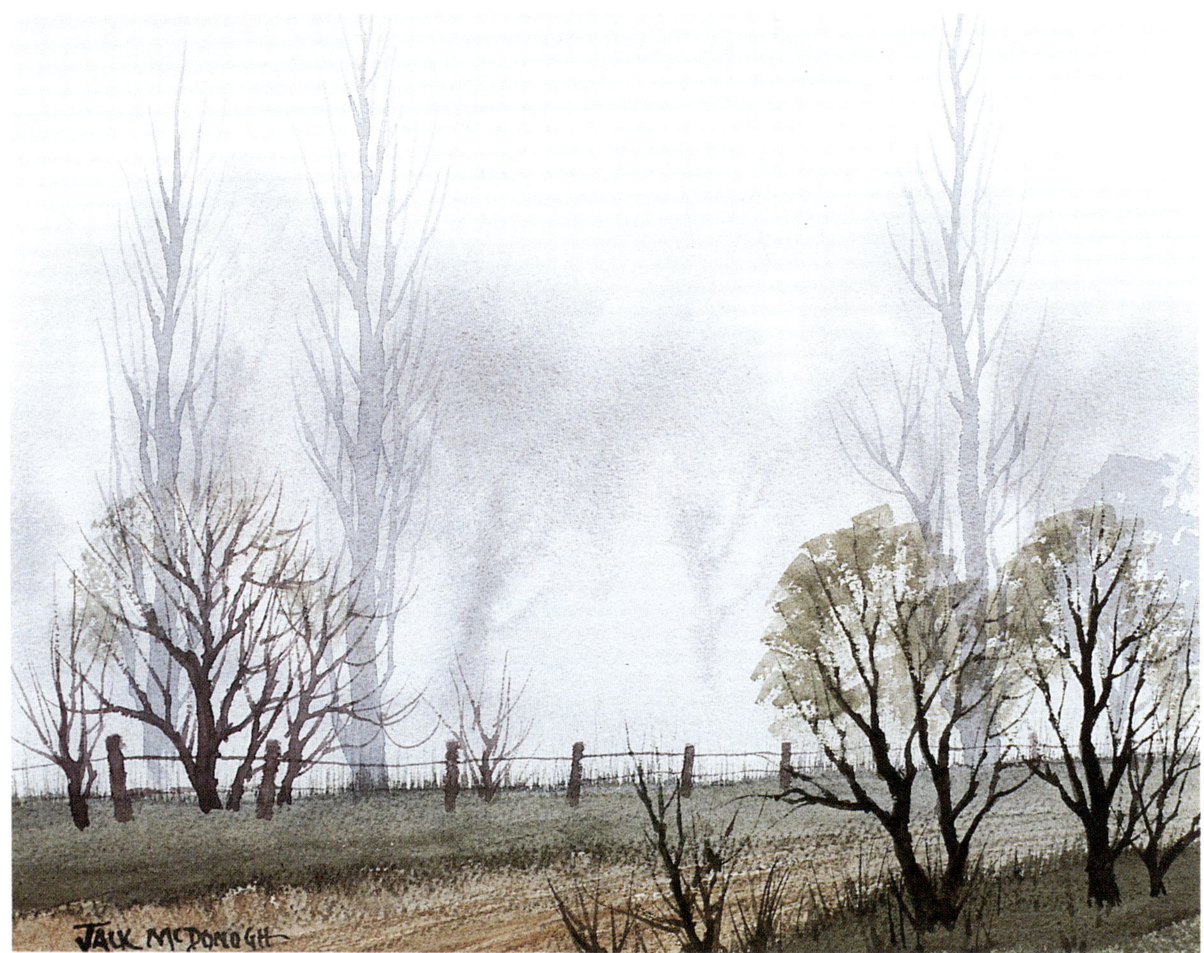

STEP 3

A Strengthen foreground grass on right hand side with a wash of raw umber and a touch of antwerp blue. Use varnish brush to indicate grassy edge. Make some textures with the razor blade.
Allow to dry.

B Paint foreground trees. Do the trunks with a thinned burnt umber. Allow to dry and add leaves with a thinned raw umber. Use the same mixture to lightly suggest leaves on left side trees.

C With a fine round brush add some strokes to the grass edges and some twiggy pieces in right foreground. Use burnt umber.

Boats in the bay

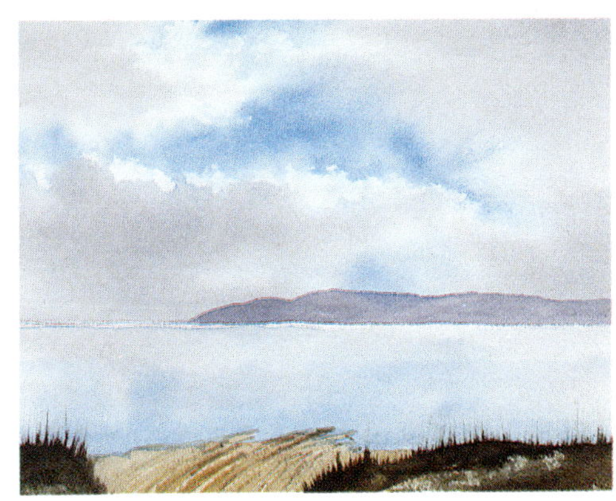

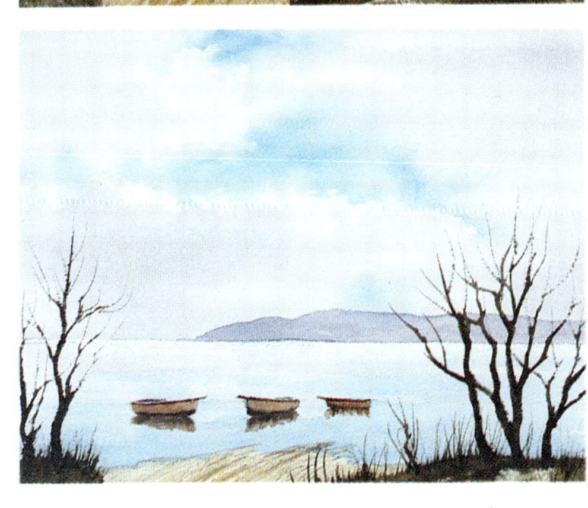

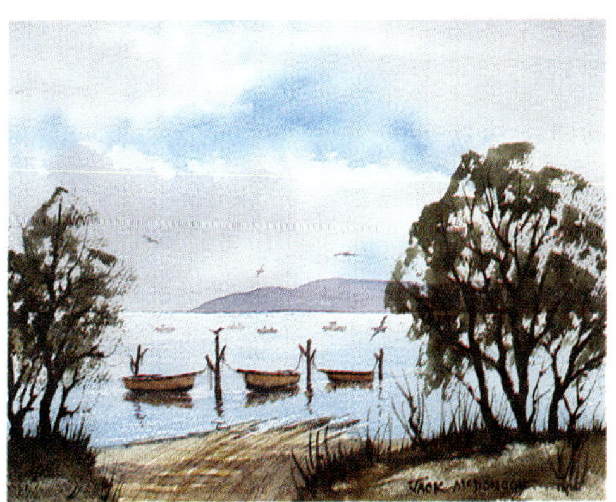

Boats in the bay

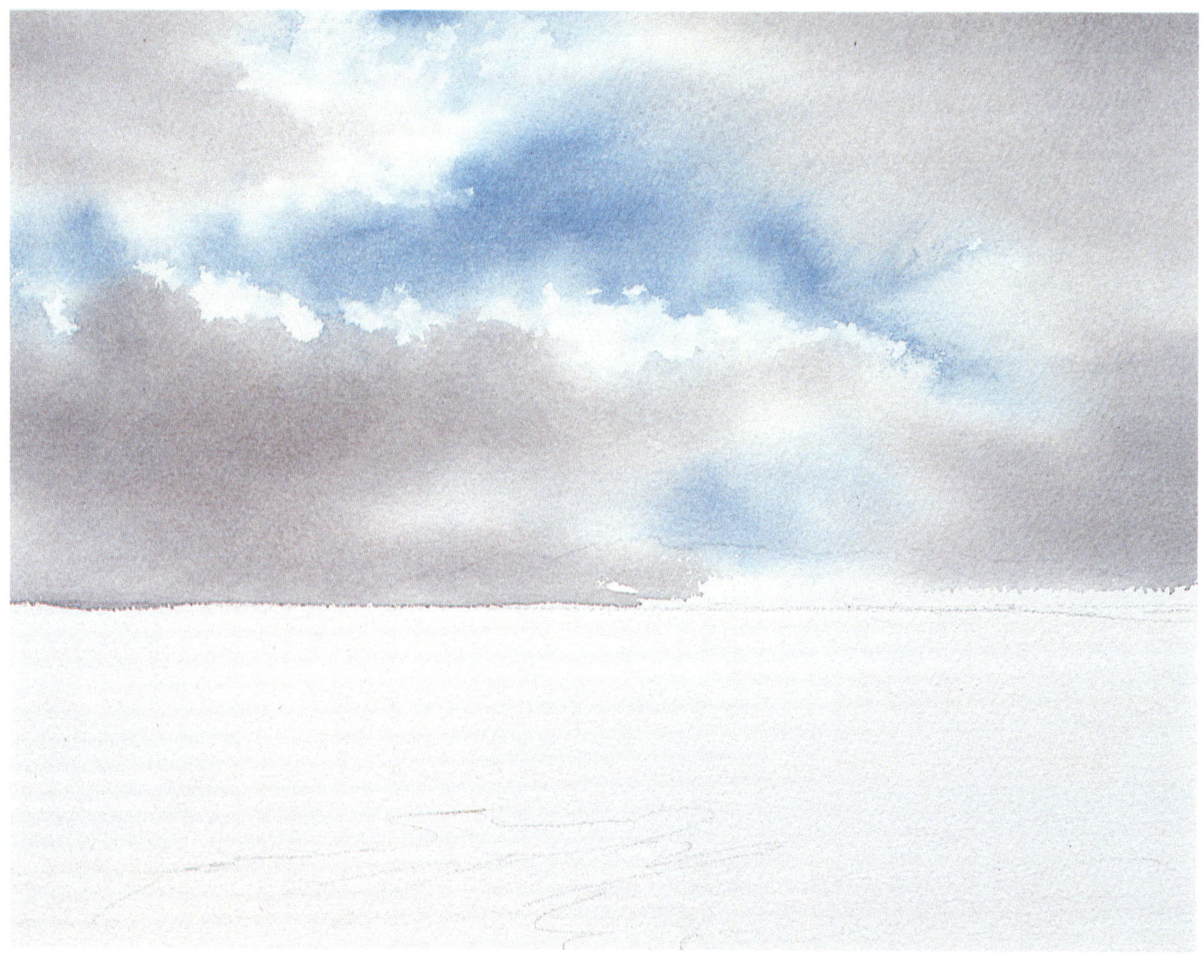

STEP 1

A Pencil outline of scene.

B Wet sky area with clear water and paint clouds with a mixture of light red and winsor blue. Use antwerp blue for sky areas.
Allow to dry.

Boats in the bay

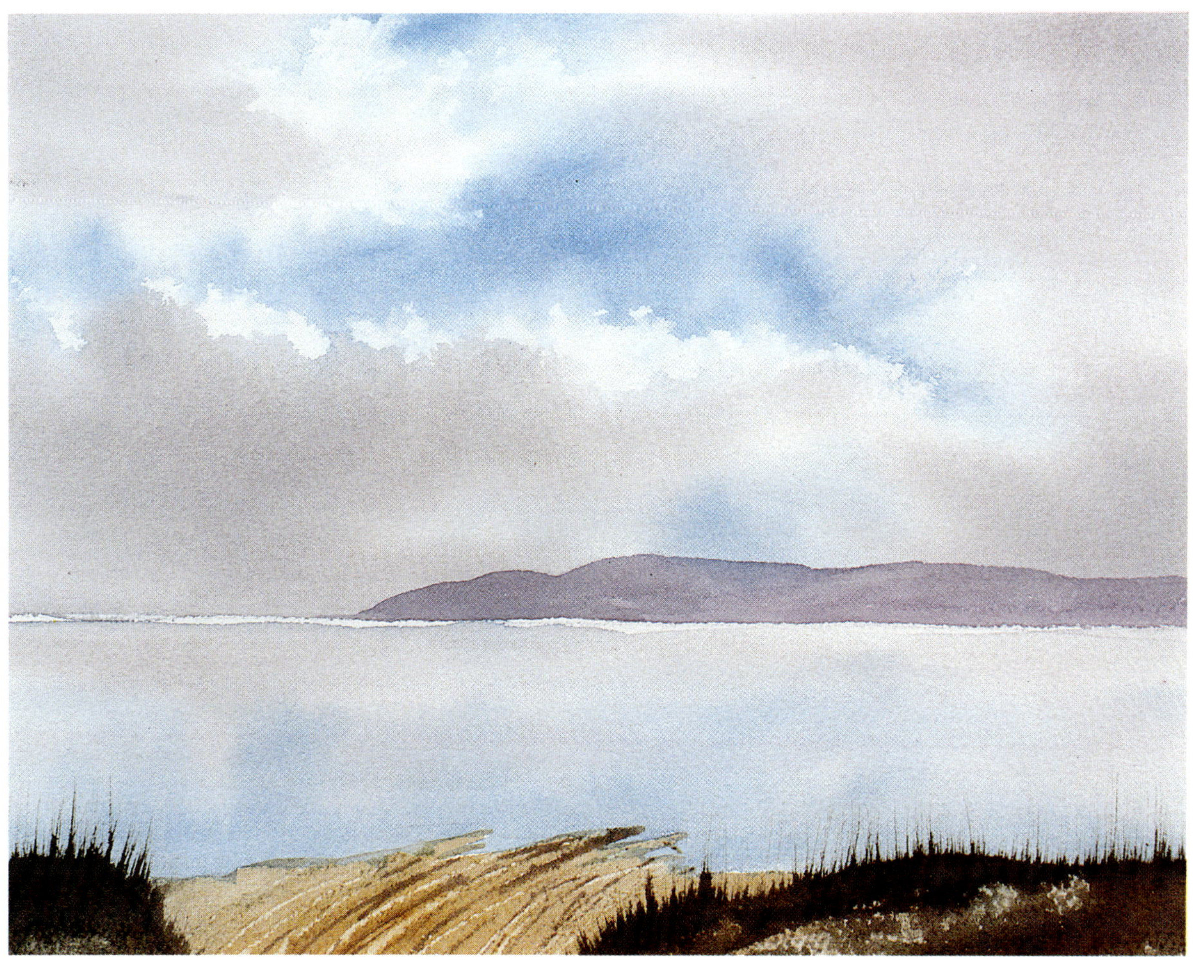

STEP 2

A Paint distant hill with cobalt blue.
Allow to dry.

B Wet water area and paint the same cloud mixture as in Step 1B onto the surface leaving white areas. While still wet paint antwerp blue into white areas and make the blue stronger in the foreground.
Allow to dry.

C Paint sandy beach with raw sienna and a touch of raw umber. Use knife strokes to show wheel marks.
Allow to dry.

D Paint foreground using raw umber strengthened in parts with antwerp blue. Use the varnish brush to indicate grassy edge and razor blade to give earth textures.
Allow to dry.

Boats in the bay

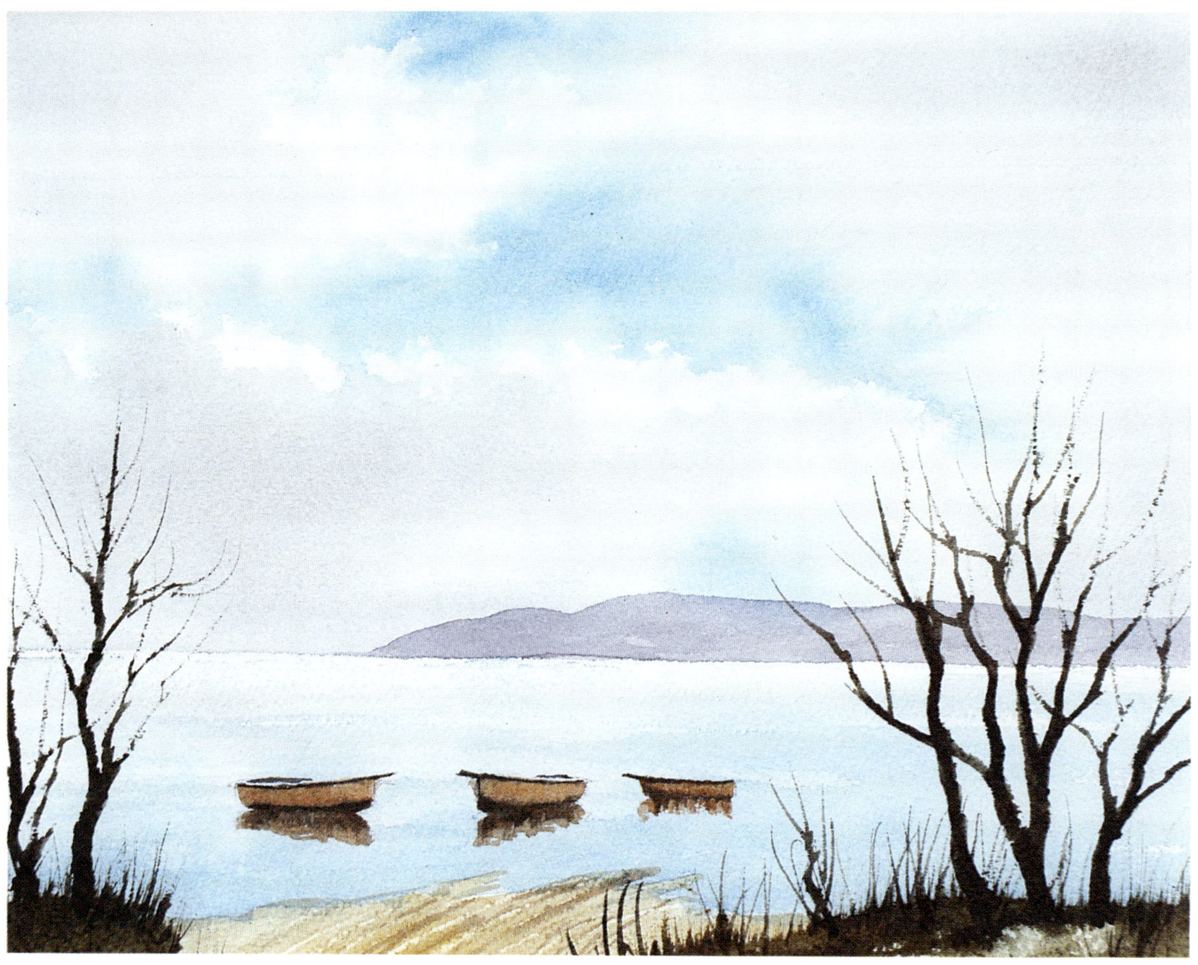

STEP 3

A Strengthen water in foreground with some strokes of antwerp blue. Allow to dry.

B Sketch boats in with pencil. Then paint using burnt sienna. Paint the reflections for the boats with the same colour and at the same time as painting the boats. Darken the water mark line with some burnt umber and add some of this colour to the reflections.
Allow to dry.

C Scrape some highlights on the water at the horizon with a razor blade.

D Paint trees in foreground using burnt umber with a touch of antwerp blue.
Allow to dry.

Boats in the bay

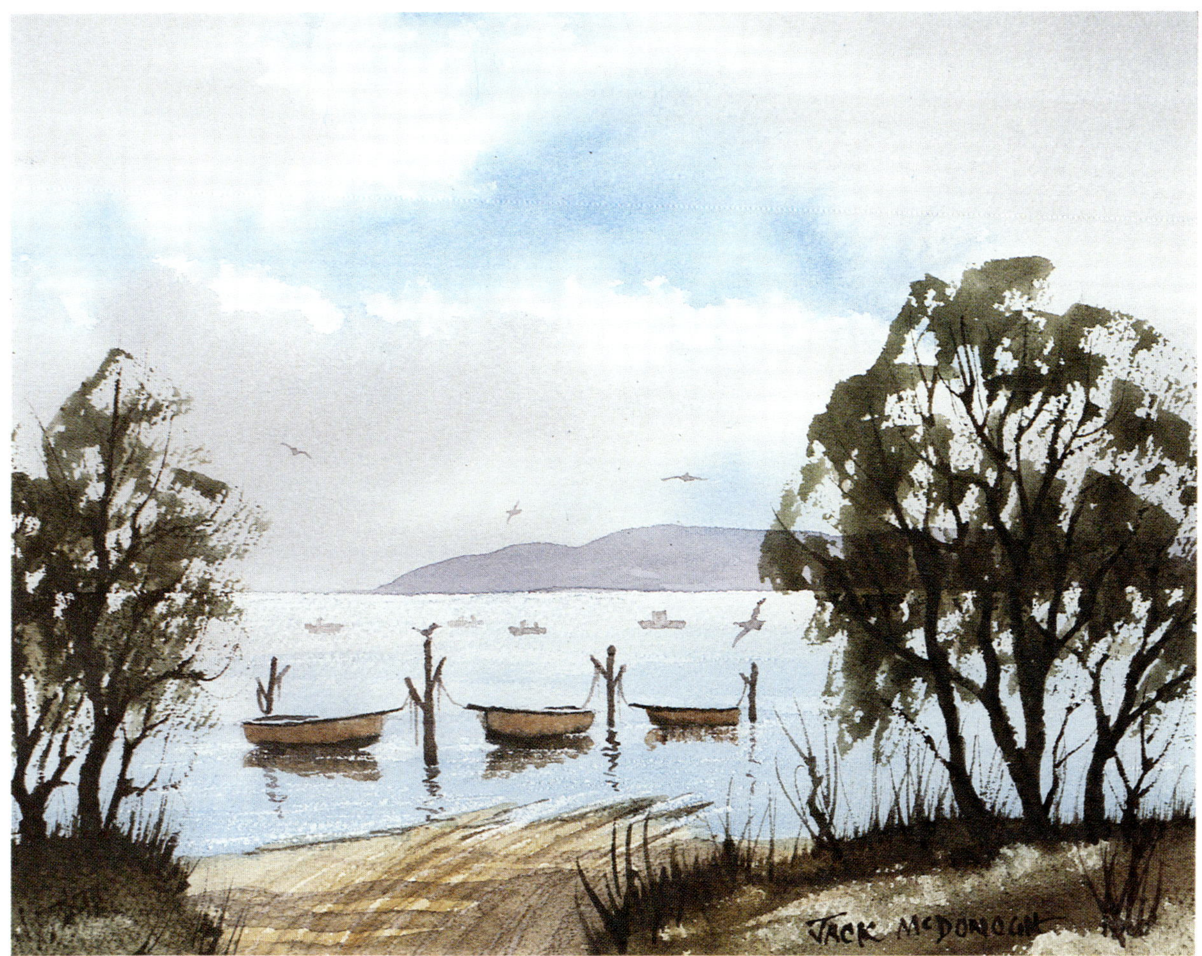

STEP 4

A Paint poles and their reflections with burnt umber.

B Paint distant boats with a cobalt blue and light red mixture.

C Paint leaves on trees with a mixture of raw umber and a touch of antwerp blue.

D Paint shadows on sandy area with a mixture of cobalt blue and light red.
Allow to dry.

E Do some scratching with the razor blade at the water's edge and near the boats.

F Paint birds with a cobalt blue and light red mixture.

G Add some more limbs to the foreground trees.

H Add some strengthening washes to leaf masses on trees with the same mixture used for the first wash of leaves.

Stormy afternoon

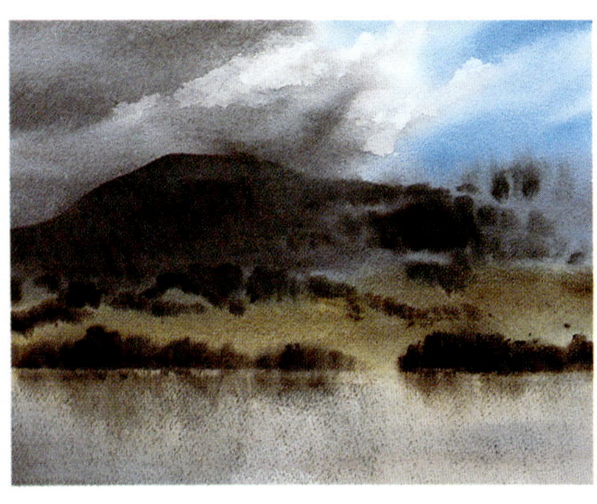

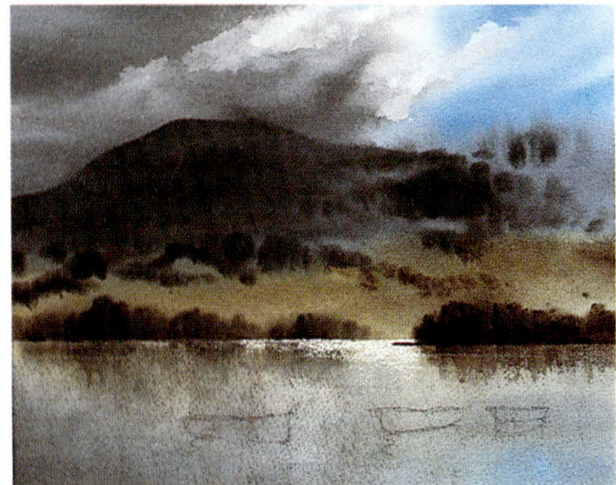

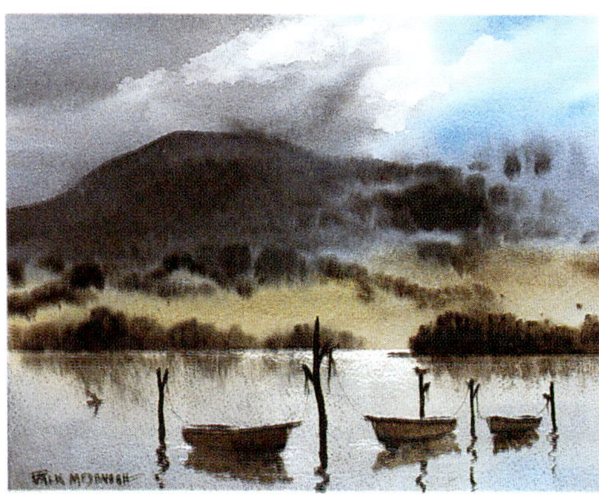

Stormy afternoon

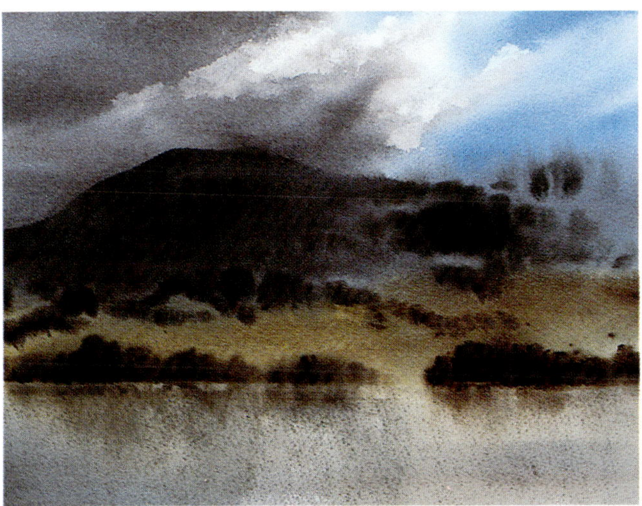

STEP 1

You will need a piece of heavy strawboard as an accessory in this step. Make it about 20 cm × 5 cm. This step is painted using the 'wet-in-wet' technique and is completed with the one wetting of the paper.

The colours are mixed on the paper. By that I mean the pigments are picked from the pans with the brush and applied directly to the wet surface. In some cases I have picked the two colours used from the pans with the same brush. This technique gives the strong colours as shown.

Do not linger too long on any one area. You can have failures with this technique but conversely you can have some wonderful successes. So be brave and go for it.

A Wet entire surface of paper.

B Pick up winsor blue and light red and paint clouds. Use antwerp blue for sky colour. Tissue edge of clouds.

C Use strong winsor blue for the mountain, thinning to the right hand side.

D Work raw umber and raw sienna into the base of the mountain.

E Use winsor blue and light red to indicate trees on the slopes of the mountain.

F Use strong burnt umber to indicate row of trees by the water.

G Make thinner use of raw sienna, raw umber and winsor blue over water area.

H With the piece of strawboard rake downwards on the surface from the base of the burnt umber trees. Repeat this raking if necessary to get the correct effect.

I When the painting is nearly dry give a firm edge to the left side of the mountain with winsor blue.
Allow to dry.

Stormy afternoon

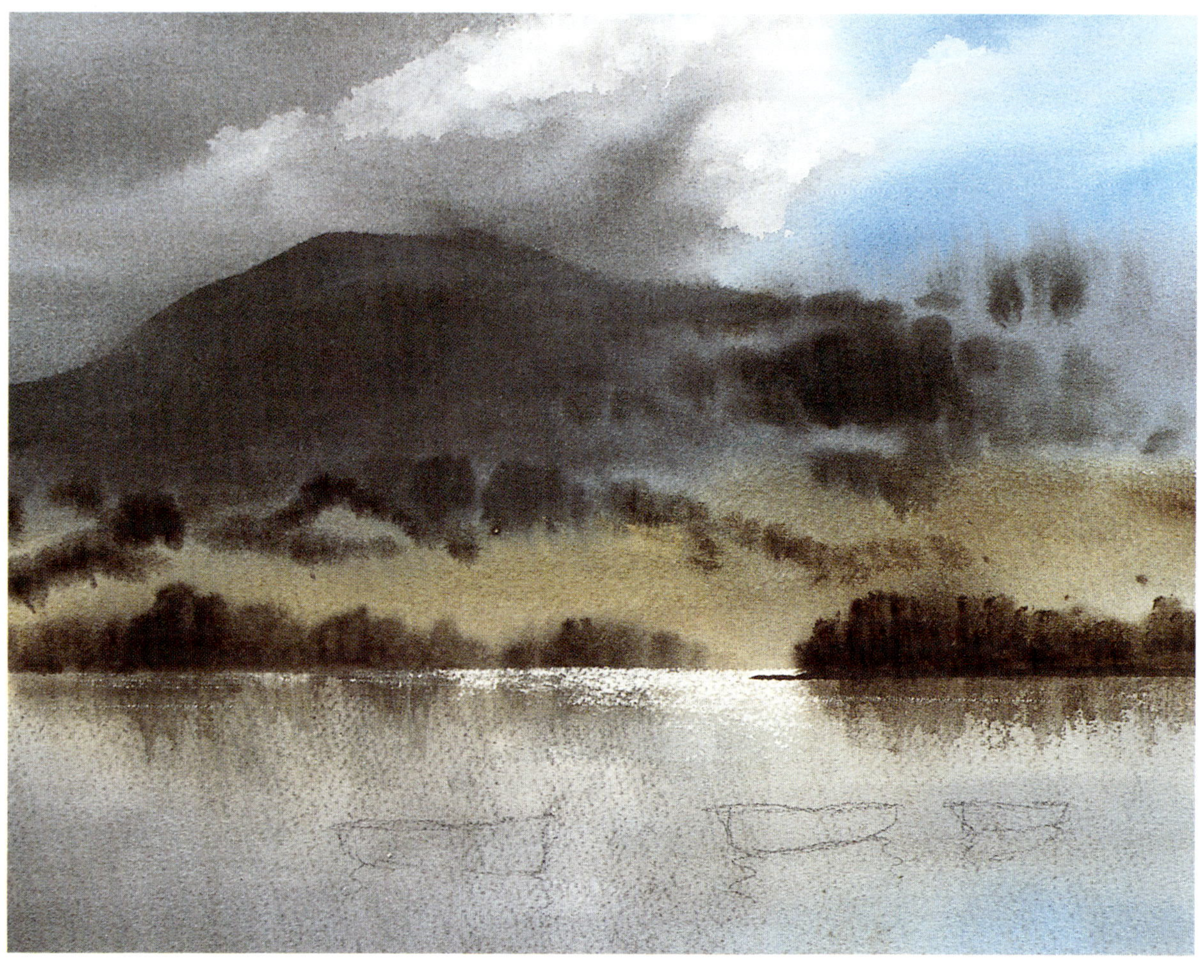

STEP 2

Check the painting within your mount. If you feel certain areas need reworking you can rewet them and repeat the process. In my case I felt the water area could do with some more colour.

A Wet water area and work a thin amount of winsor blue to left side and some antwerp blue to right side.
Allow to dry.

B Strengthen reflections on dry paper.

C Use some burnt umber to strengthen water's edge by the right hand side trees.
Allow to dry.

D Use razor blade to make the highlights on the water.

Stormy afternoon

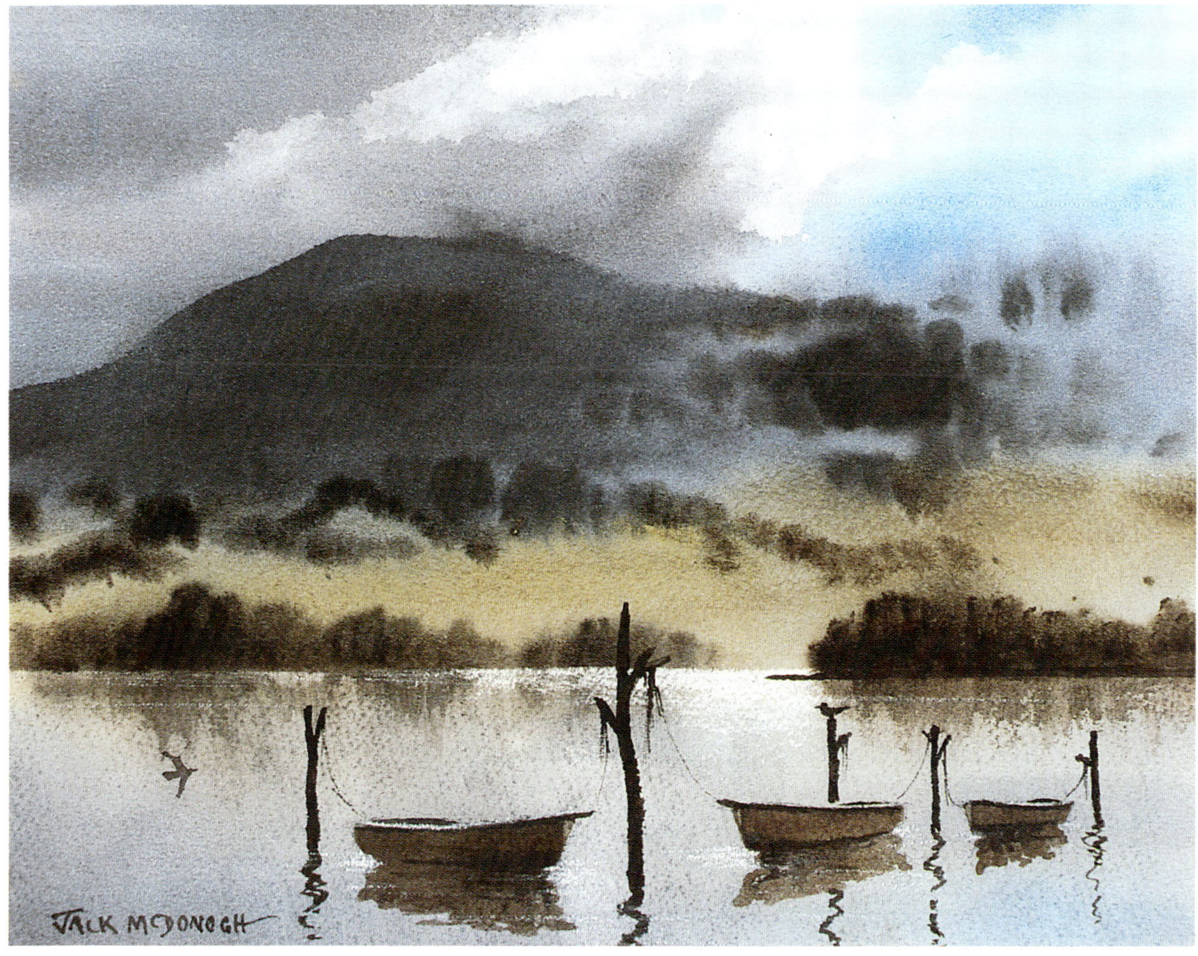

STEP 3

Check painting within the mount.

A Draw and paint boats. Use burnt umber with winsor blue at the waterline.
Allow to dry.

B Add poles and reflections—burnt umber darkened with winsor blue.
Allow to dry.

C Scratch highlights near boats with razor blade—also along the top edge of the boats.

D Paint birds in.

Summer storm

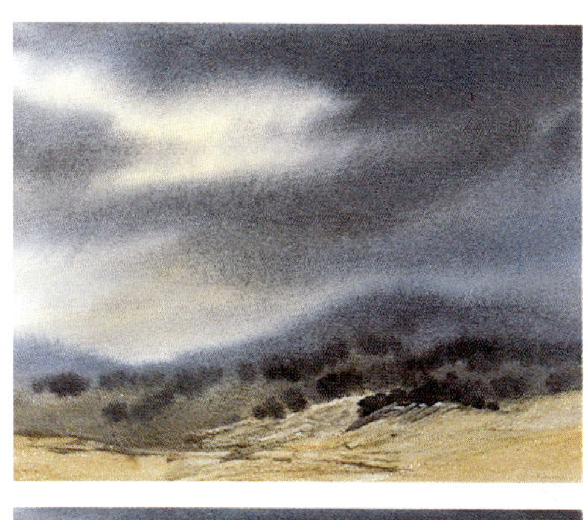

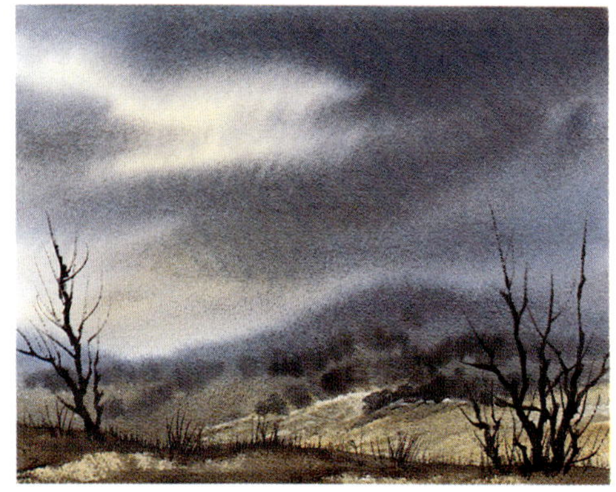

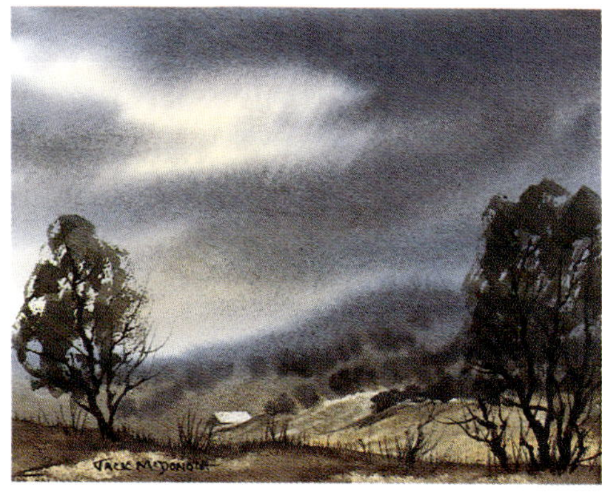

Summer storm

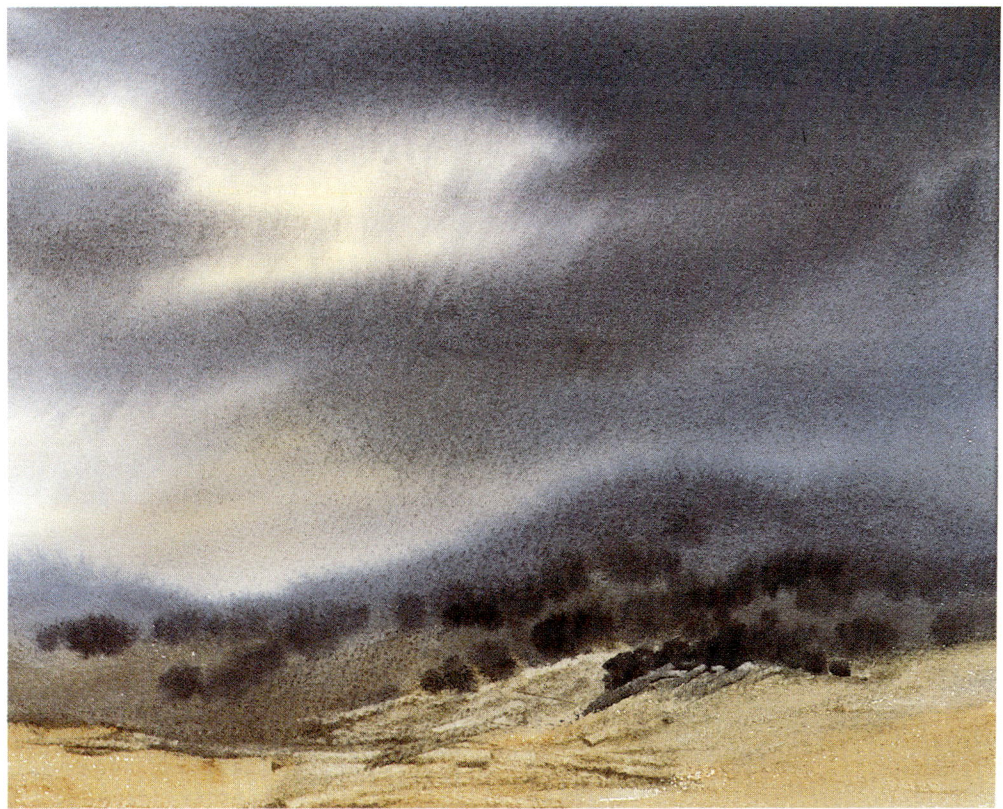

STEP 1

The 'wet-in-wet' technique is used in this painting. In this case, unlike the previous painting 'Stormy afternoon', the cloud colours are mixed in the pan. Note also that the cloud colour is mixed before wetting the surface of the paper. The raw sienna used in the sky is taken straight from the pan.

A Make a very strong mixture of winsor blue and light red ready for the clouds.

B Wet entire surface of the paper.

C Brush raw sienna straight from the pan over left side of sheet.

D Paint clouds using mixture in Step 1A.

E Hold board up vertically and tilt to get the 'run' on the clouds.

F Lay board flat and indicate hill with strong winsor blue.

G Work raw umber into base of hill, and raw sienna to the bottom of the sheet.

H Use a strong mixture of winsor blue and raw umber to indicate trees on slopes and hill.

I Use some knife strokes across foreground.
Allow to dry.

Summer storm

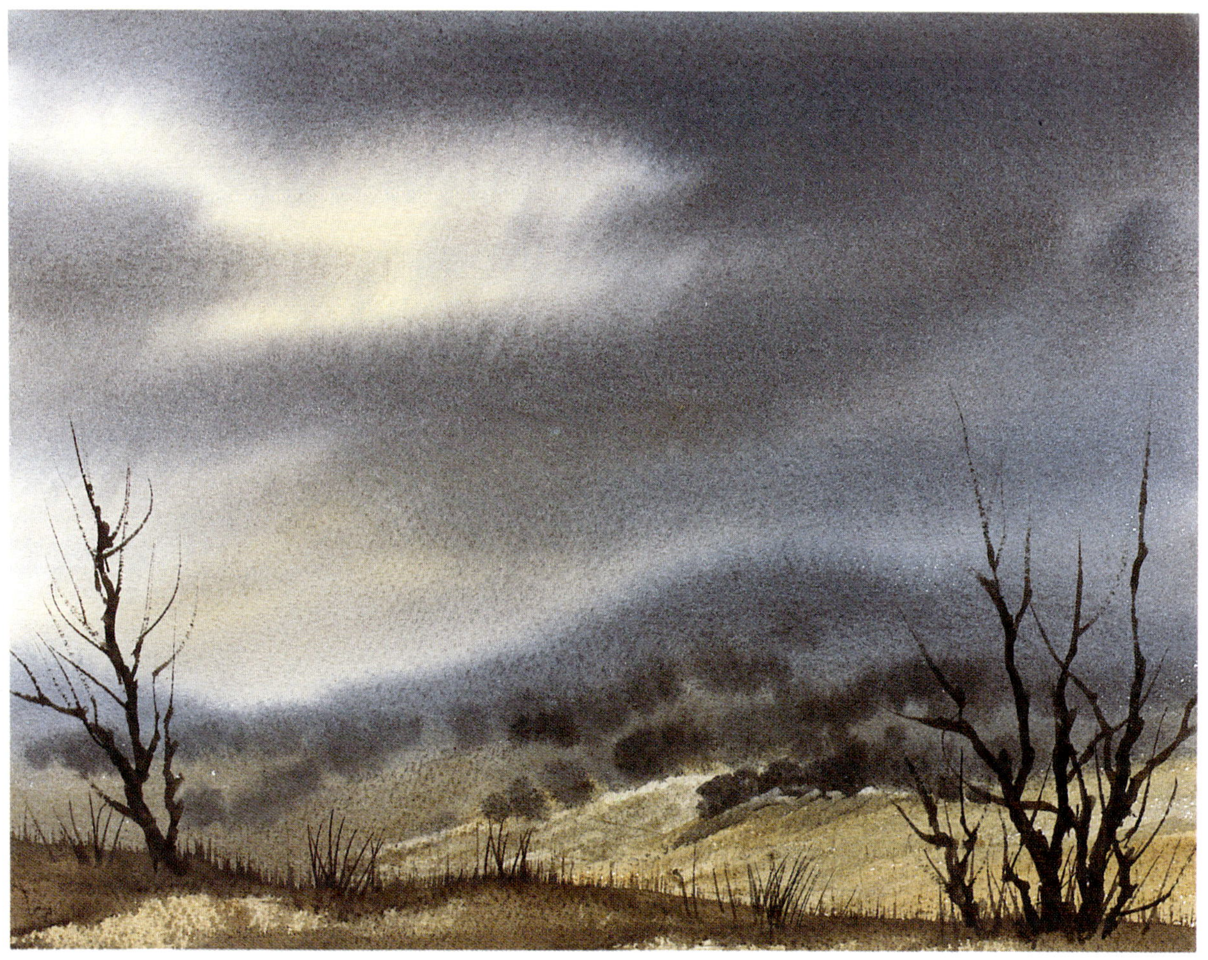

STEP 2

Check painting within the mount.

A Paint a mixture of raw umber and burnt umber over foreground. Use varnish brush to indicate grassy edge. Use razor blade to give textures to the earth.

B Indicate trees in foreground with trunks only. Use burnt umber with a touch of antwerp blue.
Allow to dry.

Summer storm

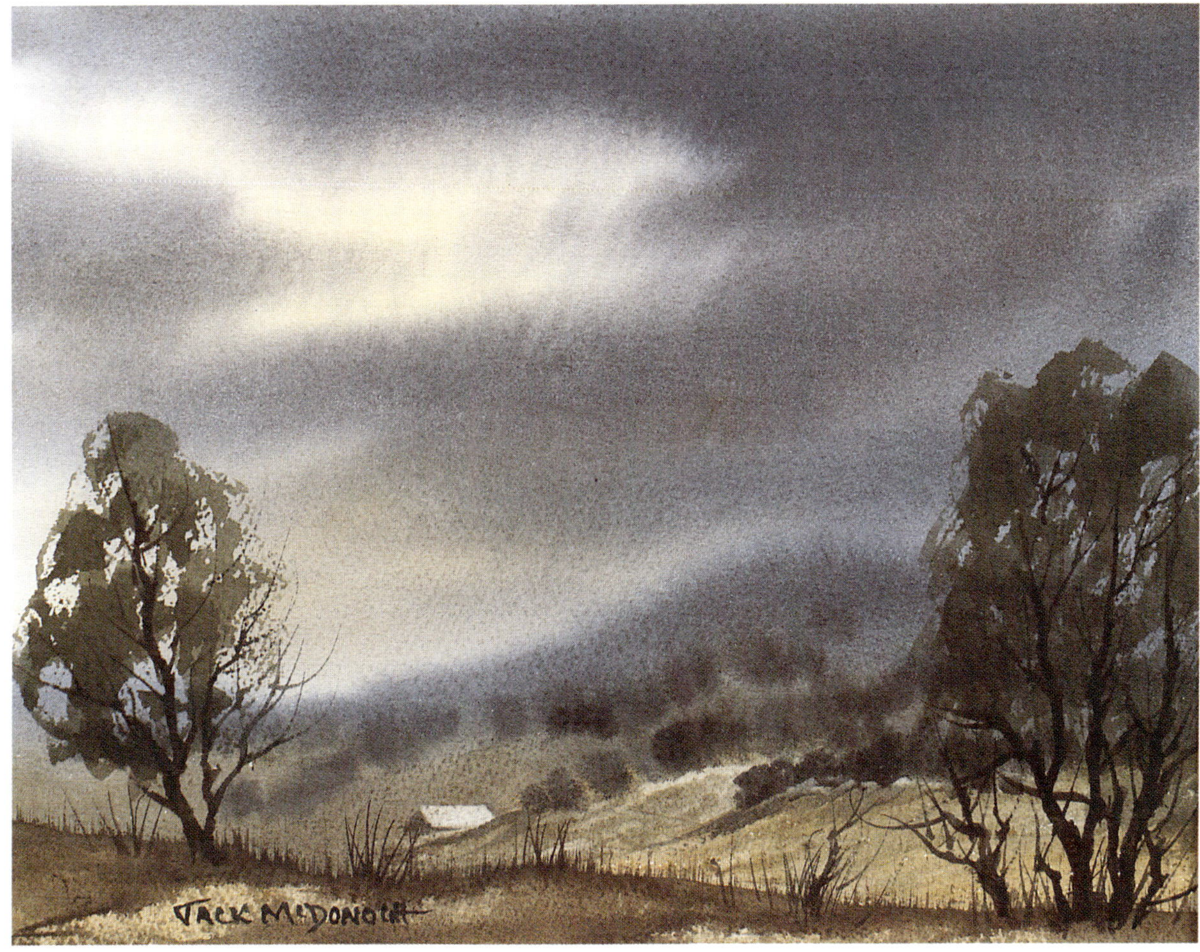

STEP 3

Check painting within the mount.

A Use raw umber with a touch of antwerp blue for leaves on trees in foreground.
Allow to dry.

B Lift shed roof by cutting the roof shape in a piece of cartridge paper and rubbing through the hole formed with a well wrung out cosmetic sponge. Dry any surplus wetness from sponge left on paper with a tissue.

C Strengthen leaves on foreground trees with the same mixture as in Step 3A.

D Indicate some more limbs in foreground trees.

The inlet at Narooma

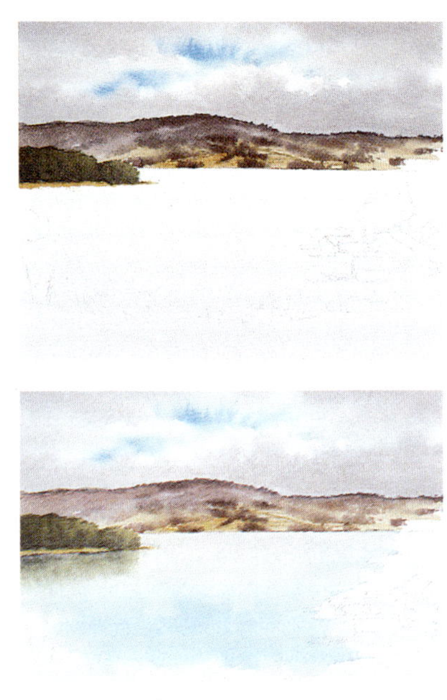

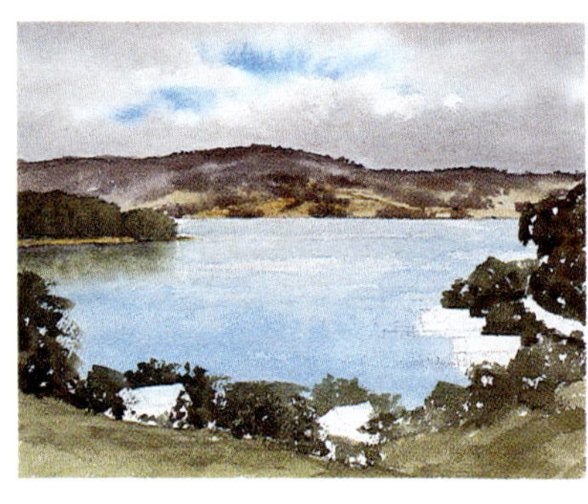

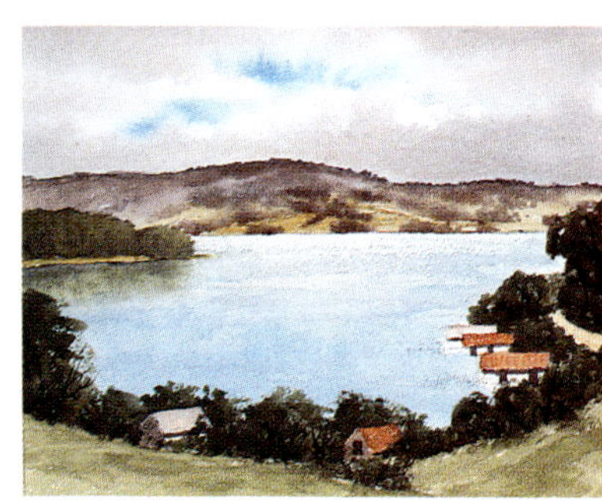

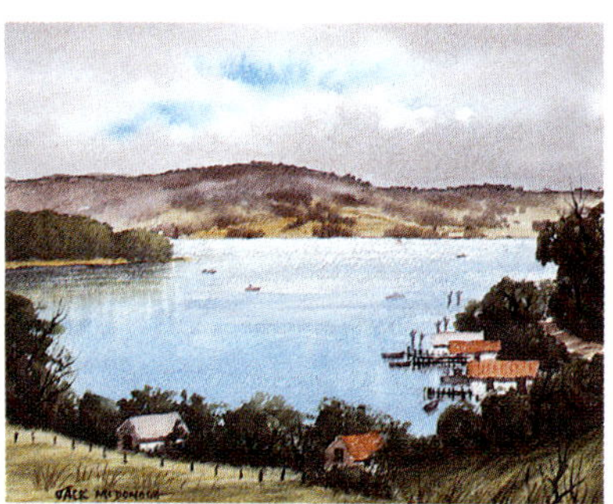

The inlet at Narooma

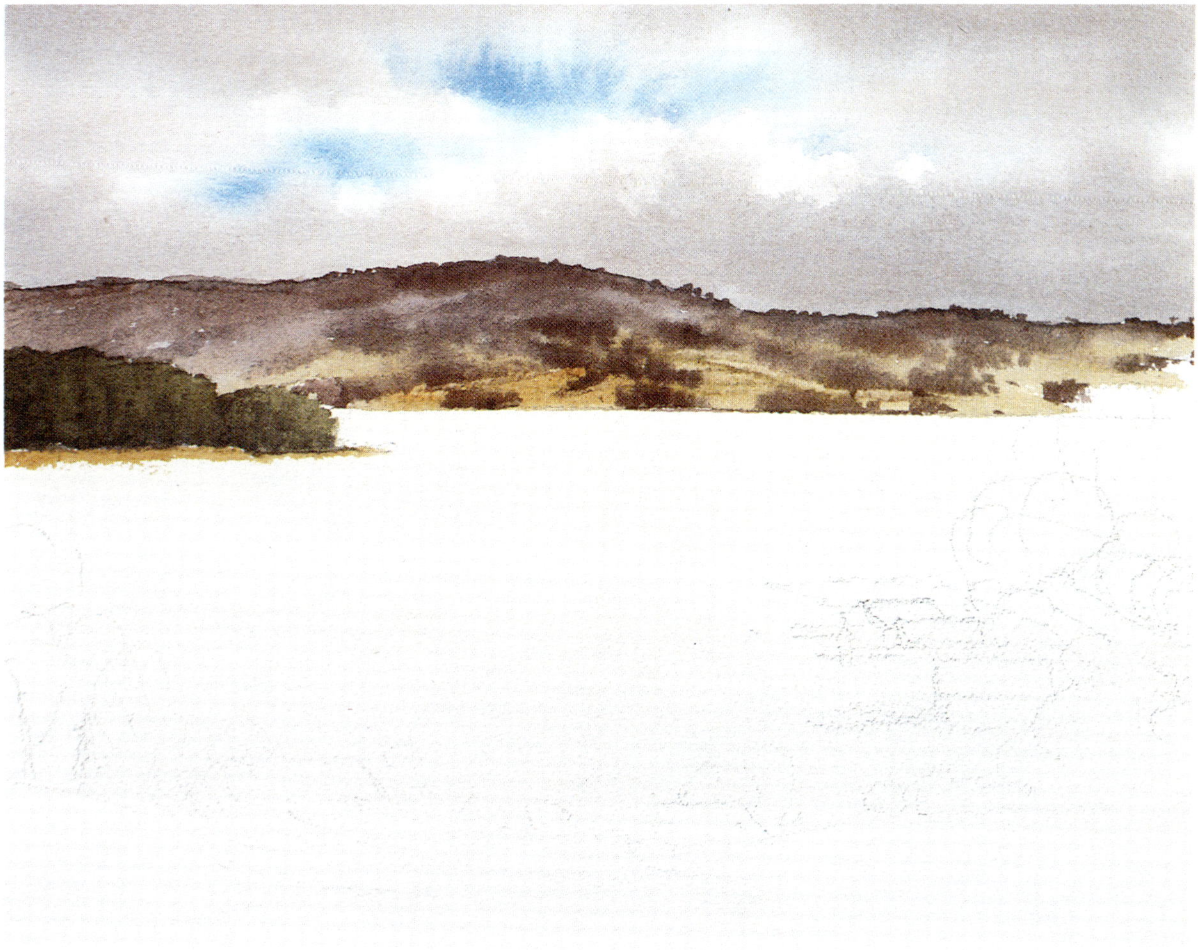

STEP 1

A Pencil outline of scene.

B Wet sky area with clear water and paint clouds with a mixture of light red and winsor blue.
Paint sky with antwerp blue.
Allow to dry.

C Paint the distant hill with cobalt blue about half way to the waterline. While still wet work some raw umber and raw sienna into the wet cobalt to indicate the grassy areas.

D While still wet work a strong mixture of cobalt blue and light red into the cobalt blue to indicate the tree areas. With the same mixture indicate some trees on the phone line and on the slopes.
Allow to dry.

E Paint the trees on the nearer left shoreline with a mixture of raw umber and a touch of antwerp blue. Work some cobalt blue into the base of these trees while wet.
Allow to dry.

The inlet at Narooma

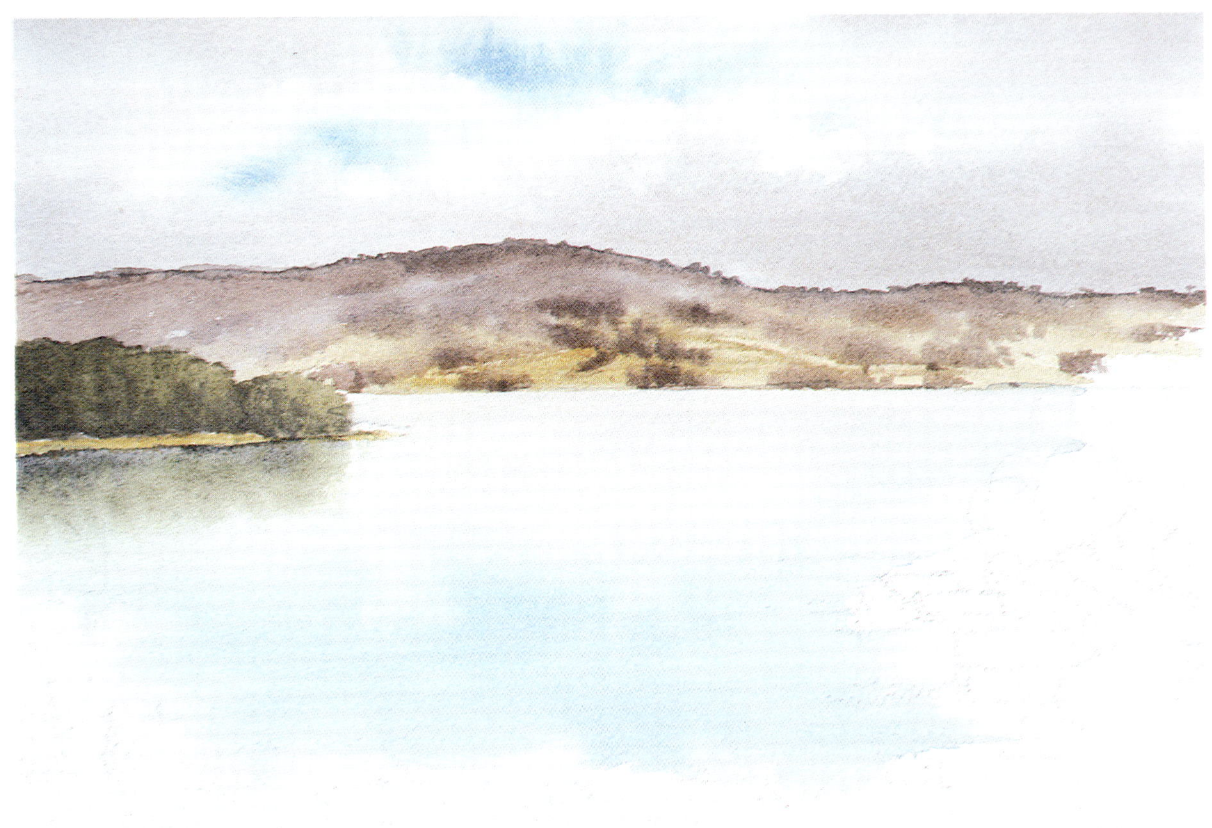

STEP 2

A Wet the entire water area. Then paint some of the cloud mixture into the wet surface near the distant shore and the remainder of the water with antwerp blue.

B While the water surface is still wet paint the reflections of left side trees with a mixture of raw umber and a touch of antwerp blue. Work some cobalt blue into the reflection at the shoreline.

C While still wet make some light vertical touches to the water with a tissue. Move the tissue downwards or toward you as you do this. Allow to dry.

The inlet at Narooma

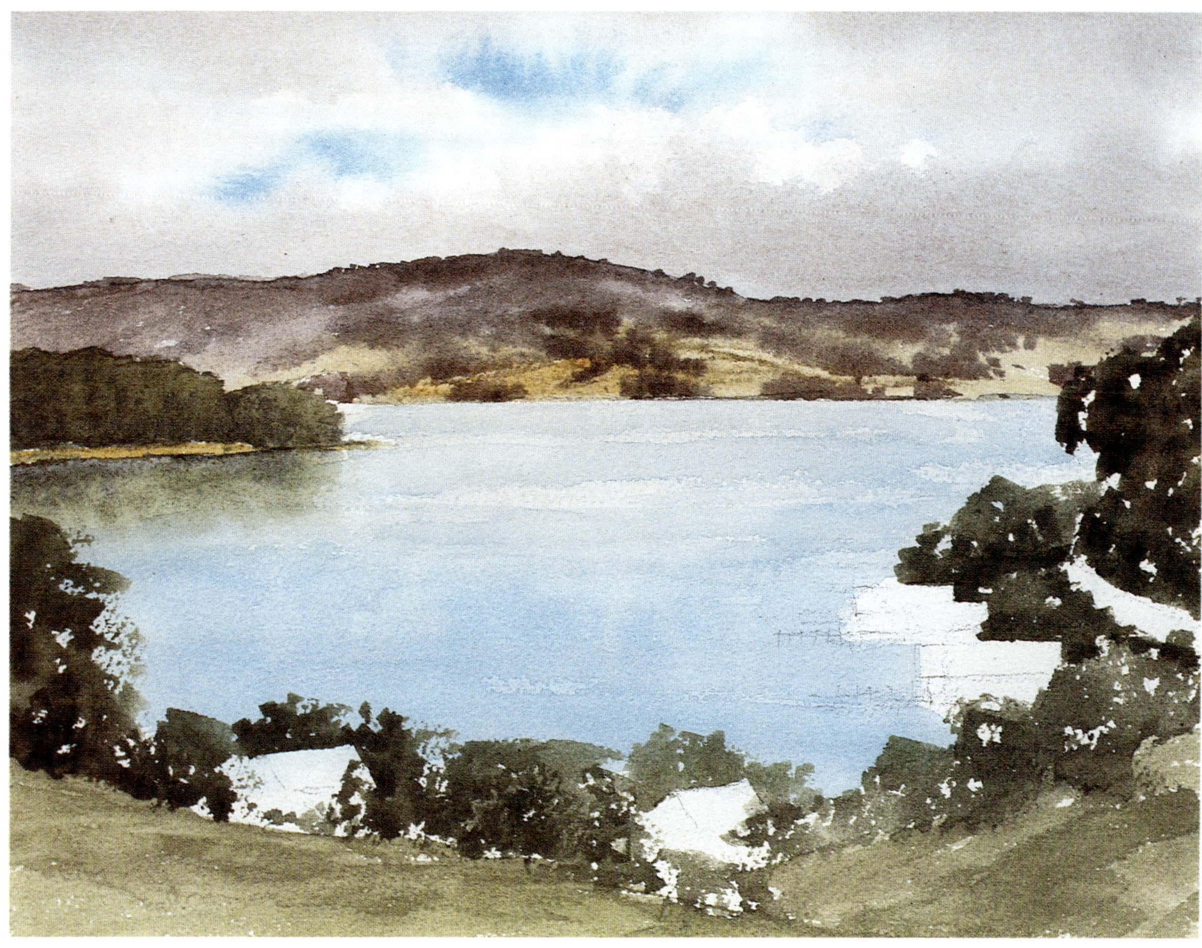

STEP 3

A Use some strokes of antwerp blue across the dry surface of the water area. Make the water darker in the foreground.
Allow to dry.

B Add trees to the picture using a mixture of raw umber with a touch of antwerp blue.

Note that the houses, boat sheds and road at the right side have all been left as white paper.
Allow to dry.

C Paint foreground grassy area with a mixture of raw sienna and a touch of antwerp blue.

The inlet at Narooma

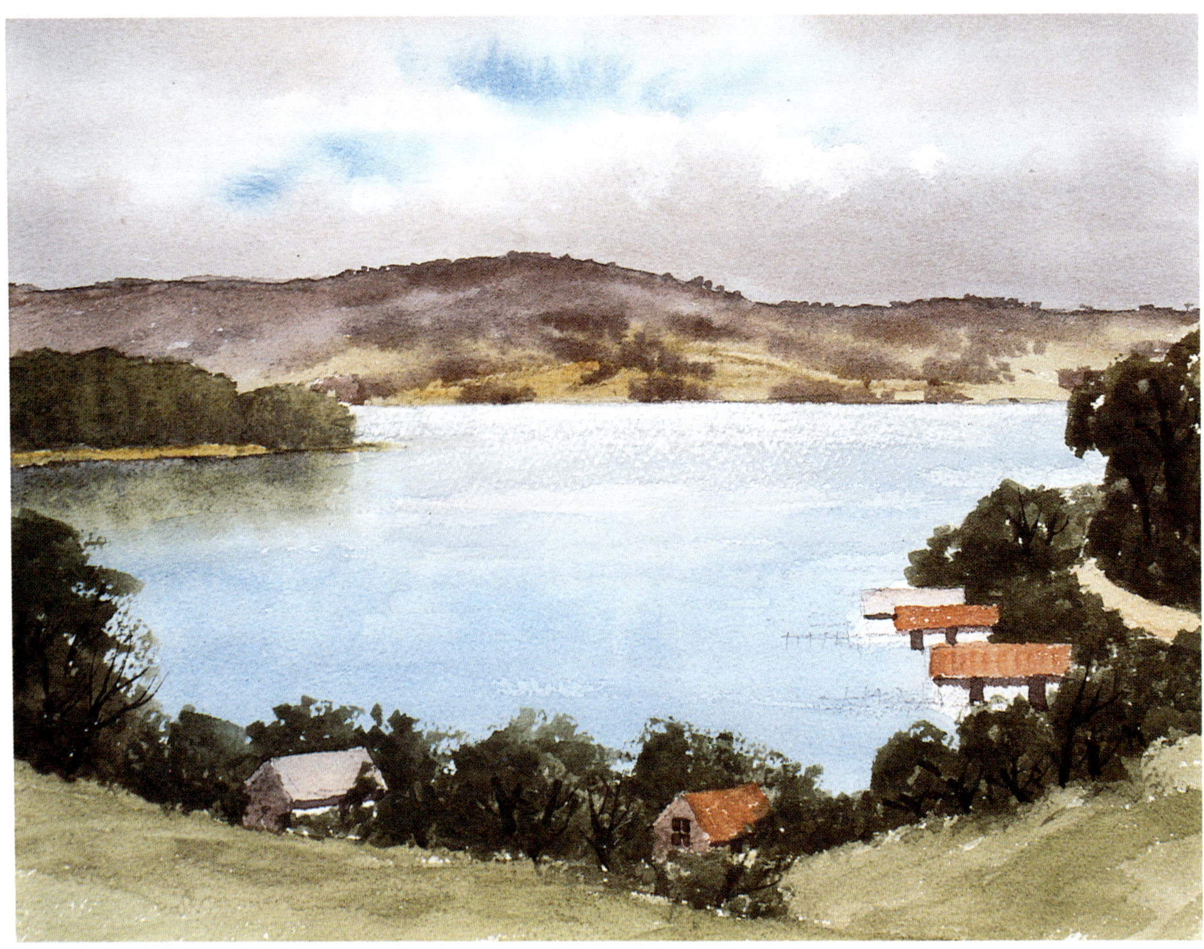

STEP 4

A Paint the road on the right hand side with a mixture of raw sienna and light red.

B Strengthen trees on shady parts with a mixture of raw umber and a touch of antwerp blue.
Allow to dry.

C Paint roofs. Two are done with a mixture of cobalt blue and light red and three with light red.

The shaded walls of houses in the foreground are painted with a cobalt blue and light red mixture. Shadows under the roofs are painted with a strong mixture of cobalt blue and light red.

D Scratch the water surface at the distant shoreline with a razor blade.

The inlet at Narooma

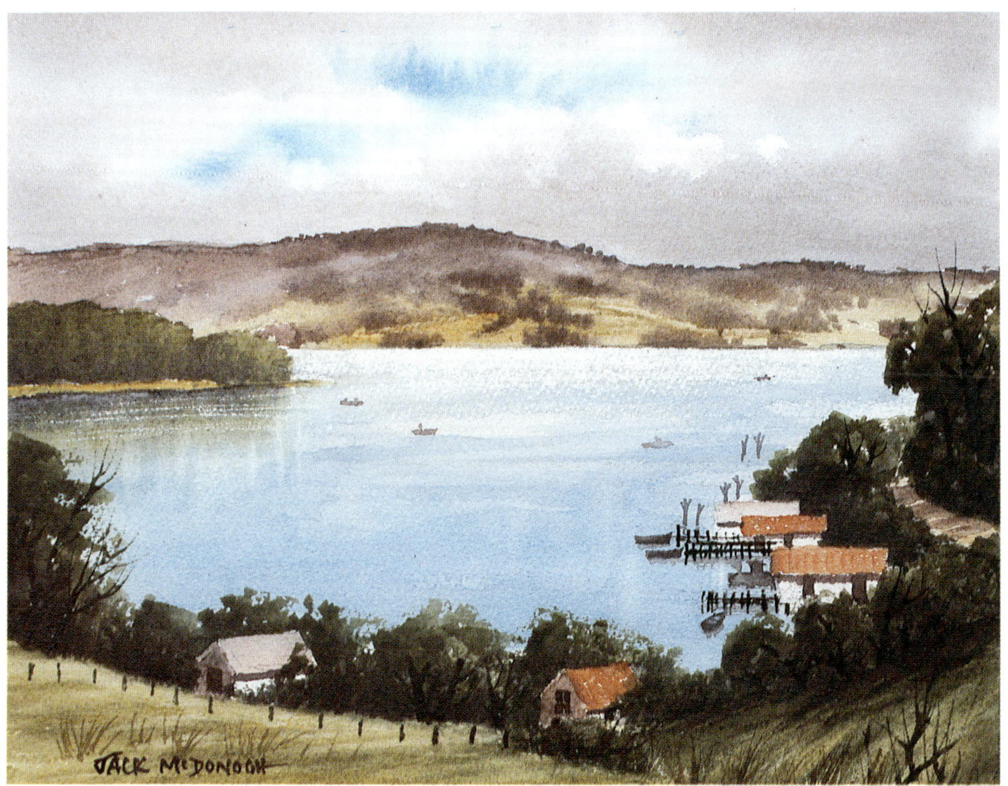

STEP 5

A Put some brush strokes of antwerp blue across the dry water surface. Allow to dry.

B Strengthen shadows on base of middle distance trees on the headland on left side with cobalt blue. Add this colour in the reflection of the trees.

C Add shadows on the road with a mixture of cobalt blue and light red.

D Add cobalt blue in shaded parts of all trees in foreground.

E Paint wharves with burnt umber and boats with a cobalt blue and light red mixture.

F Give the left side of the grassy foreground a wash of raw sienna.

G Wash some raw umber over the right side grass area in foreground.

H Do some 'lifting-off' with the lift-off brush on the dry surface of the water area.

I Paint distant small boats with a weak mixture of cobalt blue and light red.

J Paint fence posts with burnt umber.

Bathurst country

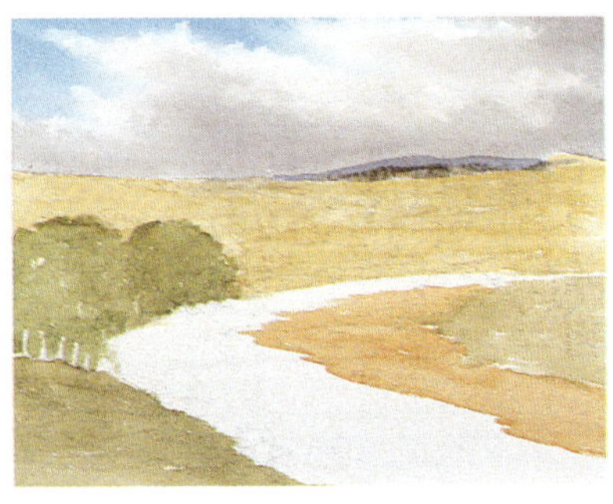

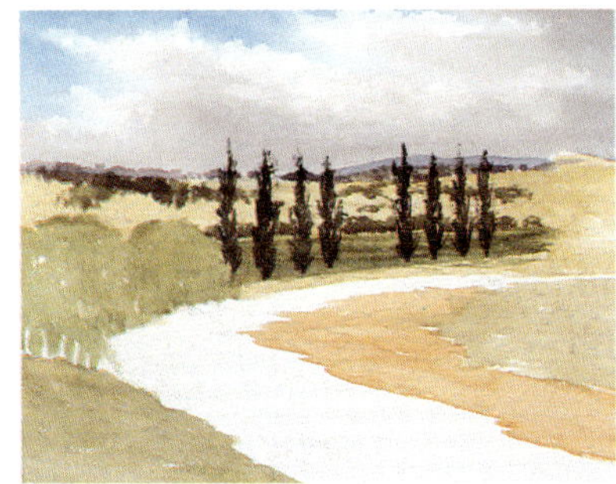

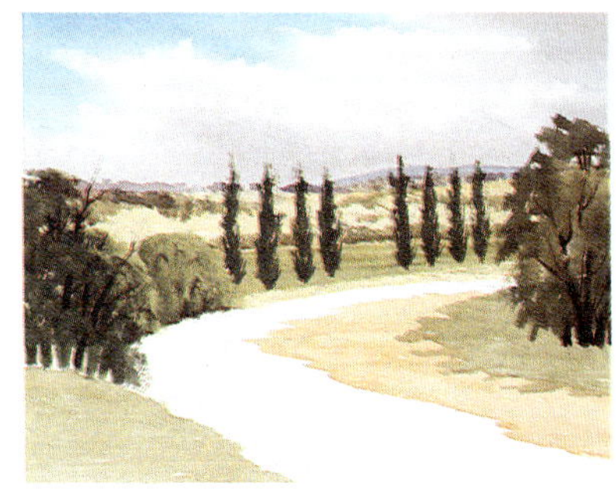

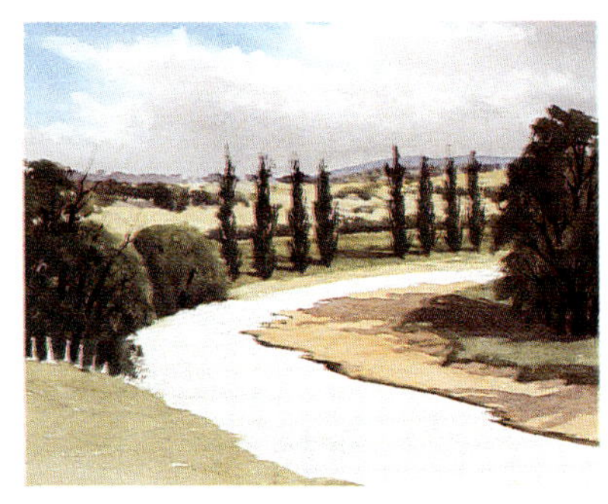

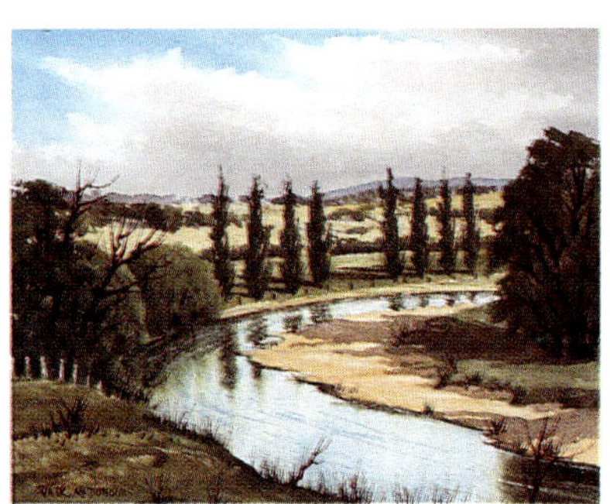

Bathurst country

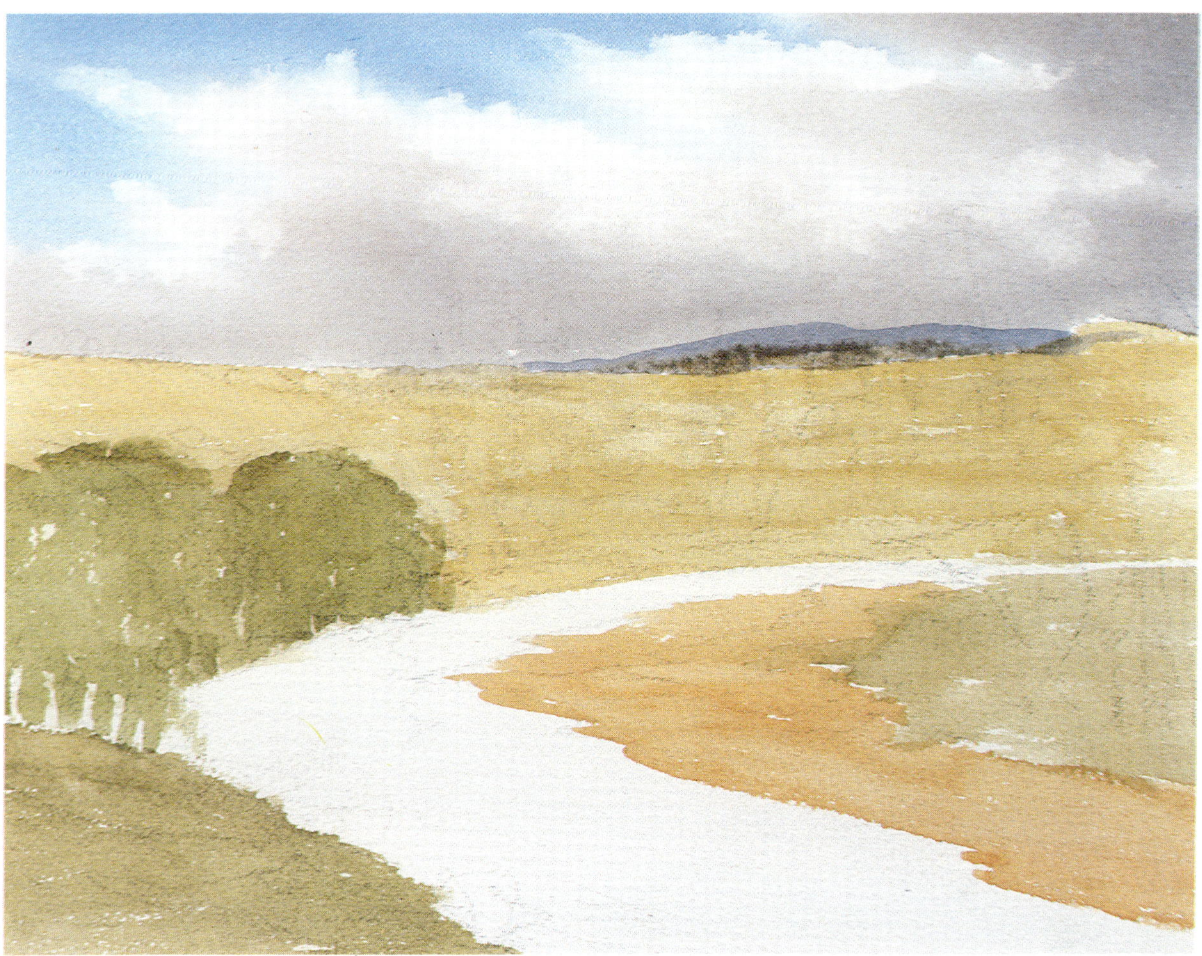

STEP 1

A Pencil outline of the scene.

B Wet sky area and paint clouds with a mixture of light red and a touch of winsor blue. Use antwerp blue for the sky area.
Allow to dry.

C Use cobalt blue for distant hill.
Allow to dry.

D Paint all grassy areas beyond the river with a wash of raw sienna with a touch of raw umber.

E Add a touch of antwerp blue to the mixture in Step 1D and paint foreground grassy areas.

F Paint sandy areas at edge of the river with a mixture of raw sienna and light red.

G Paint trees on left side of the river with a mixture of raw sienna and a touch of antwerp blue.
Allow to dry.

Bathurst country

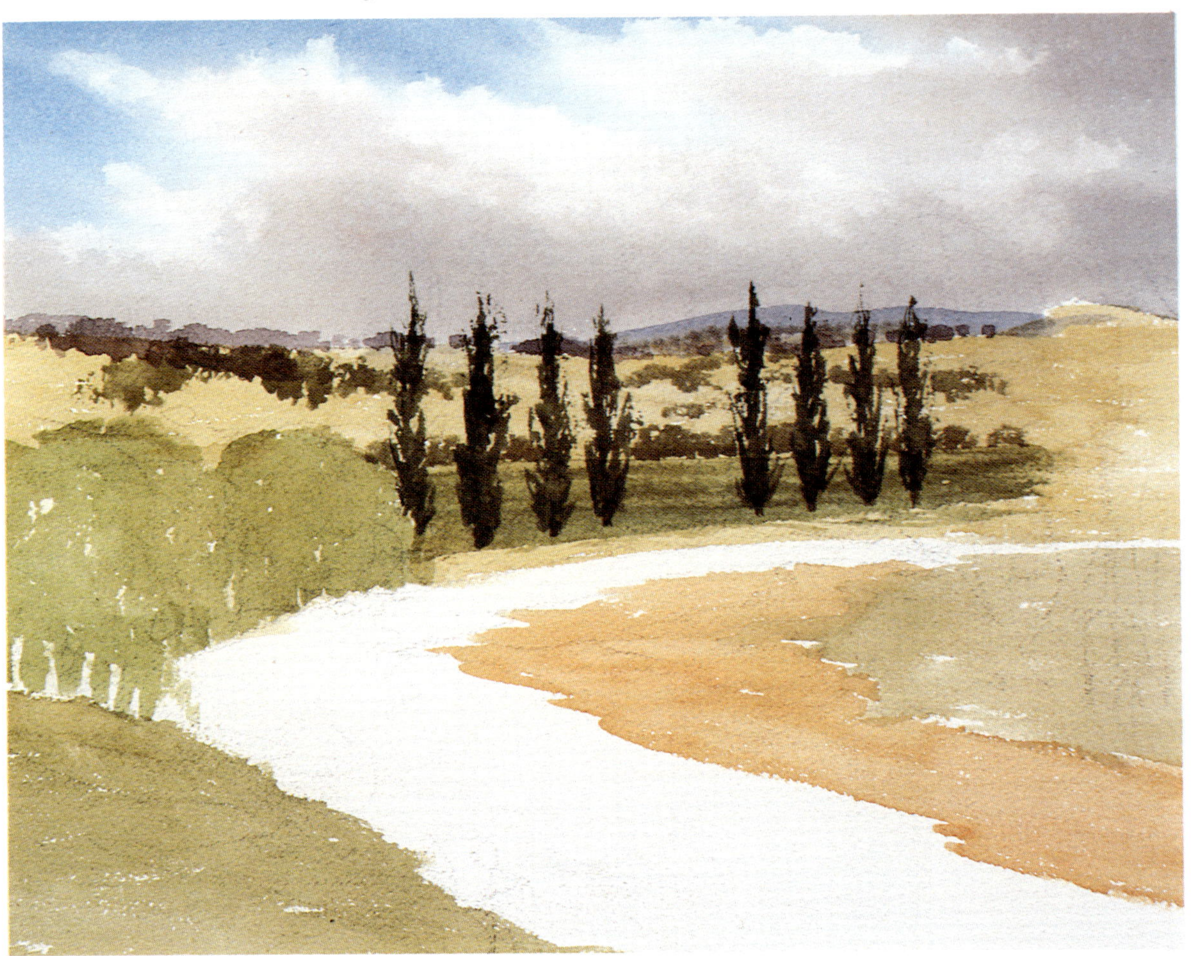

STEP 2

A Paint trees on distant hills with a cobalt and light red mixture.

B Paint a thin wash of raw sienna with a touch of antwerp blue over the field behind the poplars.
Allow to dry.

C Paint poplars with a mixture of raw umber with a touch of antwerp blue.
Allow to dry.

D Paint middle distance trees with a mixture of raw umber and a touch of antwerp blue.
Allow to dry.

Bathurst country

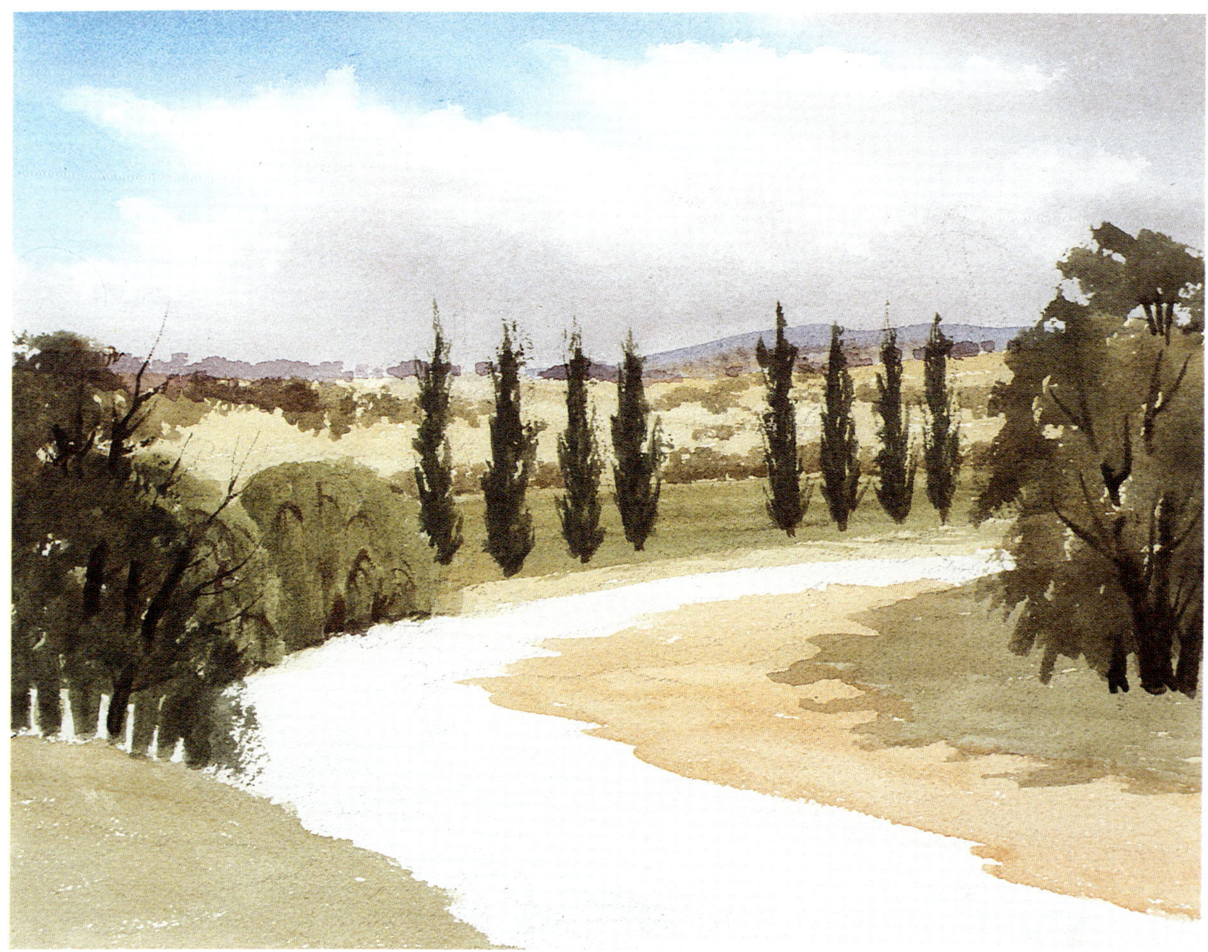

STEP 3

A Strengthen trees on the left side of the river with a mixture of raw sienna and a touch of antwerp blue.

B Strengthen grassy areas on the right side of the river with a thin wash of raw umber and a touch of antwerp blue.

C Strengthen poplars on the shaded side with a mixture of raw umber and antwerp blue.

D Paint trees in left foreground with a raw umber and antwerp blue mixture. Paint trunks and limbs with burnt umber and a touch of antwerp blue.

Work around the fence posts and leave them as white paper.

E Paint trees in right foreground with the same mixtures as in Step 3D. Allow to dry.

Bathurst country

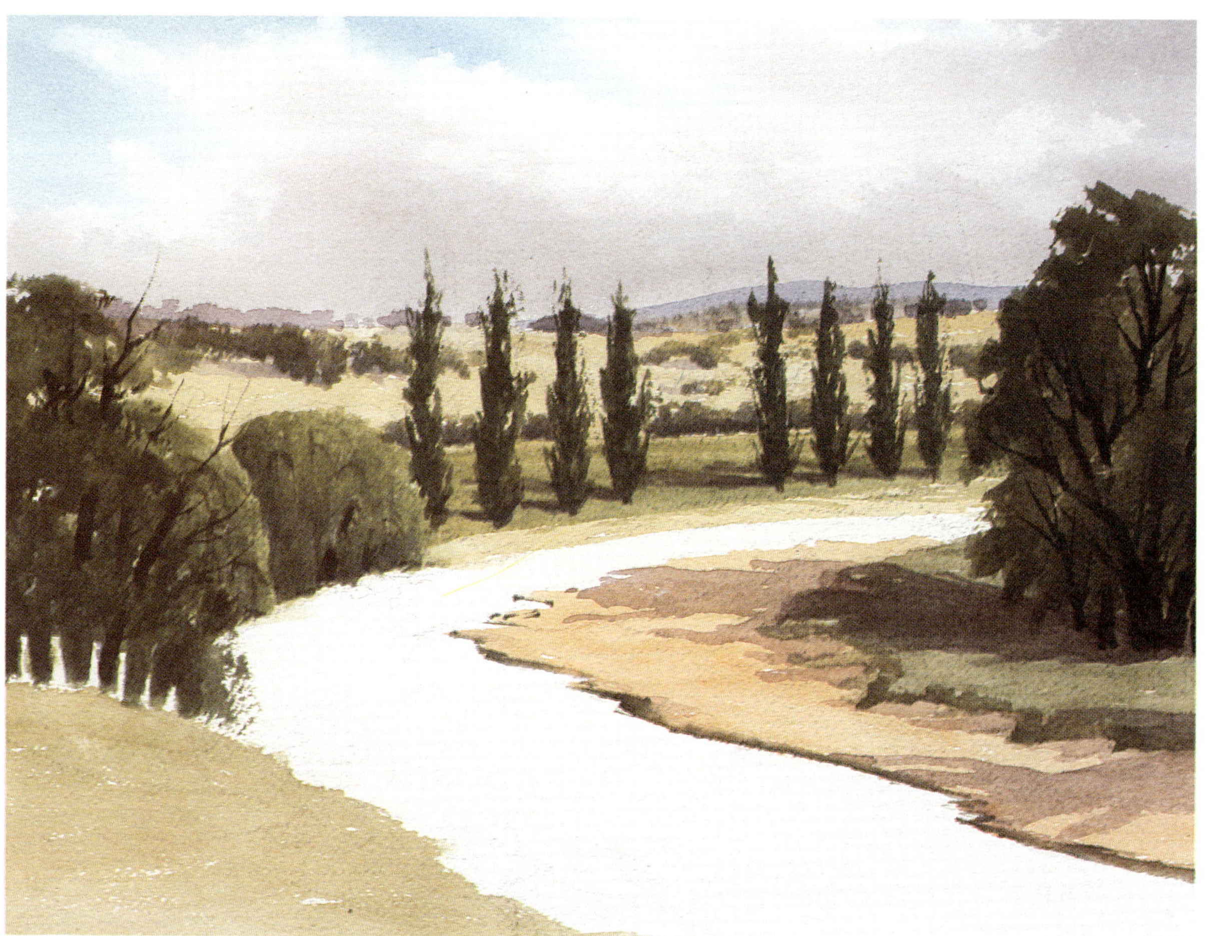

STEP 4

A Work cobalt blue into shaded side of all trees in the background.

B Strengthen trees in right foreground on shaded side with a mixture of raw umber and a touch of antwerp blue.

C Work cobalt blue into trees at the river bank on the left and then into trees in left foreground.

D Paint shade on field behind the poplars with a cobalt blue and light red mixture.

E Use the same mixture to show shadows behind trees in right foreground and on the sandy areas by the river.

F Darken sand at water's edge with some burnt umber. Allow to dry.

Bathurst country

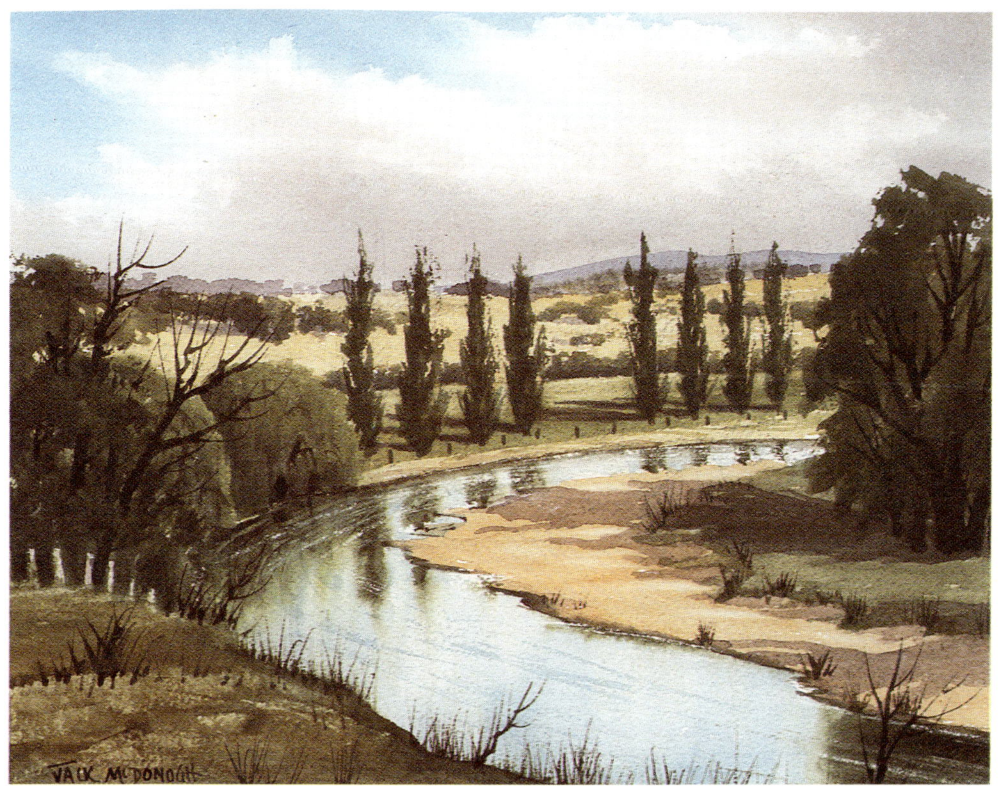

STEP 5

A Wet surface of the river area with clear water. Paint a wash of antwerp blue onto the wet surface. Make the blue stronger in the foreground. While wet paint reflections of the trees with the same colours used to paint the trees themselves.
Allow to dry.

B Scratch highlights in various parts of the water with the razor blade.

C With the lift-off brush 'lift' some highlights on the water with downward strokes.

D With a fine round brush indicate grassy edges on sandy banks some with raw umber and some with burnt umber.

E Strengthen grassy area in left foreground with a wash of raw sienna and raw umber. Use the razor blade and knife for textures and the varnish brush to indicate grassy edges.
Allow to dry.

F With a fine round brush add grass strokes and twiggy pieces.

G Add some more limbs to trees in left foreground.

H Do some 'lifting-off' on sand areas near the edge of shadows.

I Give fence posts a weak touch of raw sienna to remove whiteness.

Low tide at Nambucca Heads

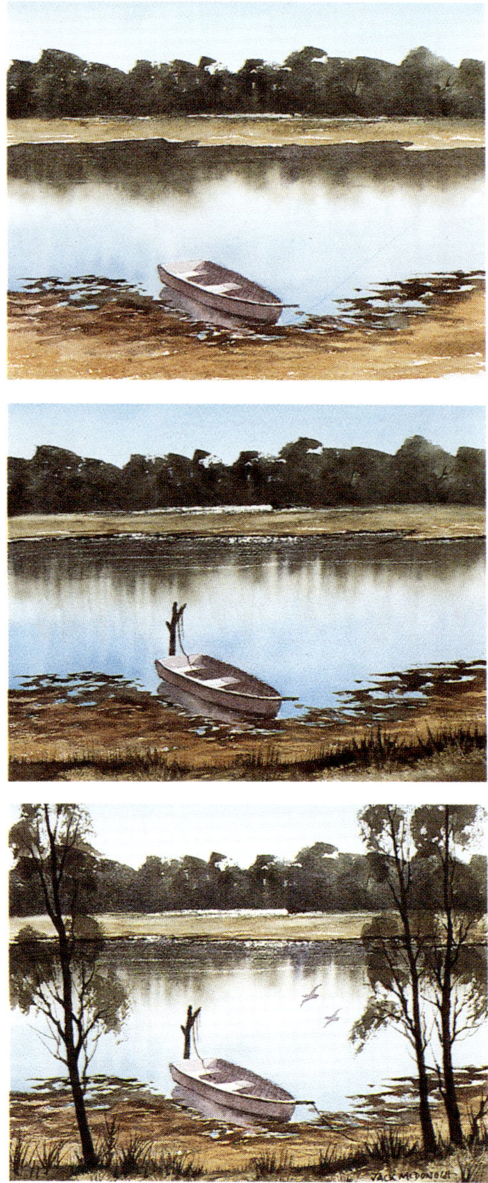

Low tide at Nambucca Heads

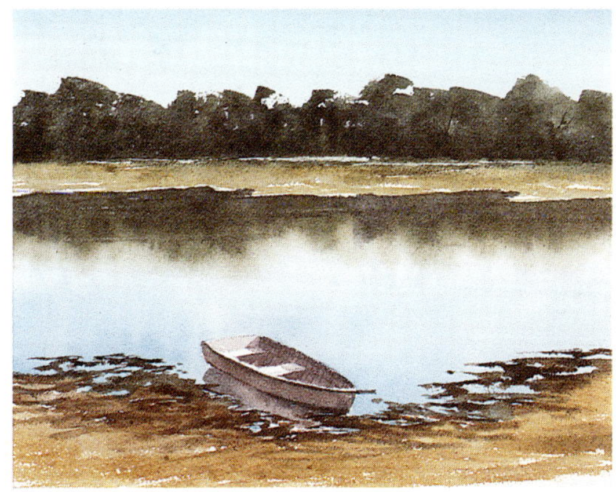

STEP 1

Because of the fact that many of the techniques used in this painting have been explained in earlier paintings I have taken the liberty of adding more painting to the first step than I usually do.

A Light pencil outline of scene.

B Wet sky area to the top of the distant shoreline and paint the sky with antwerp blue. Hold board up at a slight angle by lifting the lower edge to make the blue stronger at the top.
Allow to dry.

C Paint distant trees with a mixture of raw umber and a touch of antwerp blue. Work cobalt blue into shaded areas while wet.
Allow to dry.

D Paint distant shore with a thin wash of raw umber.
Allow to dry.

E Wet area of the water with clear water. Leaving the boat area dry, bring the wet area well into sandy foreground area. Paint antwerp blue in the wet area. Tilt board so that the blue is stronger in the foreground.

F While still wet work reflections of trees into the blue with a mixture of raw umber and a touch of antwerp blue. Tilt board so that tree reflections run downwards. Work some cobalt blue into the reflections at the shoreline. Make some downward strokes with a tissue on the water surface.
Allow to dry.

G Paint dark sandy areas in foreground over the blue with burnt umber, darken in spots with winsor blue. Paint sandy area with raw umber and raw sienna as it moves away from the dark areas.
Allow to dry.

H Paint boat using a mixture of cobalt blue and light red. Add reflection of boat with the same mixture.
Allow to dry.

Low tide at Nambucca Heads

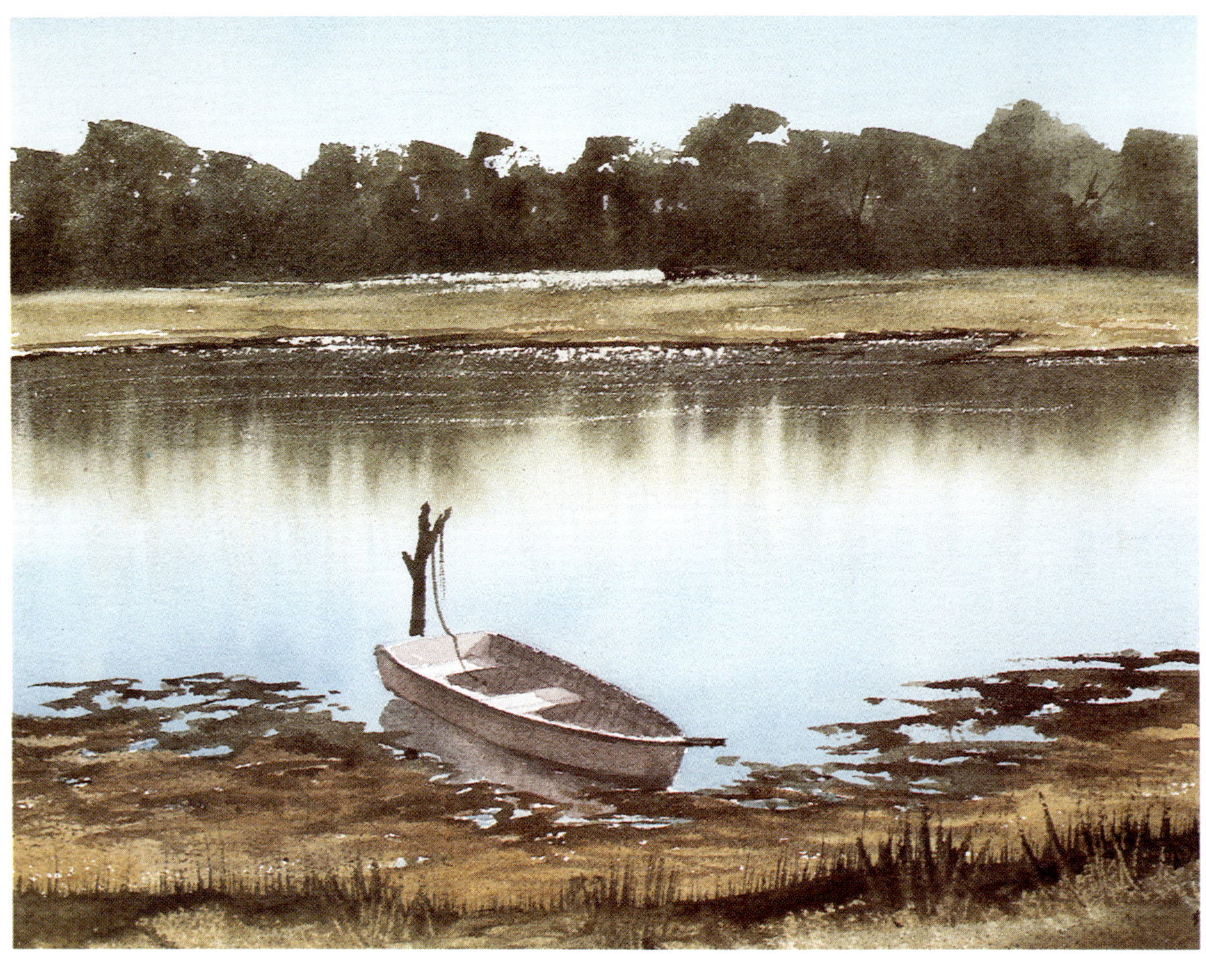

STEP 2

A Darken edge of distant shore at water line with burnt umber.

B When dry 'lift-off' lower edge of reflections of trees.
Allow to dry.

C With the razor blade scratch highlights in the water at background shoreline and make a couple of long scratches through reflections. Scratch an area of water beyond the further shoreline.

D Paint the pole with burnt umber.

E Paint foreground grass with raw umber and a touch of antwerp blue. Use the varnish brush to get grassy edge and the razor blade for textures.
Allow to dry.

Low tide at Nambucca Heads

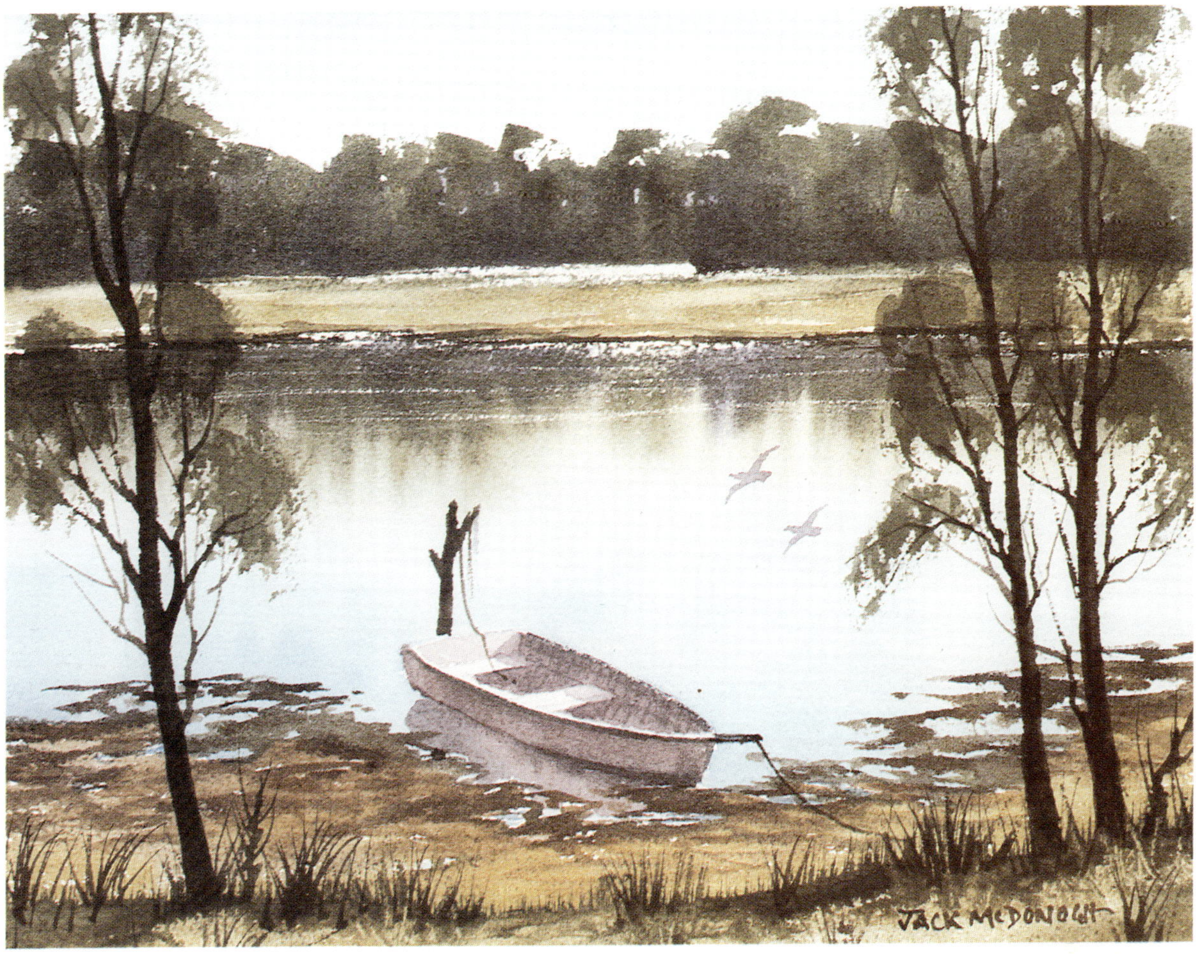

STEP 3

A Strengthen trees at back of shoreline with cobalt blue in shaded areas.

B Paint trees in foreground. Paint trunks first with a mixture of burnt umber and a touch of antwerp blue. Allow to dry and paint leaves with a mixture of raw umber and a touch of antwerp blue.
Allow to dry.

C Strengthen leaves on foreground trees with the same mixture as used in Step 3B.

D Add extra grass strokes to foreground with a fine round brush with a thinned burnt umber. Add some twiggy pieces, and rope on boat.

E Paint gulls using cobalt blue and light red mixture.

In conclusion

It has been often quoted that an artist has to paint a thousand watercolours before achieving a good one. In my early days of painting watercolours I thought this seemed a bit much. Now after many years of painting I often think the originator of the statement was being very conservative. As I always say on bidding farewell to my classes: 'The day you think you are painting perfect watercolours—give it up.' I take this advice myself as well. I'm still learning.

I'm saying this because I see this book as a help along the way to you in your chosen creative activity. Any art or craft that can be mastered quickly, to me, is not worth the time spent on it. Watercolour painting will involve you in the pursuit of excellence for all of your life.

One of the great joys that comes to the landscape artist is the fact that he or she becomes a student of nature. Wherever you may be, with or without your sketchpad, you will start to see pictures. You will find yourself painting pictures in your mind. All this study helps when you are painting again.

Let there be no doubt in your mind that paintings are not made solely with the hand, brush and pigments—your mind will never be more active than when you are involved in the planning and painting of a landscape. This can be exhausting, so don't push yourself with long painting sessions. I find after about two or three hours of painting I am mentally tired so I rarely paint for longer than a few hours.

My final advice is for you to keep practising. Study all forms of art. We all gain from each other, so I hope I've helped you in your continuing pleasure in the study and practice of painting landscapes in watercolour.